NOBODY TURN ME AROUND

Nobody Turn Me Around

A People's History of the
1963 March on Washington

———

Charles Euchner

BEACON PRESS   BOSTON

Beacon Press
25 Beacon Street
Boston, Massachusetts 02108-2892
www.beacon.org

Beacon Press books
are published under the auspices of
the Unitarian Universalist Association of Congregations.

13   12   11   10   8   7   6   5   4   3   2

Text design by Tag Savage at Wilsted & Taylor Publishing Services

SOME OF THE DIALOGUE IN THIS BOOK WAS RECONSTRUCTED WITH INFORMATION FROM INTERVIEWS AND ARCHIVAL MATERIALS.

Library of Congress Cataloging-in-Publication Data
Euchner, Charles C.
   Nobody turn me around : a people's history of the 1963 march on Washington / Charles Euchner.
      p. cm.
   Includes bibliographical references.
   ISBN 978-0-8070-0059-5 (hardcover : alk. paper)
   1. March on Washington for Jobs and Freedom, Washington, D.C., 1963. 2. Civil rights demonstrations—Washington (D.C.)—History—20th century. 3. African Americans—Civil rights—History—20th century. I. Title.
   F200.E934 2010
   975.3'041—dc22   2009046943

Dedicated to America's redeemers—

Bayard, Martin, Philip, Roy, Whitney, John, James, Joachim, Carson, Matthew, Walter, Floyd, Rachelle, Cleve, Courtland, John, Walter, Mahalia, Jim, Marian, Medgar, Daddy, Fred, Ralph, Bob, the Gadsden trio, the Children's Crusade, Lolis, Malcolm, Smallwood, Ossie and Ruby, Rudy, Matt, Daniel, Bill and Peggy, Dorothy, Andy, Wyatt, Haskell, Bernard, Joan, Patrick, Sam, Eleanor, Louis, Charlie, Cecil, Harvey, Michael, Spote, Coretta, Tom, Elliott, Michael, Dunbar, David, Harry, Odetta, Ella, Rosa, Len, Anna, Dorie, Joyce, Pauli, Daisy, Charlton, Ned, Jack, Burt, Dick, Fannie Lou, Carol, Lena, Jimmy, Robert, Ericka, Hank, Goodwin, Francis, Linda, Jerome, and countless others

—with gratitude

That day, for a moment, it almost seemed that we stood on a height, and could see our inheritance; perhaps we could make the kingdom real, perhaps the beloved community would not forever remain the dream one dreamed in agony.

—JAMES BALDWIN

I never realized it at the time, but it was time for a national conclusion. The March on Washington did not represent the opening of a new period, it represented the conclusion of the period of marches.

—BAYARD RUSTIN

To create a pointillist portrait of the March on Washington—with views of the event from perspectives ranging from sharecroppers to presidents—I used a wide range of sources. My goal has been to bring this moment in history to life, showing people, places, and events, rather than summarizing or characterizing them. Some scenes were the products of recollections of sources. Whenever possible, I corroborated the events and words of the scenes from several sources. Other scenes were reconstructed from live television and radio recordings, transcripts, and notes that participants kept while preparing for the march, while participating or observing, and immediately afterwards.

This brief narrative necessarily offers only a partial account of an event that involved more than a quarter-million people. In selecting the characters and events, I attempted to produce an account that showed the wide range of people and groups, actions and reactions, and interests and emotions.

Please see the endnotes for more on sources.

CONTENTS

The Longest March

———

ON A PITCH-BLACK NIGHT, a crescent moon barely visible in the sky, three teenaged boys walked along the gentle slopes of Highland Avenue on the edge of Lookout Mountain, then to U.S. Highway 11, north of their hometown of Gadsden, Alabama.

The oldest, a seventeen-year-old named Frank Thomas, led. The two younger ones, a sixteen-year-old named James Foster Smith and a fifteen-year-old named Robert Avery, walked ten or twenty feet behind. James and Robert tried to stay out of earshot of Frank.

Tall and lean, these boys became men during the summer. They didn't just play football in the street, act in school plays, walk up to the waterfall, or hang out on Sixth Street. They traveled the world, places like New York, Atlanta, and Birmingham. They learned from some of the legendary figures of the civil rights movement, like Julian Bond and John Lewis. They confronted the white supremacist mobs in the Gadsden demonstrations.

"Are we really doing this?" one of the younger ones said as they trudged along the road. "He's going to turn back," the other answered.

At about ten o'clock at night, the teenagers began a journey of 675 miles to the nation's capital. They carried a sign reading "To Washington or Bust." Now, after midnight, they wondered whether they would really walk to the March on Washington for Jobs and Freedom, the grand finale of the civil rights movement in the sweltering summer of 1963.

Earlier that night, they gathered at Sip Harris's nightclub, one of the regular meeting places of the Gadsden Movement. James and Robert had just gotten home from a two-week trip to New York, where they raised funds for the movement by speaking about their experiences down south. Over Cokes, they told Frank about the famous people they met. Frank missed out on New York. He wanted one last adventure before starting school again.

"The March on Washington is coming up," Frank said. "Man, I *sure* would like to go."

"Yeah, but we ain't got no money," Robert said.

"Well," Frank said, "I been thinking of hitchhiking. I want to go *bad*."

"Hey, that's a good idea. We could do that."

The conversation continued for a few hours. They debated whether their parents would let them set out on foot for Washington, D.C., without any real plan or money. They talked about how long it might take to walk. They didn't know whether they could hitchhike rides.

"It's going to take a long time," Robert said. "That's a long way."

"We have to leave now to get there in time," Frank said.

Then they stood up. Someone offered a ride to James's house in East Gadsden, then to Robert's house, near another nightclub and church where the civil rights movement gathered. It took a while to persuade James's parents, but Robert's mother said yes right away. Then they walked to Frank's house and convinced his parents.

Then they walked up the mountain road, at the foot of Lookout Mountain. The road into the mountain begins long and straight, then twists every hundred yards or so on the way up, then straightens out again at the plateau.

Good thing it was dark out and everyone was sleeping. The road to Noccalula Falls was not necessarily the worst part of town for blacks, but no white parts of town were good for blacks in the summer of 1963.

"Are we really doing this?"

"I don't know. I think so."

"This fool is joking."

"He's going to turn around."

Frank turned around.

"Come *on up*. Get *up*."

They passed a big house, set up on the hill on the left side of the road. That was the house where the most notorious killer in Gadsden's history was rumored to live.

They walked a couple hundred more feet. Robert moved out toward the center of the road. Then James moved farther into the road, to Robert's left.

Frank noticed the two drifting.

"Wait a minute," he said. "We all know where we're about to be. This ought to *inspire* us. We don't need to be afraid. Let's have a prayer."

They approached the spot where a white Baltimore postman named William Moore, resting near a picnic table by the side of the road, was shot dead on April 23. It was on the border of Etoweh and DeKalb counties. Everyone knew—or thought they knew—that the killer was the owner of the house the boys just passed.

William Moore was a marine in World War II and a former social worker, a white man who conducted a one-man campaign against racism. He protested a segregated theater in Baltimore and picketed the courthouse of his native town of Binghamton, New York. As a postman, he decided the best way to dramatize injustice was to deliver letters. He marched from Baltimore to the Maryland state capital of Annapolis to deliver a letter to the governor. He marched from Baltimore to Washington to deliver a letter to President John F. Kennedy at the White House, where a guard told him to "drop it in the mailbox." Then, in the spring of 1963, Moore decided to march from Chattanooga to Jackson to deliver a letter to Mississippi governor Ross Barnett. The letter asked the governor to "be gracious and give more than is immediately demanded of you."

Friends warned that his mission was too dangerous, and family members treated the journey as the irrational act of a deluded man. Moore went anyway. He pushed a mail caddy and wore a sandwich board reading "End Segregation in America" and "Equal Rights for All Men." When he entered Alabama, he befriended a stray dog and talked to a man at a store.

Moore settled in for the night near Reece City, about six miles north of Gadsden. He found a patch of pavement just off the highway, with a picnic table and benches under the shade of a sweeping tree. Someone shot him twice with a .22-caliber rifle. A motorist found him facedown, with stocking feet; he had a clean wound over his left eyebrow and a jagged hole on the left side of his neck. Tests showed that Floyd Simpson, the white storeowner whom Moore met earlier that day, owned the gun. No one was ever indicted for the murder.

Moore's murder brought the civil rights movement to Gadsden. The previous summer, attempts at demonstrations and sit-ins sputtered. But when Moore was martyred, organizers from the Congress of Racial Equality (CORE) and the Student Nonviolent Coordinating Committee (SNCC) moved into town. They held meetings every night and targeted the segregated establishments along Broad Street—the Princess Theater, F. W. Woolworth, White Castle, Sears, Grant's, Nelson's.

They marched through the black neighborhoods, picking up people as they went. If they started with fifty, they ended up with a hundred. One day, they reached the courthouse with over a thousand demonstrators. Hundreds got arrested that day. When parents and friends gathered outside, police chief Al Lingo ordered his men to attack with cattle prods. Gadsden became a national story.

These three boys plunged into the movement. Now, they walked all night, three dark figures silhouetted against a dark night.

The three boys got on their knees. "We were all churchgoing kids," Robert Avery later said. "Most black folk were churchgoing people. You had to be to survive."

They prayed to God, asking for guidance and protection.

"That's the first time I knew we were going all the way to Washington," Robert Avery said.

The boys got their first ride about seventeen miles from their starting point, on Highway 11.

For a brief stretch, the boys rode a bus. But that trip exhausted their travel funds and so they hitchhiked up Highway 11 until they got to Virginia, and then got rides up Highway 29 to Lynchburg. White people gave them all but the last ride. In Lynchburg, where they saw Confederate flags and effigies of blacks, a black family picked them up and took them the rest of the way to Washington.

They arrived at two o'clock in the morning on Wednesday, August 21, a full week before the march. A cop directed them to the local office of the Southern Christian Leadership Conference, where they saw Walter Fauntroy's name painted on the glass. They called Fauntroy, the local minister who coordinated Washington planning for the March on Washington, from a phone booth. Fauntroy first thought the call a prank, but Frank convinced him they were serious, so he got up and met them. Fauntroy put the boys up at a YMCA for the night and gave them jobs for three dollars a day. They stayed in the dorm of a beauty school. Settled for a week in Washington, they met all the major figures in the civil rights movement—the march's organizers, A. Philip Randolph and Bayard Rustin, Andrew Young and Fred Shuttlesworth, and the radical kids from the Student Nonviolent Coordinating Committee. Rustin gave them money to supplement their wage. He also bought them bus tickets to return home.

The Gadsden trio and hundreds of thousands of others would mass on the National Mall, before the Lincoln Memorial, to appeal to Americans for civil rights. Seventy-eight percent of Americans now acknowledged that the nation's racial problems "cannot be defended in the court of world opinion," according to a Harris poll. Something, then, had to be done. But 55 percent of whites "would mind" a black living next door, 32 percent would mind their children going to school with blacks, 23 percent would mind going to the same church, and 21 percent would mind working side by side with blacks.

Since spring, the Gadsden boys watched and participated in the movement in its busiest year.

They went to Birmingham to help Martin Luther King's assault on the most violent big-city bastion of segregation. Nicknamed "Bombingham"

—more than fifty explosions had ripped the city's homes and churches since the end of World War II, one just days before—Birmingham posed the movement's biggest test. If segregation could be beaten there, it could be beaten anywhere. King and his team started with a campaign of sit-ins, which fizzled. On Good Friday, King marched downtown with fifty others; they were arrested and jailed. In captivity, King wrote "Letter from Birmingham Jail," a document destined to be a classic statement of dissent.

Then the young people—high school kids, like the boys from Gadsden—took over the Birmingham campaign. On the first day of the "Children's Crusade," 600 were arrested; the next day, 250 more were arrested. Frustrated, police chief Bull Connor ordered his men to attack children with dogs and fire hoses, cattle prods, and nightsticks. One day, children spontaneously broke away from the march and dashed downtown, where they unfurled banners and signs. This symbolic takeover scared businessmen, who pressured the mayor to call a ceasefire and negotiate a settlement.

The Gadsden trio eagerly watched the news as 758 demonstrations took place in 186 cities, with 14,733 arrests. To track the civil rights wildfire, the Justice Department created a poster with a grid of activities across the country. "We didn't want to rely on the alarmist statistics produced by the FBI," said John Nolan, a Justice Department lawyer. "We needed honorable and legitimate data. Everything you have read about the FBI, how it was determined to destroy the movement, is true."

The Gadsden boys even traveled north to help spread the movement. As they reported what was happening in Alabama to northern fundraisers and organizers, they got firsthand accounts of the explosions in Danville and Cambridge.

For almost three years, a broad coalition petitioned officials in Danville, a tobacco and textile center on Virginia's southern border, to end segregation. The city council repeatedly rejected pleas to integrate public facilities and give blacks representation on public boards. The coalition filed a federal lawsuit in 1962 and launched a wave of protests downtown in 1963. When demonstrators blocked traffic, a segregationist judge ordered the protesters to disperse, issued a sweeping injunction against all forms of protest, and convened a grand jury that indicted protesters under the slavery-era John Brown Law. But the demonstrations continued, even after a "Bloody Monday," when police—and a gang of deputized firemen and garbage men—chased protesters into an alley and beat and fire-hosed them nearly to death. As they lay on the ground, the police posse thrashed their curled bodies. By the end of the summer, six hundred protesters were arrested and stood trial in the court of the segregationist judge Archibald Aiken.

Events in Cambridge, a declining canning town on Maryland's Eastern Shore, resulted in martial law. The Citizens Nonviolent Action Committee—the only adult-led chapter of SNCC—demanded not only an end to segregation, but also a concerted effort to give blacks better economic opportunity. Barely one in ten blacks lived in a family with a steady jobholder, most making starvation wages. When protests and counterprotests in June turned violent, with rock throwing and shooting, the governor mobilized the National Guard. In July, Attorney General Robert Kennedy brokered a "treaty" that called for the creation of a biracial human relations committee and an end to segregation in schools, housing, and public facilities. But a public referendum, scheduled that fall, endangered the few rights blacks already enjoyed. The city remained tense all year.

Violence swept the South all year. Vigilantes in Clarksdale firebombed the home of Aaron Henry, the head of Mississippi's NAACP. After a gas bomb went off in a church in Itta Bena, Mississippi, mobs threw bottles and rocks at activists spilling onto the streets. Vigilantes shot into the home of college professors helping the movement in Jackson. A civil rights worker traveling from Itta Bena to Jackson was shot in the neck and shoulder. A bomb destroyed a two-family home in Jackson. Whites in the North Carolina town of Goldsboro ran down demonstrators in a car and threw bottles and rocks. Whites in Pine Bluff, in Arkansas, attacked civil rights workers with ammonia and bottles. Someone shot into the home of an NAACP board member in Saint Augustine. When nine activists prayed in a county courthouse in Somerville, Tennessee, police allowed hoodlums into the building to beat them up.

Calls for a national demonstration swirled through the civil rights movement for years. Some wanted to bear witness, to present a "living petition" to the president and Congress. Others wanted to disrupt the politics of the nation's capital, with sit-ins at congressional offices and loud demonstrations outside the White House. Some wanted to highlight the economic plight of blacks; others wanted to focus on civil rights. James Bevel—who in the spring proposed that Americans from all over march on Birmingham—now wanted those marches to converge on Washington.

Marching to the nation's capital from far away was what these three boys from Gadsden were doing.

In the week before the March on Washington, Martin Luther King met the Gadsden boys' parents when he visited their hometown. The parents asked King to look after their children. That Saturday, King stopped by the Washington headquarters for the march, a vast warehouse at the black radio station WUST. The boys heard a commotion at the other end of the room.

They thought it might be another bomb threat. Then they heard King's baritone. King walked straight toward them. People parted.

"I just came from your home town," he said. "I have to take care of something, but I'll be back."

After twenty minutes or so, King returned and talked for about a half hour with Frank Thomas, James Smith, and Robert Avery about their dreams and the movement.

The Gadsden trio worked all week making signs. They took preprinted signs—with slogans approved by the March on Washington committee, like "We Demand Voting Rights Now" and "We March for Jobs for All & Decent Pay"—and power-stapled them to wooden staffs.

The night before the march, the trio loaded those signs onto a Hertz truck to take to a green-and-white-striped party tent on the National Mall. Back and forth they went, loading and unloading the signs with bold red and blue lettering.

On August 28, 1963, hundreds of thousands of demonstrators would carry those signs down Constitution and Independence avenues in what Martin Luther King called the greatest demonstration for freedom in the nation's history.

PART 1

Night unto Dawn

———

MARTIN LUTHER KING SAT in his suite at the Willard Hotel and read the freshly typed pages brought to him.

Out of public view, King let himself sprawl. He took off the jacket of his black preacher's suit, uncorked his thin navy blue tie, and loosened his collar.

The other members of the Big Ten—the civil rights, religious, and labor leaders who made up the organizing committee of the March on Washington for Jobs and Freedom—stayed at the Statler Hilton Hotel. The media swarmed around the Statler lobby, where tables held press releases and advance copies of speeches.

But King stayed at the Willard, Washington's most historic hotel. Back in 1867, Nathaniel Hawthorne said the Willard "more justly could be called the center of Washington than either the Capitol or the White House or the State Department." Representatives of industry and labor, abolitionists and suffragists, state and foreign government officials—*everyone*—met in the Willard's lobby.

Wyatt Tee Walker and Andrew Young, ordained ministers who had turned their lives over to serving King, sprinted up and down the stairs with new versions of his speech. They delivered revisions downstairs to King's secretary, Dorothy Cotton, who typed new drafts in a noisy room full of King's courtiers.

As advisers, Walker and Young gave King two different perspectives. Walker, the son of a pistol-toting preacher, emerged as a civil rights activist during the Montgomery campaign of 1955 and 1956. Pastoring a church in Petersburg, Virginia, he set up a local organization based on the Montgomery Improvement Association, which coordinated the bus boycott. King hired him in 1962 to manage the Southern Christian Leadership Conference. Wearing a small dab of a mustache and dapper suits, Walker took strict command. Before he arrived, the SCLC was just a loose collection of preachers, long on Jesus and short on organization, with no strategy for taking full advantage of King's star power. Walker set higher speaking fees, fixed King's schedule, shielded him from supplicants. Walker earned enmity from others in the movement—like Bayard Rustin, the organizer of the March on Washington—for his sharp elbows and ego.

Andy Young, a New Orleans native barely out of seminary, was a pious young servant with a lighter touch. In debates about a speech or march or bail payment, he would say, "Let us leave Martin to seek God's counsel on this." His light skin and accommodating words made some call him an Uncle Tom. "Andy," King once joshed, "there's not a white man you wouldn't Tom."

The March on Washington would conclude with King's address. A quarter of a million people would watch King at the Lincoln Memorial, and millions more would see him on TV or hear him on radio. All three TV networks would cover his speech live, an unprecedented event. Most Americans had heard only small fragments of King's speeches. He had never before given a complete speech for a national audience.

King wanted to deliver "sort of a Gettysburg Address"—the greatest oration in American history—but he really wanted to do more. Abraham Lincoln's words at the battleground of Gettysburg were short, solemn, modest. Ultimately, the address changed the nation's creed. The United States, once considered a plural noun, became singular. But few people heard Lincoln's address.

King's goal was to create a new civic compact. He wanted to *arouse* his audience, right away, to imagine and work for something brand new—a nation unshackled by racist laws and practices. Just as Lincoln inspired his people to press a bloody war, King needed to inspire his people to press a dangerous nonviolent war.

King needed to keep all his forces together, and the swelling ranks of new activists too—and to persuade them all to maintain faith in nonviolence as a political strategy. Two of King's closest advisers—Young and James Bevel—didn't even want to go to Washington. "Y'all are having a picnic," Bevel said. "We wanted to have a *movement*." All over the country, from New York to Savannah, from Chicago to Jackson, blacks questioned whether nonviolence could defeat an entrenched system of racism. Radical young activists wanted to confront racists wherever they were—in rural hamlets, corporate suites, congressional offices, the Justice Department, and the FBI. They questioned how long they could participate in a movement dedicated to integration and nonviolence.

Activists from SNCC and CORE—the Student Nonviolent Coordinating Committee and the Congress of Racial Equality—faced violence every day in cities like Jackson and Danville, Monroe and Itta Bena, Cambridge and Albany. As police and vigilantes beat them, FBI men stood on the sidelines taking notes. Demonstrators often spent months in jails and cattle pens, their punishment for marching for freedom. They seethed when President John Kennedy appointed racist federal judges and his administration indicted activists for peaceful protests in Georgia. The radicals—James Farmer called them the "Young Jacobins"—could follow King's message of love and reconciliation only so long before they exploded.

Many blacks in Northern cities turned to Malcolm X, the apostle of black nationalism who crackled with a message about fighting the "white devil" by "any means necessary." Now, Malcolm sat in the lobby of the Statler Hotel and railed against the "Farce on Washington" and the "Uncle Toms" who ran it. Even the organizers of the March on Washington couldn't resist the charisma of this onetime pimp and drug dealer.

The movement's old establishment—people like Roy Wilkins of the National Association for the Advancement of Colored People and Whitney Young of the National Urban League—had to play an active role supporting the grassroots activists. Wilkins and Young preferred to work within the white power structure, filing lawsuits and building jobs programs, conferring with presidents and foundations, and attending conferences. But they needed to do more, and King had to show them why.

King even needed to reach out to black segregationists—the church and business leaders who argued that battling Jim Crow was too dangerous, accepting the hoary old argument that blacks never had it so good anywhere in the world. "I glory in the name 'Uncle Tom,'" said Percy Green, publisher of the black *Jackson Advocate*. "After all, during slavery time, Uncle Tom was the only nigger eating high on the hog."

Reluctant whites, fearful and defensive, also needed to find a comfort zone to support civil rights. King would never persuade hard-core segregationists, who believed that race mixing would "mongrelize" a superior white race. But he might reach moderates—whites in affluent suburbs and members of progressive labor unions, universities, and newsrooms.

King and his aides worked on the speech for a week. They gathered at Clarence Jones's house in the Riverdale section of the Bronx and debated themes and words.

Jones, King's lawyer and fix-it man, came up with the speech's fresh new idea. Years before, Jones had met Nelson Rockefeller at the Chase Manhattan Bank to collect $100,000 for bail money. Before getting the check, he signed a promissory note. The weekend before the march, Jones remembered the experience.

That's what we have been trying to do all these years, Jones thought. *We've been trying to cash a check—a check for the basic political freedoms that all Americans enjoy—and that check gets sent back with a stamp reading* INSUFFICIENT FUNDS.

By reminding people that blacks lived in America at its founding in 1776—long before the Irish and Germans and Italians and other immigrants knitted themselves into America's fabric—King would argue that civil rights represented not a special plea but a need to square accounts with the past. The theme also evoked the pit-in-the-stomach feeling that comes from giving or getting a bounced check.

But King's speech had to go deeper. King had to provide the moral equation to right centuries-old wrongs. At the center of this appeal, always, was Christian love and reconciliation.

"Hate for hate only intensifies the existence of hate and evil in the universe," King preached to his congregation in Montgomery back in 1957. "If I hit you and you hit me and I hit you back and you hit me back, you see, that goes on ad infinitum. It just never ends." Hate distorts the mind, prevents anyone from seeing straight. Love breaks the vicious cycle. Love connects people to their strengths and nourishes others' strengths. And when people build on their strengths, they can topple tyranny.

Everyone knew that King's speech would define the March on Washington. Phil Randolph, the septuagenarian labor leader and director of this march, scheduled him to speak last. King had to make the best of the opportunity.

And so now Wyatt Walker and Andy Young burst into Dorothy Cotton's room downstairs at the Willard and blurted out a new phrase, pointed to the onionskin page with revisions in King's handwriting, and told her what words to type.

They waited for her to finish, then ran upstairs to show King the latest draft.

When they reached King, they gave him the new sheets and offered ideas about how the words sounded now.

King's speeches and sermons took a familiar shape. He started slowly, his deep baritone voice sounding mournful . . . then moved to a description of America's promise and failings . . . and eventually reached a point of ecstasy, when he revealed a new vision of racial justice in America.

King crossed out words and wrote down new phrases. After all these years of autographs and last-minute speeches and sermons, his handwriting was still as good as a schoolboy's. His tall, right-leaning letters reached high, trailed by elegant loops.

I am not un*mind*ful
that *some* of you
have *come* here
out of great *tri*als and *tribu*lation.

Surprising intonations turned his prose into poetry. His syncopation created suspense, called forth allusions to biblical and American themes.

King listened to his internal voice. He searched for phrases, images, sounds, colors, emotions. He knew his own baritone, and he wanted the words to match his voice.

As a student at Crozer Theological Seminary, Martin Luther King Jr. took eight classes in homiletics. But he really learned about speaking as a child, sitting in the pews of Ebenezer Baptist Church and listening to Daddy King and visiting ministers. They sang out their sermons in honeyed voices, then shrieked and yelled as they moved out of the pulpit and into the pews. Daddy's wild style—the "frenzy"—sometimes embarrassed young M.L. King. But he was fascinated. After church, M.L. ran home to listen to the radio sermons of Benjamin Mays, Mordecai Johnson, Howard Thurman, and George Buttrick. Before a mirror, he mimicked their words and mannerisms. He also read anthologies of their sermons, the era's self-help literature. All his life, King carried Buttrick's 1928 book *The Parables of Jesus* wherever he went.

For every speech and sermon, King drew from a repertoire of "set pieces"—fragments of arguments and visions that he crafted from the Bible, from Hegel and Buber and Niebuhr, from America's sacred documents and history, from gospel music and the preachers he heard as a boy. His favorite phrase came from Amos: "But let judgment run down as waters, and righteousness as a mighty stream."

Stitching together speeches and sermons, King always looked for the perfect ending. If you knew how to start and how to end, everything in between came naturally.

Now King wondered: Should he talk about *the dream?* Should the dream provide the emotional conclusion of the speech?

King had spoken about a dream for months. At a mass meeting in Birmingham, he sketched out a vision of an integrated society, concluding, "I have a dream tonight."

The Bible talks of dreamers. The book of Joel teaches that "your old men shall dream dreams, and your young men shall see visions." In Genesis, Joseph dreams of what will happen in the future, and his father, Jacob, rewards him with a coat of many colors. In Egypt, Joseph lands in jail, where other inmates tell their dreams. When the Pharaoh learns that Joseph has interpreted those dreams, he asks Joseph's advice.

The "American Dream"—that dizzying collection of images about family and community, flag and sacrifice, immigrants and ancestors, prosperity and ever-expanding inclusion—was a standard trope. King referred to it often.

SNCC and CORE organizers also talked about a dream as they worked in the Deep South. When King visited the site of a church burned to the ground by the Ku Klux Klan in 1962, in Terrell County, Georgia, a student named Prathia Hall started saying, "I have a dream," trancelike.

King sometimes hesitated to talk about dreams because he feared those dreams turning into nightmares. He read Langston Hughes's 1951 poem "Harlem," which asks what happens to a dream deferred. "Dreams are great, dreams are meaningful," King said. "And in a sense all of life moves on the wave of a dream. Somebody dreams something and sets out to bring that dream into reality, and it often comes in a scientific invention, it often comes in great literature, it often comes in great music. But it is tragic to dream a dream that cannot come true." King understood the dangers of dreams.

Always, King remembered the dreamlike state that strengthened his own commitment to God, back during the Montgomery bus boycott. Late one night, King answered the phone and heard a profanity-filled diatribe: "Nigger, we are tired of you and your mess now. . . . If you aren't out of this town in three days, we are going to blow your brains out, and blow up your house." Unable to sleep, King sipped coffee. Where does that hatred come from? Why is it so powerful? How can it change?

"And I discovered then that religion had to become real to me and I had to know God for myself," King remembered later. "And I bowed down over that cup of coffee. I will never forget it. And . . . I prayed a prayer, and I prayed out loud that night. I said, 'Lord, I'm down here trying to do what's right. I think I'm right. I think the cause we represent is right. But, Lord, I must confess that I'm weak now. I'm *faltering*. I'm losing my courage. And I can't let the people see me like this . . . because if they see me weak and losing my courage, *they* will begin to get weak.'"

At that moment, King heard some inner voice: "Martin Luther, stand up for righteousness. Stand up for justice. Stand up for truth. And lo I will be with you, even until the end of the world."

That was King's dream.

Two months before the March on Washington, King led the Great March for Freedom in Detroit. The United Auto Workers organized the demonstration as a trial run for the March on Washington. That march brought out a hundred thousand people—two hundred thousand, some insisted—who walked down Woodward Avenue.

King told the crowd at Cobo Hall: "I have a dream this afternoon." He described the dream . . . that one day the sons of former slaves and slave owners could "live together as brothers" . . . that white and black children "can join hands as brothers and sisters" . . . that "men will no longer burn down houses and the church of God simply because people want to be free" . . . that "we will no longer face the atrocities that Emmett Till had to face or Medgar Evers had to face" . . . that his four children will be "judged on the basis of the content of their character, not the color of their skin" . . . that "right here in Detroit, Negroes will be able to buy a house or rent a house anywhere that their money will carry them and they will be able to get a job" . . .

That day in Detroit, people cheered wildly. The theme resonated, more with each refrain. "Yeah!" the crowd shouted. "That's right!" "I have a dream!"

But the Detroit speech had a clunky feel. And the dream passage consumed four minutes. The speech in Washington was supposed to last only seven minutes. Roy Wilkins, the head of the NAACP, threatened to turn off the microphone if King spoke for more than ten minutes. If King talked about the dream, he wouldn't have time for much else.

King asked Wyatt Walker and Andrew Young what they thought.

"Don't use the lines about 'I have a dream,'" Walker told King. "It's trite, it's cliché. You've used it too many times already."

Young agreed.

King looked up but said nothing.

Years before, King came up with the refrain "Give us the ballot" for his speech for the Prayer Pilgrimage for Freedom. He showed it to Bayard Rustin. "*Martin*, the mentality of blacks today is not that they want to be *given* anything," Rustin said. "They want to *demand*." King agreed, but decided to keep the line. "It just rolls better for me," he said.

In the room next to King's at the Willard Hotel, Harry Boyte lay down in a sleeping bag on the floor. His father had recently begun work as the office manager of King's Southern Christian Leadership Conference. Harry joined his father in Washington before starting college at Duke that fall.

As he drifted to sleep, Harry heard a booming baritone from the next room. Over and over he heard the same words: "I have a dream . . . I have a dream . . . I have a dream . . ."

"He must be practicing his speech," young Harry Boyte thought.

ALL THROUGH THE NIGHT, technicians from the Army Signal Corps worked on the sound system on the platform of the Lincoln Memorial. The technicians removed the system's pieces, placed them on the ground, and tried to figure out how to rebuild it.

Someone sabotaged the $16,000 sound system—state-of-the-art electronic equipment—to derail the March on Washington. Now it had to be fixed—or else the crowd of a quarter million people would get cut off from the day's program.

Walter Fauntroy, one of Martin Luther King's oldest allies, learned about the monkey-wrenching the night before. At about eight o'clock, he got a telephone call with news that the system from American Amplifier and Television Corporation did not work.

Fauntroy was a short stocky man, with dimples and the wisp of mustache favored by civil rights ministers, always dressed in a dark suit. A Washington native, he preached at New Bethel Baptist Church, which he had attended as a boy, to a congregation that had cheered his childhood victories in speaking competitions and raised money for his education at Virginia Union University. He was named the Washington organizer for the Great March, but the New York organizers sometimes mocked him as "Little Lord Fauntleroy." But he didn't notice, or he didn't care.

Fauntroy and his staff managed ground-level arrangements—renting "Johnny on the Spot" portable toilets, supplying first-aid tents and water, and arranging for ambulance service. When the United Auto Workers delivered signs to the Washington headquarters of the march, local volunteers—and out-of-towners, like the three boys who had hitchhiked from Gadsden, Alabama—power-stapled the signs to the wooden posts. Fauntroy got the sticks, staples, and staple guns from John Hechinger, the owner of the city's big hardware store.

Bayard Rustin had insisted on renting the best sound system money could buy. To ensure order at the march, Rustin insisted, people needed to hear the program clearly. He told engineers what he wanted.

"Very simple," he said, pointing at a map. "The Lincoln Memorial is here, the Washington Monument is there. I want one square mile where anyone can hear."

Most big events rented systems for $1,000 or $2,000, but Rustin wanted to spend ten times that. Other members of the march committee were skeptical about the need for a deluxe system.

"We cannot maintain order where people cannot hear," Rustin said. If the Mall was jammed with people baking in the sun, waiting in long lines for portable toilets, anything could happen. Rustin's job was to control the crowd.

"In my view it was a classic resolution of the problem of how can you keep a crowd from becoming something else," he said. "Transform it into an *audience.*"

Rustin called Walter Reuther of the United Auto Workers and David Dubinsky of the International Ladies' Garment Workers' Union. "We expect you fellows to raise the money for a sound system—$20,000," he remembers telling them. Then he called Jack Conway of the AFL-CIO and told him to make sure Reuther and Dubinsky delivered.

"You must be able to do it for less than that," Conway said.

"Not for what I want."

Conway checked with sound experts and found out Rustin was right. To get one square mile of clear sound, you need to spend upwards of $20,000.

Three companies bid, and American Amplifier and Television got the job. AATC assembled the system on Tuesday, as crews pitched the tent for the March on Washington headquarters and laid lines for telephones and television cameras.

The evening before the march, everything was set. Walter Fauntroy, in charge of coordinating all local operations, exhaled. The speakers worked, the toilets and water systems were in place, the signs were getting stacked. "Praise the Lord," he said.

Then, at eight o'clock, Fauntroy got a call.

"We were sabotaged," Fauntroy said. "It was expertly done. We can't get this thing back in order. They knew what they were doing. Somebody has savaged it."

Fauntroy called the contractor and told him to fix it. "I can't do it," Fauntroy heard the contractor tell him. "I can't get people in here, and if I got them in here they couldn't fix in twelve hours what it took them days to set up."

Fauntroy called Attorney General Robert Kennedy. "We have a serious problem. We have a couple hundred thousand people coming. Do you want a fight here tomorrow after all we've done?"

Fauntroy then called Burke Marshall at the Justice Department. When Fauntroy attended Yale Divinity School, Marshall was at the law school. Fauntroy asked him to get the Army Signal Corps to come fix the system. A team of engineers reported to the Lincoln Memorial.

Late the next morning, Fauntroy jumped when he heard sounds echo across the Mall: "Testing . . . Testing . . . Testing . . . One, two, three . . ."

CHARISMA MEANS, LITERALLY, "GIFT OF GRACE." In the presence of a charismatic figure, people set aside their own concerns and devote themselves to the leader. Martin Luther King's charisma transformed the civil rights movement, elevating it from the most ordinary country churches to the suites of the NAACP to the White House. That charisma spread globally, too, from Africa to Vietnam, from Paris to Moscow.

King's followers believed what Johnnie Carr, a childhood friend of Rosa Parks's and a significant figure in the movement, said: "God revealed to him that he would have to lead his people. When Moses was sent to lead the children in Israel out of Egypt, God had to do a lot of things to him to make him understand that he was ready. I think that God did something to Dr. King to make him know that he was to be the leader of his people."

Establishment figures like Roy Wilkins resented the credit and attention given King. The NAACP had toiled for half a century—building organizations, raising money, lobbying politicians, filing lawsuits—before this twentysomething preacher became a global hero during the Montgomery campaign.

King's onetime assistant Harry Wachtel laughed at the unfairness of it all: "Here I am, I'm shoveling snow all along and here comes up a guy with a snowplow and he goes right through."

With this resentment came an undercurrent of gossip and criticism. King had flaws—laziness in everyday management, obsession with his media image, indecisiveness, timidity with movement rivals, obsession with martyrdom. At organizing meetings, he often nodded off, catching up on sleep lost to constant travel and speaking demands.

But to Bayard Rustin, the organizer of the March on Washington, the petty details did not matter. What mattered was the transformative power of the man.

"Martin was not really an organizer," he said. "He was an *inspirer.* Somebody else did the organizing, and I'm not talking about the people around Martin. The organizers for Martin's movement were Bull Connor and the dogs and fire hoses and nightly television. That's *witness.* [King] created a movement out of the inability of the South to behave itself.

"This is what made the SNCC kids angry with Martin. They had been in Mississippi and bitten by dogs. They couldn't get the national television. They could not get the nation's attention. Martin would come in, and in fifteen minutes the whole of America was watching. That is why they ended up cursing him and calling him Da Lawd and all that. They didn't understand the dynamic. He couldn't go anywhere where blacks were disenfranchised without becoming heroic."

King's charisma came not from his appearance. A stout man, he stood just five feet, seven inches tall and weighed about 170 pounds. Audiences sometimes saw little more than the top of his head over the podium. Even at the young age of thirty-four, his face showed strain from a life of travel and national crisis.

He moved with a workingman's grace. His body forged forward. As a young man, he loved to play pickup basketball and dance, even though his father disapproved. People just meeting King were amazed at how big his hands were. They were even more amazed by his attentiveness. His almond eyes, betraying a mysterious Asian lineage, fixed on his companions. He talked softly. He could be funny. Even when people had no real connection with King, they wanted to be part of his world.

Wyatt Tee Walker, his assistant, liked to tell the story of a trip to Nashville. When King traveled to big cities, he sought out remote little churches. On this day, King could not find a little country church he had planned to visit, so he stopped at a filling station to ask for directions. No one could help, so King drove away. Before King drove a block, a station attendant chased King's car.

"Dr. King!" he shouted as he chased the car. "Dr. King!" So King pulled over.

Breathless, the man approached the open window of the car.

"Dr. King, after you left, my brother-in-law came. I asked him. He don't know either."

Even if they couldn't help, King's followers wanted him to know they tried.

From the time he was a teenager, King carefully managed his public persona. King almost always wore black marrying-and-burying suits—in fact, five of his six suits were black—with dark ties and starched white shirts. He knew the racist stereotypes of blacks as lazy, stupid, shuffling, oversexed. Whatever the stereotype said, he projected the opposite. He wouldn't even eat watermelon in public.

Out of the public eye it was a different story. He loved the South's fatty and caloric foods—fried chicken, collard greens and rice, black-eyed peas. "Man, this food is good, man," he would say as he grabbed a piece of fried chicken. "I can't wait on *you-all*." He ate with his fingers. "He used to always have everybody rolling because you could tell that he never did learn the finer arts of eating as his mother taught him," his Morehouse College classmate Walter McCall remembered. King smoked a pack of cigarettes a day.

When he faced some problem that required the wisdom of Clausewitz or Sun Tzu, he fell into a chair and drew on a cigarette. He got quiet, disengaging from the frenzy.

King's greatest role model was his father, a strict and stubborn man who began life as Michael Luther King and preached at Atlanta's Ebenezer Baptist Church.

The elder King, a wide-bodied man with a sharp tongue, was a self-made man from south Georgia who had moved to Atlanta as a young man to escape the violent racism of his hometown and the strained relations with his father. He knew the violence of the rural South. Once, a white mob chased him down and beat him within an inch of his life. Another time, he watched a mob beat a black man to death. When he tried to stand up to racism, it only made matters worse. When he spoke up for his sharecropper father against an overseer, his father was fired and unable to find work again, fueling his anger.

Known as Michael in his younger days, he struggled to overcome his hatred of whites. Only as an adult did he let go. On her deathbed, his mother admonished him: "Hatred makes nothin' but more hatred, Michael. Don't you do it."

Michael King fled his home when his father, drunk, beat his mother and then started beating him. He got to Atlanta with nothing. By the time he was twenty he was preaching at two parishes. For eight years he courted Alberta Williams, the daughter of A. D. Williams, then the preacher at Ebenezer. When the couple wed, they moved into the family's giant Victorian house. Over time, Daddy King became one of Atlanta's most powerful blacks, a fiery preacher who battled segregation and demanded hard work and toughness.

Daddy King always expected his oldest son to follow him into the pulpit. After traveling to Berlin, Daddy King decided to change both father and son's names to honor the founder of Lutheranism. Martin Luther's most famous statement, challenging the pope's entrenched power—"Here I stand; I can do no other"—could be King's living epitaph.

As a young man, King showed little promise of greatness. He was earnest and hardworking but unremarkable. Professors at Morehouse College remember a student with serious deficiencies as a writer, too shy to become a campus leader, and burdened by his father's expectations. Psychological testing "did not show much promise," one professor said later. "He did not distinguish himself as a top-flight, outstanding student," said Louis Chandler, who taught public speaking at Morehouse. King did not even defend himself. "Someone would come up and knock the devil out of him," Chandler recalled. "Instead of fighting back, he wouldn't. Not that he was a coward, but he just didn't believe in it." His brother A. D. fought for him.

Could King be a great man? "We had no idea, but suppose we hadn't worked on his English or he hadn't worked on his English," his teacher Brailsford Brazeal said later. "We wouldn't look back on his speeches as masterpieces."

King considered medicine and the law. "I had doubts that religion was intellectually respectable," he said later. "I revolted against the emotionalism of Negro religion, the shouting and stamping. I didn't understand it and it embarrassed me." When he announced that he would go into the priesthood, his father exulted. Holding off the decision as long as possible helped King put some distance between himself and his demanding father.

Even when he was working hard at Morehouse, professors and classmates thought King might be nurturing serious ambitions. "He was storing up information," his classmate Herman Bostick said. "He was getting knowledge. He was drawing what he could from his teachers, their way of looking at life, their philosophies of life, to the end of developing his own philosophy of life." Already, Bostick remembered, King had developed an interest in Gandhi.

When he got to Crozer Theological Seminary, outside Philadelphia, he was transformed. For the first time in his life, he lived with whites. He shed a hatred of whites that had smoldered his whole life. Crozer was more cosmopolitan than anything King had seen. Students came from Greece, China, India, England. King knew he had to study harder than ever to keep up. If he caught up to his peers at Morehouse, he sprinted ahead at Crozer.

"You could see a change in him after a couple days," his friend Marcus Wood remembered. He started dancing and playing pool—pursuits that Daddy King viewed as sinful—and dating women. He fell in love with the daughter of the school's cook, who was white. And he excelled in homiletics.

King's first direct challenge to segregation came at a restaurant in Maple Shade, New Jersey. When King and some friends from Crozer asked for service, a restaurant worker brandished a .45. One member of the group, Walter McCall, sued the restaurant. The case died in the grand jury when white witnesses refused to testify.

As a Crozer student King proclaimed that he wanted to do great things. And he started to talk about becoming a martyr.

"We weren't interested in talking about him being a martyr," Wood said. "He said about the martyrs [that] their philosophy lived on after they died.

The white boys would say, 'You're not going to be no martyr. You go down south they're going to hang you on the highest hill.' We would say, 'You don't know how God's going to lead you—you may want to be a martyr but your life is in God's hands.'"

By the time King finished at Crozer and enrolled in a doctoral program in theology at Boston University, he had a mission.

In September 1951, he drove his brand-new car—his father's present for getting through college without getting a woman pregnant—through Virginia. He arranged to stay in a guest room at a Virginia Union University dormitory. A graduate seminary student named Wyatt Tee Walker asked a freshman named Walter Fauntroy to entertain him. The two stayed up late talking about civil rights. Fauntroy said, "He taught me about satyagraha," Gandhi's strategy of refusing to submit to a regime's unjust laws and practices. "He said we as an oppressed minority can win freedom with the same tactics. He was very clear about that. I was fascinated because I was tired [of being told] I can't drink water from the same fountain."

In Boston, Martin Luther King met Coretta Scott. Coretta, who studied voice at the New England Conservatory, vowed never to marry a minister. But, she recalled later, "I found out that you don't marry ministers. You marry the man." Before they wed in 1953, King insisted that she sacrifice her career in music to focus on her full-time job as a pastor's wife. Coretta idolized him and forgave his long absences, and when he spoke, she thought, "His words flowed from some higher place. . . . Yea—Heaven itself opened up and we all seemed transformed."

King was twenty-six years old and had pastored at the Dexter Avenue Baptist Church in Montgomery for one year when Rosa Parks refused to move to the back of a private bus there on December 1, 1955. Parks had recently attended a weeklong seminar on activism at the Highlander Folk School in Tennessee and vowed to "do something" to promote civil rights.

Because he was new in town and had not yet made any enemies, King was selected to lead a massive boycott against the bus company. Over a year, King rallied the city's blacks to stand together as the Montgomery Improvement Association organized car pools to jobs and stores.

At first, protests demanded not an end to segregation but more courteous treatment, hiring blacks as drivers, and seating on a first-come, first-served basis. In June, the federal district court declared segregation on buses unconstitutional, and the Supreme Court affirmed the ruling in November. The boycott ended in December.

King's commitment to nonviolence also matured. In the early stages of the protest, Bayard Rustin lived in King's basement and advised him on strategy. When he arrived, gunmen guarded King's house and pistols lay on chairs inside. Rustin told King that if he was going to lead a nonviolent movement, it had to be completely nonviolent. By the time of the Supreme Court decision, King had become the nation's—maybe the world's—leading apostle of nonviolence.

The NAACP claimed credit for the victory, because of its role in that court case. But the real victory was the black community's ability to sustain a nonviolent protest campaign for a whole year. Two years before, a Baton Rouge minister named T. J. Jemison had led a successful bus boycott. But that campaign ended in two weeks—not enough time to build a movement. Montgomery became the laboratory for the civil rights movement; nonviolent direct action became the movement's DNA.

Nonviolence, in fact, became something like a religion to King's legions. "When I started reading Gandhi and Tolstoy," said James Bevel, one of King's lieutenants, "I thought, 'Oh, Christianity makes *sense*.' It's just like *geometry*. In high school I could always make As in geometry. You can't miss. You add this, you add this, you add this, and you're going to get *this*. It's like a law. You can't miss with this. If you maintain the integrity in your heart and honestly do your work, and your motive and intention is right, and you go and seek what's just, there is no way for you not to achieve your objective."

Nonviolent disobedience forces supporters of unjust laws to explain themselves. "For the first time, you force the community into a *dialogue* and everyone has to start talking. What is truly the rightness and wrongness? . . . We never met a white merchant in private who agreed with segregation. . . . Okay, since nobody agrees with it, what's holding it up? Why are we doing this? [Merchants said,] 'I don't agree, I don't agree,' and yet everyone comes and bows."

The waters of racism could be virulent, violent, terrorizing; but the undercurrents, which pulled along the less fanatical segregationists, could be even more powerful. Nonviolent direct action forces these contradictions into the open by provoking police to arrest activists. When enough people refuse to abide by unjust laws, those laws crumble. All regimes—royal, authoritarian, theocratic, democratic—maintain power only when people submit to that power. When they withdraw their consent, regimes need to change the rules or give up power.

Most people in the black community could not embrace nonviolence completely. "Nonviolence is okay as a tactic but damn it as a philosophy of life!" said C. B. King, a participant in the Albany Movement. "I personally never accepted it as a philosophy of life but [it] was the only tactic that black people could have used that would be effective. We weren't ready for anything else," said Albert Cleage. "The fact that it fit into the framework of traditional Christian interpretation and Gandhi made it acceptable to churches and to Christian people who weren't capable of going into any laborious criticism or philosophy." Brailsford Brazeal, one of King's teachers at Morehouse, put it simply. "The alternative was to get beaten up or thrown in jail and railroaded into long sentences."

Whether it was a complete, infallible system or simply the least worst strategy, nonviolence became the essence of the movement.

After Montgomery, King struggled to find a vehicle for his calling. He created the Southern Christian Leadership Conference in 1957 and spoke at three major demonstrations in Washington—the Prayer Pilgrimage of 1957 and the rallies for integrated schools in 1958 and 1959. He traveled abroad. After years of his father's prodding, he moved back to Atlanta to become co-pastor of Ebenezer Baptist Church. The sit-ins of 1960 and the Freedom Rides of 1961 almost passed him by. In 1962 he organized a massive assault on segregation in Albany, Georgia, and in 1963 an even more ambitious assault on segregation in Birmingham.

King gave speeches practically every day. In 1963, he traveled 275,000 miles, the equivalent of eleven trips around the earth, and delivered more than 350 speeches.

The NAACP's Roy Wilkins complained that King only talked but never *changed* anything.

"Martin, if you have desegregated *anything* by your efforts, kindly enlighten me," Wilkins said.

"Well," King said, "I guess about the only thing I've desegregated so far is a few human hearts."

Now, for the first time, King had the chance to desegregate a national audience of human hearts.

A. PHILIP RANDOLPH FACED ONE SIMPLE CHOICE in organizing the March on Washington. The first option was to rally unprecedented numbers of blacks and their allies and sympathizers, demonstrating the broad appeal of a civil rights reformation. The second option was to rally a few thousand hard-core activists to mount a direct assault on the White House, Justice Department, and Congress.

Randolph never carried off a massive national demonstration as he threatened. In 1941, Randolph organized an all-black march to pressure President Franklin Roosevelt to ban discrimination in war industries. In

1942, he called for a mass rally for national legislation to abolish the poll tax. Randolph threatened a march in 1944 during the filibuster of a poll tax bill. In 1948 he called on blacks to rally and disobey the draft as long as the military was segregated.

In each instance, Randolph called off the marches. His allies, including Bayard Rustin, bitterly denounced his decisions. They accused him of a loss of nerve and wondered whether he really believed in mass action. But Randolph always said he wanted to work within the political system. Protests were a means to the end of getting government to negotiate. Blacks and workers, he said, "can only hope to achieve a status of equality, freedom and dignity within the framework of democracy with its institutions and heritage of civil and human rights."

By the late 1950s, after *Brown* and Montgomery, the civil rights movement had a historic chance to mobilize, march, and agitate for full citizenship.

In 1957, Bayard Rustin organized the Prayer Pilgrimage to Washington, which brought thirty thousand people to the Mall. The featured speaker, Martin Luther King, overwhelmed the crowd with his "Give Us the Ballot" speech. In 1958 and 1959, Rustin organized the Youth Marches for Integrated Schools. King spoke then, too.

The idea of a mass demonstration in the nation's capital continued to intrigue Phil Randolph. The centennial of the Emancipation Proclamation offered a historic moment to challenge the nation about the problems of racism and discrimination.

In the fall of '62, Stanley Aronowitz, a staff member for the Amalgamated Clothing Workers union, undertook an undercover operation for a march. Aronowitz barnstormed the nation to canvass the most radical labor unions for money and ideas. Bayard Rustin told Aronowitz to find out their views of a mass demonstration—and whether they would donate, say, $5,000 in "dues."

By going to the old Communists and socialists, Aronowitz later recalled, Rustin hoped to "outflank Kennedy's labor connections" and King's moderate, nonviolent SCLC. If Rustin went to Kennedy's backers, they would report to the president. Later, in fact, when the United Auto Workers joined the march effort, UAW people fed inside intelligence to the White House. In the earliest planning stages, in 1962, it was better to steer clear of Kennedy's financial and political network.

Aronowitz reported the results of his fund-raising tour. "If you do a march, it can't be for freedom," he told Rustin. "It has to be for jobs."

Rustin agreed but fretted that Martin Luther King would only participate in a march for civil rights. King, he knew, was reluctant to participate in any mass demonstration. *What if it fails? What if nobody goes? What if we antagonize President Kennedy?*

In December, King asked Kennedy to issue a new emancipation proclamation on January 1, 1963, the hundredth anniversary; Kennedy said no. King considered re-creating the walk of Lincoln's secretary of state, William Seward, to deliver the proclamation. He never did.

While King pressed Kennedy, Bayard Rustin went to Phil Randolph's office in Harlem. Accounts vary. Some say Rustin suggested staging an Emancipation March for Jobs to demand a new minimum wage, job training, and an end to workplace discrimination. Other say Randolph suggested the march, jokingly.

Blacks made up 22 percent of the nation's jobless—with twice the nation's overall jobless rate—and 36 percent of the long-term unemployed. Technology threatened to eliminate entry-level jobs. "The march of technology," Randolph said, "is liquidating unskilled and semiskilled jobs"—about two million a year. Blacks were shut out of apprenticeships and were typically the last hired and first fired. The gap between the black middle class and working class grew; 20 percent of the black population made $7,000 a year or more and 60 percent made $3,000 or less.

Randolph asked Rustin to outline a plan for a march. Rustin recruited Tom Kahn and Norman Hill—the first a lanky white organizer who initially got involved in socialist politics at Brooklyn College, the second a small but powerful black organizer who worked for CORE—to work with him. In early January, they produced a three-page memo:

> We envision a two-day action program divided as follows:
>
> a) A Friday in June—a mass descent on Congress and a carefully chosen delegation to the White House. The objective in Congress would be to so flood all congressmen with a staggered series of labor, church, civil rights delegations from their own states that they would be unable to conduct business on the floor of Congress for an entire day. Just as these delegations would present, in part, our list of legislative demands, so would the White House delegation seek to put before the president, as leader of his party and as Chief Executive, our proposals for both legislative and executive action.
>
> b) A Saturday in June—a mass protest rally with the two-fold purpose of projecting our concrete "Emancipation Program" to the nation and of reporting to the assemblage the response of the president and Congress to the action of the previous day.

On March 7, Randolph spoke to the Negro American Labor Council, the federation he started to expand his base as his own Pullman union declined. But the delegates showed little enthusiasm. Randolph succeeded on March 23 when the NALC executive board endorsed the Emancipation March and Mobilization for Jobs in July.

Randolph asked other civil rights leaders to join. SNCC said yes. CORE, with its fiery leader James Farmer, also agreed. The young people in SNCC and CORE grew excited about the prospect of a national showdown, on Capitol Hill and the White House, on civil rights.

Planning continued, haltingly, all spring. In April, Roy Wilkins of the NAACP and Whitney Young of the Urban League rejected pleas to participate. Wilkins said he was preoccupied planning a conference, with President Kennedy a keynote speaker. Young expressed concern that political activism would endanger his organization's nonprofit tax status.

Randolph struggled to get an answer from Martin Luther King, who was running the Birmingham campaign. Randolph eventually enlisted Fred Shuttlesworth to push his friend. At one point Shuttlesworth told King that if he did not agree to be a cosponsor, he, Shuttlesworth, would.

For King, a decisive moment came on Good Friday, during the Birmingham campaign, code-named Project C (for "confrontation"). King debated with his aides—James Lawson, Ralph Abernathy, James Bevel, Diane Nash Bevel, Andrew Young, C.T. Vivian—about what to do.

Rustin joined the group's regular planning meeting on Good Friday. Two discussions took place at the same time—how to confront Birmingham's power structure, which had flummoxed Project C, and how to use Birmingham to take the movement to a national audience.

"There was a need to bring the activities to a conclusion, to summarize them with some major effort," Lawson remembers. "'Culmination' and 'conclusion' were some of the words we used. Martin King did get persuaded that we should go to Washington out of that strategy committee."

James Bevel—the mastermind of the Birmingham campaign, the man Martin King called a "genius"—had his own idea for a March on Washington.

Rather than just show up *in* Washington, Bevel wanted to walk 1,200 miles from Birmingham. He wanted people from cities all over America, in fact, to make similar pilgrimages. Bevel drew lines on maps, showing possible routes to Washington from Birmingham, Boston and New York, Detroit and Chicago, Richmond and Chapel Hill. As they walked, the marchers would pick up new demonstrators, just as Gandhi did on his 1930 march to the sea.

Logistics posed challenges—Who would feed the marchers? Where would they sleep? How would they deal with violent attacks and unfriendly sheriffs?—but Bevel thought his many-streams march would create a national sensation. "The worst thing they could do is put us in jail," he said, "and we've all been in jail."

King felt an urgency to act. "More than ever before is this national determination and feeling that time is running out," he told an adviser named Stanley Levison, in a conversation wiretapped by the FBI. "We are on the threshold of a significant breakthrough and the greatest weapon is mass demonstration. . . . We are at the point where we can mobilize all this righteous indignation into a powerful mass movement."

The mere threat of a march, he said, "might so threaten the president that he would have to do something." Thinking expansively, King imagined simultaneous protests and work stoppages all over America while the Washington demonstration took place.

Still, King would not commit to Phil Randolph's march. At one point, King's younger brother, A.D., called Cleveland Robinson, a burly, mostly blind labor leader from Jamaica who worked with Randolph's Negro American Labor Council, and told him to leave King's name off the list of sponsors.

On May 15, Randolph announced an October Emancipation March on Washington for Jobs. "He who would be free," Randolph said, quoting Frederick Douglass, "must himself strike the first blow." Randolph made a calculated decision to announce first and get support later. The NAACP and Urban League were conspicuously absent from the list of sponsors.

The next day, the Reverend George Lawrence vowed that protesters in Washington would "tie up public transportation by laying our bodies prostrate on runways of airports, across railroad tracks, and at bus depots."

Then two events, 982 miles and four hours apart, made some kind of coming together inevitable. On June 11, President Kennedy delivered a prime-time address on civil rights. Kennedy's speech, the most important presidential address on civil rights in a century, gave activists hope.

Hours later, just after midnight, a Ku Klux Klansman named Byron De La Beckwith murdered Medgar Evers, the NAACP's man in Mississippi. Evers, a powerfully built, charismatic figure, brought hundreds of young people into civil rights. Evers was shot when he returned home in Jackson after a long day. The assassination traumatized the movement in the Deep South. After his funeral, Evers's followers insisted on marching down North Capitol Street, past the State House. Police blocked their way, arrested the marchers, and carted them off to jail. Some demonstrators attacked police with rocks and bottles. President Kennedy pleaded for a cooling-off period. More than a hundred thousand people promptly protested in thirty cities.

As these events shifted the tectonic plates of civil rights that summer, Phil Randolph reached out to the labor movement. He lobbied fellow members of the AFL-CIO executive board, all white, but only Walter Reuther of the United Auto Workers said yes. George Meany, the president of the AFL-CIO, rejected participation in the march. He grumbled about Communist infiltration of the march and about embarrassing President Kennedy.

President Kennedy called Randolph and asked him to call off the march. But it was too late. Tens of thousands of people already were demonstrating on any given day. They needed a national outlet.

Finally, Randolph called the leaders of the major civil rights organizations, the "Big Six"—Roy Wilkins of the NAACP, Martin Luther King of the SCLC, Whitney Young of the Urban League, James Farmer of CORE, Jim Forman of SNCC—to meet at the Roosevelt Hotel on July 2 to get firm commitments and make a press announcement.

When they went to the Roosevelt Hotel, Randolph and Rustin knew Wilkins and Young would resist supporting Rustin as an organizer. Rustin had three strikes against him—he was a onetime Communist, a draft dodger, and a homosexual. But Randolph promised Rustin he would stand behind him.

Before the meeting, Rustin later recalled, Wilkins confronted Rustin.

"I don't want you leading that March on Washington, because you know I don't give a damn about what they say, but publicly I don't want to have to defend the draft dodging. I know you're a Quaker, but that's not what I'll have to defend, I'll have to defend draft dodging. I'll have to defend promiscuity. The question is never going to be homosexuality, it's going to be promiscuity and I can't defend that. And the fact is that you were a member of the Young Communist League. And I don't care what you say, I can't defend that."

And then he paused.

"I'm going to fight against you."

Rustin had a chance to respond, but he knew he would not persuade Wilkins.

"I'm not going to argue with you," Rustin said. "I don't think those things can be defended by you. They can only be defended by a unified collective leadership."

"Do you think your buddy Martin is going to come out publicly and defend you? He won't."

"Why don't you talk to him?" Rustin asked.

Wilkins stared at Rustin.

"He wouldn't dare talk to me," Wilkins said. "He couldn't talk to me in any such depth. He's a political *idiot*."

To start the meeting, Phil Randolph outlined his dream of a national demonstration. Randolph also said he wanted Bayard Rustin to run the march. Wilkins and Young objected. Farmer and Lewis expressed support. King was silent.

"I will not press Bayard on you gentlemen as the leader of the March on Washington," Randolph said. "I will take it."

Relieved, everyone agreed Randolph was the right choice. For one thing, he was the only one without a major organization to run. And he had the respect of most people in the civil rights, labor, and peace movements.

"But," Randolph said, "I will take it under one circumstance, and that is that I will be free to choose my own deputy, and my deputy is going to be Bayard Rustin."

That plan—the elder statesman as director, the controversial organizer as the details man—broke the tension. Randolph got his deputy, but Wilkins warned Randolph that he was responsible for any controversy. He had to take the heat. And he had to control his protégé.

When the Big Six finished, Phil Randolph told Rustin the news. Rustin immediately approached Wilkins.

"Did I hear that right? You're going to let me organize this thing?"

Wilkins said yes.

"Can I get a memo, outlining our understanding?"

Wilkins said yes.

The Big Six agreed to invite labor and religious groups to join the march—eventually making the group the Big Ten. It would be a broad coalition, not just blacks, demanding jobs and freedom. They also agreed that they would not engage in civil disobedience. The march would make a public plea for civil rights, not stage an assault on the White House or Congress. There would be no sit-ins or blockades—nothing that didn't get the okay of police and other authorities.

Rustin set the date for Wednesday, August 28. He estimated that he would need two months to organize. The march had to take place in the middle of the week so preachers could bring their flocks without missing Sunday services. Congress would be in session during the week. The event might include a march down Pennsylvania Avenue, demonstrations on Capitol Hill, and the flooding of congressional offices with petitioners. The details would be sorted out later.

Within days, Rustin drafted a plan. He addressed a wide range of issues —the logistics of staging a march on the National Mall, bringing in a hundred thousand protesters by buses and trains, rallying the army of the unemployed and poor, enlisting unions and churches, raising money with celebrity events and button sales, coordinating media relations, pressuring the president, finding the best loudspeaker system, dealing with critics in government and the media, finding portable toilets, bringing in water trucks and tapping into fire hydrants, and training police in nonviolent methods of crowd control. Also included: fending off charges of Communism, providing protection for buses traveling from the South, mediating disputes among local civil rights leaders, and countering subversion by the FBI.

On the same day that he sent his memo to the Big Six, Rustin got a call. The sweet-tempered Roy Wilkins had replaced the hard-edged Roy Wilkins.

"That's a masterpiece of organizing," Wilkins said. "You'd better get down here so we can talk about how you're going to get some money."

Wilkins gave him $5,000 to start work. The Reverend Thomas Kilgore of Friendship Baptist Church agreed to rent them a dilapidated five-story brownstone in Harlem. The paint crumbled, the windows jammed, and the building retained the summer heat. But for two months, it would be home.

TWENTY-FOUR BUSES IDLED on 125th Street near Seventh Avenue in New York City. The silver buses carried massive banners on their sides: MARCH ON WASHINGTON FOR JOBS AND FREEDOM.

It was two o'clock in the morning. For two hours, a total of forty buses came to collect passengers in Harlem. Bus captains, wearing yellow ribbons, walked around with clipboards, conferred among themselves, talked with bus drivers, and answered questions.

Cabs and cars, their lights brightening the early morning hours, dropped off marchers. Friends and family stopped by to wish the demonstrators a good trip. Marchers milled around looking for bus assignments, taped to the doors of the buses. When marchers discovered they were assigned buses without air conditioning—or with groups of old people—they maneuvered to change buses.

"You've got to switch me to Bus Ten. It's the swingin' bus. There's nothing but old ladies on this crate."

"Hey, is this bus air-conditioned?"

"Where can I get seat reservations?"

William Penn, a young man masquerading as Inspector Clouseau—

caterpillar mustache, a black beret, wraparound sunglasses, and an air of entitlement—got kicked off the bus twice. The bus captain, George Johnson, intercepted him and told him to leave. He walked out of sight and came back a few minutes later. On his third try, he announced that he had traded seats with another marcher.

"All right, all right, I've had it," George Johnson said. "Get on your buses and stay there. No more switching. We are leaving."

The bus captain's seriousness provoked the comedians on the bus. "Yessir, *anything* you say, *sir.*" "Don't you fret now, Mr. George." "Don't be upsetting yourself, boss." "You *knows* I always listen to you, captain, *sir.*"

Outside the bus, the perfectly attired members of the Nation of Islam sold copies of *Muhammad Speaks,* the official publication of the Black Muslim movement. The tabloid's front page screamed: NATION OF ISLAM OFFERS HEARST $100,000 TO PROVE CHARGE—a response to the *Los Angeles Herald-Examiner*'s sensational story alleging that the founder of the Nation of Islam was white.

A young reporter for the *Village Voice,* Marlene Nadle, approached the Muslims. "Are you going to Washington?" she asked. "No, ma'am, I have to sell papers. *You* people go to Washington." An older Muslim standing outside the buses told Nadle he would have gone to Washington had the Muslim leader, the Honorable Elijah Muhammad, given his blessing. But he was staying home.

The riders on Bus 10 did not think the march would do much good. Many were embittered by a recent standoff with Mayor Robert Wagner at City Hall and another protest at the city's Board of Education headquarters in Brooklyn. For forty-four days—until police routed them, cutting the chains that bound them to fencing and carrying them away in paddy wagons—demonstrators occupied Wagner's office demanding equal opportunity for blacks and Puerto Ricans in public construction projects. At first Wagner benignly allowed the protesters to settle in. But he grew impatient as the smells of unbathed protesters overwhelmed the office and protesters petitioned the March on Washington committee to condemn the mayor.

One marcher, sympathetic to both integrationists and black nationalists, said the march wouldn't do any good but he wanted to go anyway.

"It's like St. Patrick's Day," he said. "I came out of respect for what my people are doing, not because I believe it will do any good. I thought it would do some good in the beginning. But when the march started to get all the official approval from *Mastah* Kennedy, *Mastah* Wagner, *Mastah* Spellman [archbishop of New York], and they started setting limits on how we had to march peacefully, I knew that the march was going to be a mockery, that *they* were giving *us* something again.

"Well, if the white man continues to sleep, continues to ignore the intensity of the black man's feelings and desires, all hell is going to break loose."

Bus 10 carried reporters from the *Village Voice* and *New York Herald Tribune,* as well as a TV reporter and cameraman from French television. The French reporter looked for French-speaking passengers to interview. *Pourquoi voyagez-vous à Washington pour les manifestations? Croyez-vous que le congrès passera la législation pour les droits civils?*

The bus hissed and pulled off the curb, south toward the Lincoln Tunnel and New Jersey Turnpike. Forty-nine people—twenty-seven of them white, twenty-two black—settled in for the ride.

Someone asked Frank Harman, a young white man, why he wanted to go to the march and why he wanted to volunteer for the Peace Corps in Nigeria.

"I want to go to help these people because they are human beings," he said.

Wayne Kinsler, a nineteen-year-old black arrested at a City Hall sit-in, responded: "If this thing comes to violence, yours will be the first throat we slit. We don't need your kind. Get out of our organization."

Frank Harman was confused. "What's he talking about? What did I *say?*"

"We don't need any white liberals to patronize us," Kinsler said.

"We don't trust you," someone said from a few seats away.

"We don't believe you are sincere."

"You'll have to prove yourself."

The Peace Corps volunteer held his ground: "I don't have to prove myself to anyone except myself."

The abuse continued. "We've been stabbed in the back too many times."

"The reason white girls come down to civil rights meetings is because they've heard of the black man's reputation of sex."

"The reason white guys come down is because they want to rebel against their parents."

But nobody challenged a slight white man named Jim Peck, also taking the trip on Bus 10.

Jim Peck, a child of privilege who went to Choate and Harvard, dropped out of college after one year to join the pacifist movement during World War II. Peck was one of the leaders of the 1961 Freedom Rides. From the beginning of the trip, Klansmen aboard the bus taunted the riders—

"Nigger!" "Nigger lover!" "Black bitch!" "Damn Communists!" The racists on the Greyhound bus punched and kicked two black students. When Peck and a college professor intervened, the Kluxers punched them in the face, kicked them in the guts, then stacked them like kindling on the back seats. "Ain't nobody but whites sitting up here," one said as he took a seat in the front of the bus. "And them nigger lovers . . . can just sit back there with their nigger friends." When the bus arrived in Birmingham, a mob awaited. Freedom Riders walked toward the station and into a gruesome beating. One group dragged Peck into a corridor and kicked him, hit him, and slammed him with pipes and oversized key rings, before finally leaving him unconscious. Hours later, Jim Peck woke up alone in the station.

So nobody challenged Jim Peck's credentials to be on Bus 10. Not a nineteen-year-old black kid who had just emerged from a sit-in in the comfort of a liberal mayor's office. Not anyone.

As the bus roared south on the New Jersey Turnpike, among a line of hundreds of yellow school buses and silver charter buses with banners reading FREEDOM NOW and MARCH ON WASHINGTON, the noise swelled. Finally, drowsy passengers told everyone to be quiet, get some sleep. After a few retorts, all was quiet.

Bus captains were instructed to teach their passengers about nonviolence, implore them to avoid any conflict at the march. Ignore it when someone shouts, "*Nigger!*" Ignore it when someone strikes you. Let the cops and the National Guard—and the Guardians, a corps of a thousand retired cops trained by Bayard Rustin himself—isolate the troublemakers. But no one on this New York bus needed, or wanted, any instruction on nonviolence.

Mao Tse-tung had endorsed the march the week before. Roy Wilkins, the head of the NAACP, quickly rebuked Mao. "We await the opportunity to send our felicitations to Chinese citizens," he cabled Mao, "gathered in a huge demonstration in your nation's capital to protest living conditions under your government." But the kids in the movement, having read Fanon and Camus and Mao's Little Red Book, were fascinated with the ideal of revolution. They romanticized Mao's revolution. And they dreamed of a massive movement of people of color—black, brown, yellow—across the globe.

"A Chinese-African alliance seems to me the most obvious thing in the world," announced Omar Ahmad, a budding scholar of world affairs.

"If we cannot solve this domestic race problem," George Johnson said with the authority of a bus captain, "we, as a nation, cannot survive."

E. F. Karman, a thirty-five-year-old Peace Corps volunteer, showed off.

"You'll have to define your terms," he said. "Do you mean that in the context of 1870 or 1910 or what?"

Wayne Kinsler ignored Karman: "Well, if it comes to that, I'll take Chinese imperialism before Western imperialism."

George Johnson talked about President Kennedy's civil rights bill, which would ban discrimination in public accommodations.

"I don't think the civil rights bill will get through," he said. "I have no faith in the white man. Even Kennedy and Kennedy, Inc., isn't doing this for humanitarian reasons but for political ones. CORE has been criticized for its new tactics of civil disobedience. Well, as far as I'm concerned, anything done to get our rights is okay. It's remarkable that the Negro has taken it this long."

"The white power structure," Omar Ahmad said, "has bred a new Negro. And he is angry and impatient. It's not just the Black Muslims. It's the man on the street. Come back to Harlem some night and listen to what's being said on the street corners. The cops go through and you can see fear on their faces. This isn't Birmingham. If anyone starts anything, we won't be passive."

Even on a bus of know-it-alls, fear lurked. When the bus pulled into a rest stop in New Castle, Delaware, on the infamous Route 40, Dorothy Jones fretted.

Jones was a fortysomething personnel worker for the City of New York.

"Lord, I hope we don't have any trouble down there," she said. "That would just maybe show that we're not ready for responsibilities."

The debate inside Bus 10 continued, as hundreds of buses bearing marchers streamed together, all rumbling and hissing and squeaking to Washington, D.C.

A TARMAC FULL OF C-82s—"flying boxcars"—awaited crews to fly them to the nation's capital to battle rioters. The U.S. Army's Eighty-second Airborne Division, based at Fort Bragg, the most integrated place in all of North Carolina, was ready for action.

The previous day, army officers instructed more than two thousand soldiers about their mission in Washington, D.C. They examined maps of the National Mall, running from the Washington Monument to the Lincoln Memorial. The soldiers loaded C-82s with guns and ammunition and food, and then began the military's age-old game of "hurry up and wait."

The planes were designed to carry tanks, but the army had no plans to bring tanks to the capital for a civil rights rally. The C-82s would get packed with cargo, with enough room to carry troops to Washington.

The army's plan, in the event of a civil disturbance, was to roar 320 miles north into Andrews Air Force Base in Maryland and then send soldiers to the Mall by helicopter to battle the violence. The soldiers would break the mob into wedges, isolate and subdue the most violent elements, and protect the peaceable protestors.

Already, Fort Bragg had sent thirty helicopters to Washington. The Pentagon also announced that three thousand army and marine troops from Fort Meade, Fort Belvoir, and the Quantico marine base in Virginia would be available to respond to riots—in addition to a thousand troops already in the Washington area.

To Major Daniel Boatwright, the plans did not make any sense. When the colonel gave orders the day before, he cracked jokes. "You folks be careful who you shoot," he said, "because my mother and grandmother are in the crowd."

In fact, much of Major Boatwright's extended family would attend the March on Washington. Members of the Abyssinian Baptist Church in Harlem, where pastor and congressman Adam Clayton Powell preached and presided over one of black America's greatest political machines, the Boatwrights were veterans of demonstrations, boycotts, and sit-ins. The family moved to New York from Georgia in 1943 because, in the words of Major Boatwright's sister Violet, "we were seeing so much abuse, we had to leave." They moved north the way immigrants come to America—one by one, with the early migrants establishing a base and later sending for the others.

When Major Boatwright's commanders focused on the potential for a riot by the marchers, he was incredulous.

"The people on the march, they weren't going to be troublemakers," he said. "It was the outsiders, the agitators, who caused problems. We were pointed in the wrong direction. We should have been worried about the people on the side, but we really didn't think about those. The intelligence was very poor. We were thinking of a mob or people massing and going into D.C. to start something."

The soldiers at Fort Bragg were part of Operation Steep Hill, a joint battle plan of the White House, the Justice Department, the Pentagon, and the Washington Metropolitan Police. As the flying boxcars sat on the warm tarmac, the other parts of the operation—National Guard, Washington police, volunteer Guardians—began to deploy on the old bog of the capital city.

———

GOING TO THE MARCH WAS A BIG DEAL to people throughout the South who had never ventured beyond the "Iron Curtain"—the isolated reaches of the old Confederacy, where blacks lived in shacks, often in captivity to sharecroppers, with limited access to the schools, jobs, credit, and cultural resources that other Americans took for granted.

"This is *major*," said Bernard Lafayette, one of King's closest advisers in Selma. "Some people have never gone to Washington before. We realized we could get some attention from federal government. This gave us hope that we could be heard. We also had faith in the masses of people in the United States that if we would dramatize our problem, they would insist that the government take action.

"The whole idea of Martin Luther King *calling for a march* and their being *able to respond!* Some people knew that if their bosses found out they went, they risked losing their jobs. But this was a way of taking a stand."

To get courage, blacks went to church. Churches were, in fact, the center of the civil rights struggle. Breaking away from white churches in the 1800s—creating black churches, with their own music and liturgy—took a spirit of defiance. Once they had their own churches, free from the demands and influences of whites, blacks could be themselves. In their everyday operations, churches taught management, rhetoric, organizing, recruiting, fund-raising, and music. When Southern states banned the NAACP, the black churches kept organizing—even with hundreds of church bombings and burnings. Churches made every stage of the modern movement possible, from Montgomery to Birmingham.

Two days before the march, activists gathered at Selma's Tabernacle Baptist Church, a brick structure with Doric columns, to rally support for the march and urge parishioners to register to vote, over and over again.

James Pritchett led the crowd in song. Then Father Charles McNeece of St. Elizabeth's Catholic Church spoke about the campaign for voter registration. Hundreds went to get registered, but only a few were allowed. Those who attempted to register risked losing homes and jobs, as well as vigilante attacks.

The crowd murmured as Pritchett exhorted, *Never mind that they turned you away. Never mind their abuse of literacy tests. Never mind the false statements about criminal records. Keep coming back until they let you sign up.*

Albert Turner, the president of the Perry County, Alabama, voters' league, spoke next.

"The first person to die for the country was a Negro," he said. "If we are not citizens and have no rights, why do we pay taxes? They put dogs on you and the next day you go downtown and spend one dollar to help the man who put the dogs on you."

Think of the power in this group! Five thousand Negroes in Perry County are over twenty-one years old! They could register to vote! Until Negroes have a say in who's mayor, chief of police, and governor, you won't have anything!

"If you are treated right one time, there is *no turning around.* If you ever find out how good things are out there, *look out,* things are going to be rough."

The crowd shouted its approval.

"It won't be long now! Things are beginning to roll!" the Reverend Turner cried. "If I get anything, it will have to come from *you.*"

Negroes need to stay together and be proud to be black, to be full citizens and to be able to vote.

"What will you give for freedom?"

"Blood!"

"They may take my life, my family, but they can't take what I know."

The Reverend L. L. Anderson took over the pulpit to talk about the March on Washington.

"When I get to Washington, D.C., I'm going to stick out my chest and represent the Negroes in Dallas County."

"Do you love God?"

"Yeah!"

"Do you love America?"

"Yeah. Yes!"

"Are you willing to die?"

"Yeah. I am!"

"The Negro and the white man are brothers. The white man can't do everything. We're going to help him."

THE ONLY PERSON ALLOWED A GOOD NIGHT'S SLEEP on the eve of the March on Washington was Asa Philip Randolph.

Randolph stood above all the factions and feuds of the movement. An unapologetic socialist, he still escaped attacks from mainstream politicians. Randolph's courtly ways, and his complete faith in friends and colleagues, set him apart.

From a young age, Randolph looked and sounded like a distinguished man. Tall and bronze-skinned, he was balding and graying, with just a small tuft of hair on his forehead, by his thirties. He wore the finest clothing he could buy—dark three-piece suits, usually wool, with dark homburg hats. His baritone spilled out in resonant British trills, which he had cultivated as a performer.

But Randolph's statesmanlike aura went beyond looks and sounds. To Randolph, anyone in the loose coalition of labor and civil rights—with one exception, the Communists—was basically good. Even in the midst of disagreements, Randolph remained serene. As a young man, Bayard Rustin joined the youth arm of the Communist Party for three years. Randolph told him he was making a mistake, that the Communists did not really care about blacks but wanted to exploit civil rights for their own purposes. When Rustin left the Communists, Randolph embraced him. Later, Rustin attacked Randolph for canceling protests in 1948. The two did not speak for three years, but when Rustin approached him again, Randolph said, "Bayard, where have you been? I haven't seen you around lately."

When rumors circulated about Martin Luther King's womanizing, Randolph told Bayard Rustin: "Bayard, you tell Dr. King, 'You know, they accused Jesus of having relationships with Mary and Martha. You must remember that.'"

Randolph also refused to believe the rumors about Rustin—even when those rumors were confirmed, again and again. "He thought people were lying that I was gay," Rustin laughed. "He could not *face* it. He was in that sense a mother. He never did anything wrong. The difference between Mr. Randolph [and others was that he] was incapable of looking at another woman."

Randolph did not care about foibles or gossip. He cared about alliances and action.

Randolph learned about race when he was nine. A gang of white hoodlums threatened to kidnap and lynch a black man in jail, and his father, the Reverend James Randolph, joined a black posse to surround the jail and fend off the mob. His mother sat by the window all night with a shotgun on her lap, prepared to use any means necessary to protect her home and children. That night, no lynching took place. But even though he was painfully conscious of race, Rev. Randolph did not see blackness as either superior or inferior. God and Christ, he told his son, have no color.

At the age of twenty-one, Phil Randolph moved to New York, where he found a calling onstage. He won starring roles in *Othello, Hamlet,* and *The Merchant of Venice.* Acting taught Randolph how to attract and hold the attention of a crowd. Randolph adopted his powerful voice in those roles, but left the theater when his father objected. He turned to politics, developing his own stump speeches about labor, race, Communism, war—every topic in the news those days. He became a soapbox newsreel.

Randolph gained a larger following as the founding editor of the *Messenger*, a journal of news and commentary on race, labor affairs, and politics. It was the only independent publication for blacks and rivaled the *Crisis*, the publication of the NAACP.

Randolph's first efforts to organize—first waiters on a steamship then porters at an electric utility—failed miserably. Then, for twelve years, starting in 1925, Randolph battled the Pullman Company for the right to organize its workers. At the time, Pullman employed more blacks than any other company. When Randolph started his drive, porters made $67.50 for three or four hundred hours of work a month, with no paid vacation or benefits. Porters also had to pay for their own uniforms and got wages deducted when anything got stolen on their watch.

The Pullman Company responded with righteous anger. One Pullman executive called Randolph a "wild-eyed uppity Negro hustler who never made up a Pullman berth in his life." Over the years, Pullman fired eight hundred porters in retaliation for working with Randolph. The company also started its own company union. Pullman goons beat organizers, mob-style, and threatened worse if they didn't stop organizing. When intimidation failed, the Pullman Company attempted to bribe Randolph, sending him a blank check in return for halting his organizing drives. Randolph made a photostat and sent the check back. Randolph could fight back when he needed to. He had his own heavy, a burly Republican machine politician from Chicago. When a minister had second thoughts about letting Randolph's union meet at his church, Milton Webster told him: "If we don't meet in this church this Sunday, you're going to find all those stones in the middle of the street."

The union finally won recognition in 1937. Within years, wages more than doubled and working conditions improved. Porters finally won pay for their five hours of work preparing berths for customers, which previously came before they punched in. Randolph was the greatest star in black America —called "St. Philip of the Pullman Porters" and the "Black Messiah."

With the Brotherhood of Sleeping Car Porters firmly established, Randolph decided to hold a massive march on Washington in 1941.

Randolph envisioned a column of ten thousand black men—or more, as many as one hundred thousand—marching down Pennsylvania Avenue, carrying banners (WINNING THE WAR FOR THE NEGRO IS WINNING THE

WAR FOR DEMOCRACY), shouting slogans ("We die for our country! Let us work in our country!"), and singing labor songs ("Which Side Are You On?"). President Franklin Roosevelt would look through the White House windows to see the greatest gathering of blacks ever—all protesting *his* administration. Plans called for long lines of marchers walking to the muffled drums of a funeral procession.

Randolph's 1941 march was the first major demonstration planned for the capital since the Bonus Army disaster, when 17,000 veterans of World War I, impoverished by the Great Depression, sought advance payments of their pensions in 1932. They had camped out on the Anacostia Flats for two weeks when President Herbert Hoover ordered the military to clear them away. Douglas MacArthur, the army chief of staff, led an attack on the veterans in their tents, driving them from the city.

Washington had been the scene of four other marches before the Bonus Army. In 1894, Jacob Coxey brought in an "army" of about four hundred demonstrators to demand a $500 million jobs program. Suffragists gathered in 1917 to demand the right to vote. In 1925, 25,000 hooded members of the Ku Klux Klan rallied to protest the influence of Catholics on American politics. Only once did the rallies work. Suffragist protests of Woodrow Wilson's inauguration brought police reprisals—arrests, jailings, hunger strikes, force-feeding—that rallied public support. Usually, though, rallies just created historical footnotes.

Blacks had never massed together for a major protest. Before Randolph, the civil rights movement remained torn between Booker T. Washington's conservative approach (creating a vibrant culture of education, business, and faith while accepting white dominance) and W. E. B. Du Bois's "talented tenth" (forging a black leadership class from the best and brightest of all blacks). Randolph believed in the power of the masses, which included not only educated and professional people but also factory workers, longshoremen, sharecroppers, porters, and the unemployed.

"Nobody expects ten thousand Negroes to get together and march anywhere for anything at any time," Randolph said. "In common parlance, they are supposed to be just scared and unorganizable. Is this true? I contend it is not."

To claim the citizenship that was their birthright, Randolph understood, blacks needed to get in the streets. To be free, Randolph said, blacks must overcome "the slave psychology and inferiority complex in Negroes which comes and is nourished with Negroes relying on white people for direction and support."

Randolph believed—more than anyone else in civil rights or labor—that a mass demonstration would change the psychology of both blacks and whites. Blacks would gain pride, a sense of brotherhood that comes from marching with countless others. Whites—and the political system they controlled—would feel apprehensive about disorder and bad public relations. Some might even be impressed enough to support civil rights.

A march down Pennsylvania Avenue would be Roosevelt's greatest humiliation as president—greater, even, than the Supreme Court's rejection of a dozen New Deal programs and Congress's rejection of his bid to pack the Supreme Court. This humiliation would be global. These black marchers would not just battle Roosevelt's administration; they would embarrass America before the whole world.

To organize marchers, Randolph deployed his Brotherhood of Sleeping Car Porters. Local union leaders and porters spread the word as railroad cars clacked from place to place. In the weeks before the march was to take place, Bayard Rustin hitchhiked up and down the East Coast to rally union locals, churches, and universities to march.

Franklin and Eleanor Roosevelt implored Randolph to call off the demonstration. A wartime march would be too disruptive. What signal would a hundred thousand angry Negroes send to the world when the United States was fighting abroad for democracy?

Roosevelt called Randolph and his supporters, like the NAACP's Walter White, to the White House.

"What do you want me to do?" the president asked.

"Mr. President," Randolph said, "we want you to do something that will enable Negro workers to get work in these plants."

"Why, I surely want them to work, too," Roosevelt said. "I'll call up the heads of the various defense plants and have them see to it that Negroes are given the same opportunity to work in defense plants as any other citizen in the country."

"We want you to do more than that. We want something concrete, something tangible, definite, positive, and affirmative."

"What do you mean?" Roosevelt asked.

"Mr. President, we want you to issue an executive order making it mandatory that Negroes be permitted to work in these plants."

The president wondered aloud whether Randolph could get a hundred thousand Negroes to march on Washington. Walter White said he could. Mayor Fiorello La Guardia, called to the White House to help the president confront Randolph, told Roosevelt to find a solution that would satisfy the organizer.

So on June 25, 1941, just days before the planned march on Washington,

Franklin Roosevelt signed Executive Order 8802, formally mandating equal opportunity in defense industries. And Randolph called off the march.

Randolph made a habit of planning and canceling marches—four in the 1940s—and his supporters attacked him for losing nerve. But to Randolph, the primary purpose of any political action was to achieve specific goals. To march after achieving those goals would risk his credibility in future bargaining. So the larger goal of demonstrations—changing the psychology of blacks and of the nation as a whole—had to wait for another day. By 1963, the civil rights movement convulsed the country. Never before had so many people taken to the streets or gotten arrested for any cause.

Now Randolph was ready for one last hurrah.

AFTER A TRIP OF MORE THAN 2,700 MILES—days of singing, playing the slots, eating at an Iowa commune, debating civil rights and nonviolence, speculating about the revolutions in Africa and legislation at home—the bus from San Francisco encountered turbulence in Hagerstown, Maryland.

One of the black riders got off to buy a pack of cigarettes. Locals pelted him with racist taunts. When he climbed back aboard the air-conditioned Scenicruiser, he faced a full-scale attack from other riders for venturing off the bus and risking racial conflict.

Hagerstown was one of those Northern towns, about an hour and a half north of Washington, that still embraced segregation.

A moviemaker named Haskell Wexler was on board. He brought along a sound person named Nel Cox, and they moved around the bus the whole trip, gathering dozens of hours of footage for a documentary. Now Wexler stood between two bickering freedom riders, near the front of the bus. He captured their argument on film.

Wexler and his assistants jokingly call the plump woman with porcelain skin, wearing a dress and bright lipstick, the Fat Arm. "That arm filled the whole frame," Wexler said, "so we called her the Fat Arm."

"That's not our job at the present time," she told the man who got off the bus. "And the thing of it is, we are on an *action* project, however *informal* it may be. And you *don't,* on action projects, decide to take off and do something *on your own.* If you had thought that it was a good idea to do something like this, *the thing to do* would be to have called a meeting and ask everyone to talk about it and make a decision about it. And then if you had *still wanted* to do it on your own, then it would be strictly on your own *without* any identification . . ."

Heads moved back and forth as if watching a tennis match.

Several seats behind the argument, the Jazzman sat back. "I don't want anything to do with Hagerstown," said John Handy, a thirty-year-old saxophonist who traveled all over playing in the same clubs as Louis Armstrong and Charles Mingus and Dizzy Gillespie. But he grew up under segregation and had no desire to experience blatant discrimination. "That's ugly," he said. "I'm from Dallas, so I know what *that's* like."

After ten minutes spent debating the propriety of buying cigarettes as an *action,* everyone else on the bus cried for mercy. *Oh, forget it! Let's just drop it!*

The bus from San Francisco, organized by CORE, had left California on the previous Saturday morning. People gathered in the basement of the Third Baptist Church and listened to instructions. A local civil rights lawyer named Fredericka Kunstler welcomed the marchers and warned them to obey their bus captain. She emphasized the movement's strategy of nonviolence. No one knows what's going to happen at the march, she said. Whatever happens, *don't fight.*

The bus traveled more than 2,700 miles over four days, through towns like Reno, Salt Lake City, Rock Springs, Cheyenne, North Flats, Omaha, Davenport, Chicago, Pittsburgh, and Hagerstown. Some of the freedom riders were active in the local CORE chapter. Most were not.

The trip started with friendly chatter.

"You know," a young woman said, chuckling, "a friend of mine said that when you get back, when someone offers you a bus ride to heaven you won't want to take the trip."

"I think I'm *acutely* aware," the Fat Arm said, "of the fact that this thing has been going on. I wanted to get into the full swing of it and do something about it and so I'm making this bit of a contribution."

A young Chinese man named Franklin Chung talked about the growing tensions between Asians and blacks. The problem started when the YMCA in Chinatown sponsored a basketball team and recruited blacks to play. Quite simply, the YMCA team wanted ringers.

"And the thing is, they got along pretty good. They were taking them to the clubs, taking them out to supper, and late at night they're walking with them in Chinatown and they're the closest of friends. Then pretty soon, the girls started admiring them because they're physically . . . *above* the Chinese, you know?

"When this happened, I heard from a friend of mine, you know, 'The word is *out,* the word is *out,* we don't want any more colored boys in, you know?' And lo and behold you don't find any colored boys in Chinatown anymore."

He laughed.

Across the aisle, a middle-aged black woman with salt-and-pepper hair—the Realist—debated the philosophy of nonviolence with the Fat Arm. The Realist spoke in a soft New York accent.

"Suppose you are in a *situation*," the Realist asked, "where someone's going to attack your husband, maybe to take his money, maybe to . . . attack *you*.

"These kinds of situations *occur*. Would you stand by and let someone attack your husband or would you pick up the nearest stick to hand and bang the other guy over the arm, over the head, *anything* to knock him out of commission so he does not destroy your husband?"

The Fat Arm leaned on the seat in front of the Realist.

"I would *hope*," she said, "that my actions *would* be nonviolent ones." She spoke in an earnest whine. "I would hope that—possibly I might try to restrain a person because I'm not always certain that I don't—"

The Realist tilted her head, sat still. She wagged her finger and looked up. "I'm not saying *kill* him," she said. "I'm saying knock him out of commission so he can't kill or hurt your husband."

The Fat Arm was stuck.

"I'm *not* certain that I might *not* try something like that. I'm *not* certain that I *don't* approve of that sort of action, a restraining action. There are some pacifists who do, there are some pacifists who don't." She paused, looking for the right balance of resolve and modesty. "But I would *sincerely* hope that I would *not* pick up the nearest stick handy."

The Realist looked up again, her eyebrows raised, to push the matter.

"Well what *would* you do?"

That debate ended with that rhetorical question. Soon, a young woman approached Haskell Wexler, the documentary filmmaker.

"There's someone in the back you *must* talk to," she said. "An old man who's *really* lived."

Wexler turned his camera on Joseph Freeman.

Freeman was a retired janitor and carpenter who lived in a veterans' home north of San Francisco. Mostly bald, Freeman had a soft, almost perfectly oval face. In his late sixties, he had almost no wrinkles. He wore a white collar shirt and puffed on a pipe as he looked out the window. He spoke in a low, gravelly voice.

"When was the last time you were in Washington?" the young woman with horn-rimmed glasses asked.

"*Ohhhh*," he rumbled, "1919."

On July 21, 1919. He was working as a packer, after getting home from service in World War I. Near Centre Market, on Seventh and Pennsylvania Avenue, soldiers and sailors attacked blacks. They called for revenge for attacks on white women in the previous month. The riot involved thousands of soldiers and other angry whites. They pulled a black man off a streetcar on G Street and beat him. They attacked other blacks near the National Park, where the Washington Senators played. When they spotted a black person they called out, "There he goes!" Then the mob chased the black man and beat him.

"I was coming from home one evening and I didn't know anything about it and several men jumped me and attempted to drag me up in an alley and said they were going to kill me," he said. "I got away from them. And I outran them, I guess."

He paused. "So this time I won't be afraid, as I was then, 'cause I know there will be over one hundred thousand people listening."

After you outran the mob, what happened?

"I left that same day. I didn't know where I was going. I was trying to get away from those people that were trying to kill me. They ran me down to the railroad yard and I got on a freight train. I didn't have anything but the clothes on my back. And I stayed on the freight train. And it was going west and so I eventually hoboed my way all the way to California."

He looked into the distance. "Lucky the freight was going *west*." Another pause: "And not *south*." He chuckled.

The Old Man said he was going to the March on Washington because he hadn't contributed anything to the movement.

The bus stopped at a small town in Wyoming. Joe Freeman stood on the sidewalk and puffed his pipe and waited for the other marchers to finish eating at a diner. He talked about his service in two world wars.

"In the First World War, I taught," he said. "We had quite a number of men who were illiterate and semiliterate, and I taught the three Rs. The second war, I taught industrial math and bridge building and carpentry."

Back on the bus, he continued his story. He talked about facing punishment if he ever complained about discrimination. Join the NAACP, you're a *subversive*. Challenge a firing, you're a certifiable subversive. Try to appeal, and that proves the point.

"We brought these things as far as we could—we had hearings before the civil service commission and various committees that they sent out from Washington. But the point is that you were judged guilty and you had to prove your innocence. . . . You were appealing Caesar unto Caesar, appealing to the very people who had already found you guilty. So you can see what kind of a chance you had."

He never held any job longer than two years. Last fired, first fired. Anytime his past activity came up—challenging discrimination on the job, belonging to the NAACP, *subversive activity*—he was let go.

"Every time I'd get a job I was a marked man. I'd get a job as a dishwasher. The FBI, they kept a close check on everybody that was fired from a civil service position. And they'd go to your boss and say, 'Listen, this man is supposed to be subversive.' Of course, your boss, he didn't know what the hell subversive meant. He said, 'Well, I can't have you here, you're in trouble with the FBI. It isn't good for my business.' Said, 'I'm sorry but you'll have to get you another job.'

"So that's the way it was."

When Haskell Wexler decided to shoot a documentary, he had no idea what he would see. On the bus, Wexler could not always hear what his subject was saying. "The bus makes noise, and I don't like to be physically close to the person. I don't like to point the camera close to people's faces. A lot of times I don't really hear. They talk to the sound person, not the camera." Wexler would not know what sounds and images he had captured until he got back to his studio in California. Then he would cut and arrange his film until he created something wholly new.

A pioneer of cinema verité, Wexler rejected any idea of absolute truth. "You're not recording reality," he says. "You're recording stuff that you can use to make a statement."

"WHAT'S GONNA HAPPEN WHEN BIG BUBBA gets you?"

Bill Perry and his wife, Peggy, and their friend Reggie Gammon were driving down Route 40 in Maryland, after a night of drinking wine and debating whether to go to the March on Washington, when the gallows humor began.

Bill Perry was a black poet who worked as a trade magazine editor to pay bills. Peggy, his white wife, was involved in the NAACP and knew everyone in the New York civil rights scene. Reggie Gammon was a black painter who worked for an ad agency.

The three drove in Bill's 1963 black Volkswagen bug—a brand-new car, which even had a *gas gauge*. As they traveled down the New Jersey Turnpike, they saw buses and cars merging together, on the way to Washington. The sight of all those other marchers—waving, smiling, honking—cheered them. But they still feared the worst.

At the Perrys' Second Avenue apartment in Greenwich Village, the three had debated until three in the morning over whether to go to the March.

Bill feared venturing into white Washington. The word on the street, in the Village anyway, was that white cops were going to beat on black protesters. It happened everywhere else, why not Washington? The last time he spent any time in Washington—when he worked in the Department of the Navy, from 1947 to 1950—the city was as racist as any in the South. "It was very, very, very segregated, not the kind of place you pop in on a train," he said. Until recently, one hotel had borne the sign "No Niggers or Dogs."

Newspapers speculated wildly about the possibility of violence at the march. A Bill Mauldin cartoon showed long lines of blacks marching toward a powder keg labeled "Washington, D.C." If the march turned into a melee, how would the police respond? Would the military get called in? Would white vigilantes descend on the marchers? Would the marchers fight back?

Bill feared even venturing out of Greenwich Village. As half of an interracial couple, he found the antagonism in Harlem as bad as anything they saw in white neighborhoods. Greenwich Village was more open, but Fourteenth Street was a kind of DMZ. Going north of Fourteenth Street was inviting trouble. When Bill and Peggy went to Harlem to see friends, they went by car to avoid the glares along the way.

The trio also feared traveling along Route 40, the only way to get through Maryland. Everyone knew Route 40 was full of Mrs. Murphys—those small-time businesses, lunch counters and gas stations, where the people snarled at blacks passing through. They'd sell you food, but you had to take it out.

When African diplomats complained that Washington restaurants wouldn't serve them, the Kennedy State Department pressured the restaurants to serve Africans. Later, when CORE activists wore African dress for a "freedom motorcade," many restaurants moved to desegregate. But not all. Somehow it was okay to refuse service to American blacks as long as African diplomats got served. Which just created confusion. When the ambassador from Chad was refused service and assaulted, the restaurant owner said, "He looked just like an ordinary Nigra to me." When the State Department's chief protocol officer told President Kennedy about conditions on Route 40, Kennedy interrupted. "Can't you tell these African ambassadors not to drive on Route 40? It's a hell of a road. I used to drive it years ago. But why would anyone want to drive it today when you can fly?"

After hours of debate, Peggy announced that the three of them had to go. Bill said he'd go if Reggie agreed. They napped for a couple of hours, so they could start in daylight. At five thirty they got in the VW Bug and drove south.

Until the middle of August, organizers discouraged driving to the march.

But buses were in short supply. In Northern cities like New York and Chicago, march organizers booked all the Greyhound and Trailways buses, as well as the fleets of schools and churches. In other cities, many bus companies refused to rent buses to marchers.

Bill grew up in New Rochelle—the same suburb, in leafy Westchester County, where TV's Rob and Laura Petrie lived—so he didn't have to deal with racial slurs and colored water fountains. He went to integrated schools and even integrated dances. His dad, the first black postal worker in town, built a protective shell around the family.

His first experience with legal racism came when he want to St. Paul's, a prep school in Lawrenceville, Virginia—with black seating in theater balconies, segregated bus stations. Fear started to permeate his life. "Black folks disappeared in the South, and if you disappeared, no one would find you," he told his friends. "So you travel in groups."

Once the trio got to Washington, they asked people on the side of the road where to go. The Washingtonians pointed them to Connecticut Avenue, where they met up with a New York delegation at a church. They knew a few people. For the first time since they decided to go, fear faded. The churchyard was filled with people, including some interracial couples. They recognized faces, from picketing Woolworth and from the NAACP and church meetings.

A teenager led the group down Connecticut Avenue, for the two-mile walk to the Washington Monument.

"Look *straight ahead*," he said.

No one knew whether vigilantes or cops would attack the marchers. So they walked scared and determined.

"It was a group mentality," Bill said. "If we stayed together, didn't allow anyone to separate us and stayed focused, one step at a time, if we had to go through a gauntlet we could get to the Washington Monument and be safe."

When Bill Perry told his mother he planned to march, she shook her head. She and her friends considered the whole idea crazy. Perry was thinking of those older people, shaking their heads, when he saw a woman standing by the side of the road.

Dressed all in black, with high-topped shoes, the woman looked directly into his eyes and nodded. The message was, *Y'all are doing the right thing.*

Bill told Reggie and Peggy about it. "I *know* that's what she was saying to me."

Everything was quiet, on that road to the march. Peggy and Reggie and Bill talked, but quietly. They heard the soft padding of feet underneath, but not much else. *Pad, pad, pad.* They looked down the road as it bent, after Dupont Circle, and saw a long river of people. Some people cried, softly.

Somehow it seemed like a strange dream, eerie because it wasn't a nightmare. A surge of excitement marched along with the fear.

This is not the Washington I know. What's going to happen? Is someone going to start something? Look ahead. Look straight ahead. Keep going. Keep going.

ALL NIGHT, PROTESTERS STAGED a vigil outside the Justice Department. They held candles and chanted and raised signs: "We Demand an Honest Investigation" and "Even the Federal Government is a White Man."

Jesse Mae Christian—part of a group of twenty protesters arriving on Tuesday—sat on the grass in front of the Justice Department. "This is just like my house," she said. "People are so nice." She and others from Albany sat outside all night to protest a federal indictment against their leaders for picketing a grocery store in the southwest Georgia town. And in the morning, they formed a tight circle and walked. They sang:

> *Paul and Silas were bound in jail,*
> *had no money to get their bail,*
> *keep your eyes on the prize. Hold on!*

An old black man sat on a park bench nearby: "They say the March on Washington is silly. It's no sillier than Hiroshima."

The Justice Department operated in a five-story Classical Revival building with a limestone facade and a million square feet of space inside. An imposing structure fronted by Greek columns—located between the White House and Capitol Hill—the building was designed to provoke awe and trembling. But the demonstrators would have none of that.

Demonstrators distributed a fact sheet listing "hundreds, if not thousands, of extreme violations of federal laws [that were] being perpetrated against Negro citizens residing in the southern states."

A few hecklers accosted the demonstrators. James Pruitt, who had just done hard time in Mississippi for his activism, ignored them. "I was told not to fight back against that kind," he said. "We'll just notify the nearest policemen that these guys are looking for a fight."

Sheila Michaels, a staffer for SNCC in Atlanta, was walking near the Justice Department, saw the pickets, and decided to join. To her, "Washington was a mausoleum." The demonstration at Justice offered some excitement.

She saw Bob Moses, the quiet but charismatic leader of SNCC's effort in Mississippi, wearing overalls and a T-shirt, carrying a sign reading: "Without Justice, What Is Government? Robber Band Enlarged." The DOJ protesters needed more bodies, so she stayed around for a while.

Government workers stayed away and police cordoned off the streets. She approached the Department of Justice.

The year before, she was part of a group that Stokely Carmichael organized to sit in at Robert Kennedy's office. The group protested the jailing of three students on criminal anarchy charges in Louisiana. The students talked with Burke Marshall, Kennedy's top civil rights adviser, for an hour, then started the sit-in. Very civilized.

The organizers of the March on Washington agreed that the march would not include a direct challenge to the White House or Congress. There would be no marches along Pennsylvania Avenue. There would be no effort to force an audience with Strom Thurmond or James Eastland or other segregationists. Everyone would be polite.

But the young people gathered outside the Justice Department had to show their outrage at recent events in Georgia.

Just weeks before, the Justice Department had indicted nine protesters in Albany for perjury. The case began when protesters picketed segregated businesses downtown, including a grocery store owned by a man named Carl Smith. Smith had served on a jury that acquitted a white man accused of shooting a black youth. Justice gathered thirty thousand pages of evidence and convened a grand jury to prosecute the nine protesters for tampering with a jury. When the grand jury did not indict, the Justice Department charged the defendants with perjury for denying they remembered events associated with the protest.

In Americus, Georgia, four men faced the possibility of execution for their part in protesting segregation and canvassing for voter registration. Violence began when more than one hundred young people were arrested for picketing and sitting in at a segregated movie theater.

The Americus troubles began on August 8, when two hundred young people marched from Friendship Baptist Church protesting the exclusion of blacks from a public pool. Police confronted them. The cops fired fifteen warning shots. Then, when the protesters sat down on the road, police dispersed the crowd with clubs and a cattle prod. At this point, some protesters fought back with bottles and rocks. In the melee, a state trooper broke one protester's leg with a baseball bat and a local cop shot and killed a black walking through a white neighborhood. Police arrested seventy-seven protesters. Twenty-four protesters and seven police were treated for injuries.

The Sumter County prosecutor, which had jurisdiction in Americus, charged four of the protesters with "seditious conspiracy" under the 1871 Anti-Treason Act.

A few times that summer, protesters gathered at the Justice Department to rally against the Kennedy administration's accommodating stance toward old Southern pols, the appointment of avowed racists as judges, and the inaction of the FBI.

Even while protesting, Bob Moses quietly worked with the Justice Department.

"We weren't *partners,*" Moses said. "They weren't sharing with us their strategy, and we weren't planning our strategies around our knowledge of what they were doing. But we were running on parallel tracks, trying to approach the same problem from the bottom as opposed to the top. Part of the work with the Justice Department was really understanding how the government worked and taking advantage of it."

Talks with Justice officials produced an important literacy program, then loosed money from foundations for field organizers. As they worked with the government, the activists also protested. "There were lawyers who wanted to sue, and I signed my name to some of those suits. That gets publicity. The other kind of work doesn't. I just came to see it as part of the turf, as part of what's involved. So I picketed and afterwards I went in and talked with Burke."

These behind-the-scenes relationships gave the movement resources and protection during its most dangerous moments. When mobs attacked protesters and sheriffs looked on with bemusement, the activists could call the Justice Department. "When I put a call in, it immediately changes your status," Moses said. "It's a different story. Whatever [the segregationists] do, they can't do it in isolat[ion]. Someone is going to know, and that makes a difference.

"The movement was really a coalition of the bottom and the top. In order for the top to listen—the executive or the judiciary or the Congress—you needed the pressure from the bottom."

So, earnestly, these representatives of the bottom assailed the top. And they meant it. But they would also combine forces with the top. The middle —the masses of indifferent politicians, businesses, and journalists—was the real target.

———

JUST AFTER TWO O'CLOCK ON THE MORNING of the March on Washington, Bayard Rustin called John Lewis.

"We've got a problem," he said. "The Catholic Church is upset—and so is the administration."

The speech John Lewis planned to deliver—the speech he had been practicing for days—was "inflammatory." Rustin told Lewis that there was no reason to worry, but they had to revise the speech right away.

John Lewis had been the chairman of the Student Nonviolent Coordinating Committee for just a few months. SNCC was the most radical of all the civil rights groups—a radicalism forged by fighting the toughest racists in the Deep South. SNCC and the Congress of Racial Equality divided up the South and organized in places where blacks had never been organized before—where blacks had little or no contact with the outside world. People attempting to vote came home to find out they were fired from jobs and kicked out of their homes.

Dark, stocky, intense, straightlaced, Lewis deviated from SNCC's growing hedonism. People like Stokely Carmichael and Jim Forman were not only committed to the movement, but also part of an emerging youth movement. They made wild claims, laughed all night, drank, courted the media, slept around (black and white together), and turned movement politics into a Dionysian crusade. Close quarters and intense challenges drove activists into each other's arms. White shirts and ties, print dresses, and short, straightened hair were giving way to jeans and colors and Afros. But Lewis held to the old, more earnest image.

Lewis had been involved in the movement since he was a teenager. He helped organize the Nashville sit-ins, he went on the Freedom Rides, and he traveled all over the South organizing. He was arrested two dozen times. The pressure almost broke him. In August 1962, he pleaded with Jim Forman to reduce his role. "For the last few months I have been under a great deal of mental stress, sometimes physically exhausted," he told Forman in a letter. "The spirit is willing, but the body is weak."

But now, he was the organization's leader.

Patrick O'Boyle, the archbishop of Washington, had agreed to deliver the invocation at the beginning of the March on Washington's afternoon program. But O'Boyle, who had a close relationship with the Kennedy administration, objected to several lines of Lewis's speech.

O'Boyle did not like the first sentence of the second paragraph: "In good conscience we cannot support the administration's civil rights bill, for it is too little and too late." He also didn't like the line "for the first time . . . the revolution is at hand." And he did not like a section about civil rights protesters staging their own version of Sherman's March to the Sea.

But the line that most infuriated O'Boyle was a reference to patience. "To those who have said, 'Be patient and wait,' we must say that 'patience' is a dirty and nasty word," Lewis's text said. "We cannot be patient, we do not want to be free gradually. We want our freedom, and we want it *now*."

Lewis held firm, telling Rustin he would deliver the speech as written or not at all. His allies were more blunt. "Over our dead bodies," Stokely Carmichael said.

The problem started hours before, when Courtland Cox, a march staffer on loan from SNCC, saw a table in the lobby of the Statler Hilton with the texts of other speeches to be given at the march. "Why isn't John's speech there?" he asked aloud. Then, without talking to anyone, he got a copy and took it to be duplicated. He came back a half hour later with copies of John Lewis's speech—which was not really John Lewis's speech, but a manifesto of the Student Nonviolent Coordinating Committee that Lewis would deliver on behalf of the group. Cox put the Lewis speech on the table and walked away.

"Now we'll get the attention we deserve," Cox said.

The copies disappeared in minutes. One copy fell into the hands of O'Boyle. One fell into the hands of Burke Marshall, an assistant to Attorney General Robert Kennedy.

Walter Reuther, destined to play the "bad cop" in the controversy, discovered a copy of the speech when he left the Big Ten's last planning meeting before the march. Reuther's assistant, Jack Conway, saw a piece of paper on the floor. It was Lewis's speech. When Conway and Reuther read it, they were shocked by the language and immediately called Roy Wilkins, who said he too had seen a copy and was disturbed. Then Reuther took a copy to Martin Luther King.

"Well, John Lewis can't make that speech," King said. "This is completely contrary to everything we are doing."

To other march leaders, the biggest problem was Lewis's apparent opposition to Kennedy's civil rights bill. The major objective of the march, after all, had become to pressure Congress to pass the bill. The Big Ten, in fact, had spent hours discussing what to do in the event of a Senate filibuster—hoping to schedule the march to coincide with a filibuster. SNCC and CORE had even pushed for demonstrations on Capitol Hill to pressure Congress to pass the bill.

O'Boyle was in his room at the Mayflower Hotel, with thirteen other clerics, writing a statement announcing their withdrawal from the March on Washington. Reuther called O'Boyle.

"I hear you are preparing a statement," Reuther said.

"I sure am," O'Boyle said. "And in about ten minutes I will be finished and we are going to give it out to the press and the Catholics are going to be pulled out of this March because we can't have any part of a demonstration in which one of the speakers advocates open revolution."

Reuther convinced O'Boyle to wait. He would convene a group of march leaders and persuade John Lewis to cut the offensive language.

After a phone call woke him at around two o'clock, Bayard Rustin got involved. He left a note and then called Lewis in his room. Rustin told him about the archbishop's anger—especially over Lewis's rejection of more patience.

"This is offensive to the Catholic Church," Rustin said.

"Why?" Lewis asked, perplexed that such an idea would become a point of contention.

"*Payyyyy-tience*," Rustin said. "Catholics believe in the word *patience*."

At first, Lewis agreed to rewrite that passage. But when he met Rustin and others later that night, Lewis stood firm. Lewis's SNCC colleagues—Jim Forman, Stokely Carmichael, Courtland Cox—aggressively rejected any changes.

By threatening to pull Catholics out of the march over the Lewis speech, O'Boyle became an instant enemy of the young people in SNCC. A plump and balding old man, with a reputation as an authoritarian, he was cloistered in the world of celibacy and seminaries. He had never exposed himself to violence the way the protesters did in Albany and Savannah and Jackson and Mobile.

But O'Boyle had earned some civil rights credentials of his own. He desegregated the Catholic schools of Washington before *Brown v. Board of Education*. Under his direction, the Catholics had arranged for the feeding and housing of anyone who had to sleep over following the March on Washington. On his own terms, O'Boyle was a friend of the movement.

Mathew Ahmann, designated to speak for the Catholics at the march, was sympathetic to John Lewis. He went to O'Boyle and pleaded to give Lewis the right to express himself his own way.

"There was no agreement over what each of the [leaders of the march] can say," he told O'Boyle. "In fact I haven't seen anyone else's speech, and I don't think anyone else has seen mine. I don't think it can be changed." Boycotting the march over a few words, Ahmann argued, would make the Catholics look bad.

O'Boyle held his position. And he had the backing of President Kennedy's Irish mafia.

Ahmann, aware that he was angering Church colleagues, grew angry himself. *Who do these guys think they are? They wouldn't even agree to sponsor the march, and now they're telling someone from another organization what he can and cannot say?*

Lewis's speech was the product of many minds at SNCC. Lewis wrote the first version by himself. It was a sermon by a small-town Negro preacher, full of the overwrought metaphors of the pulpit: "our cup of bitterness runneth over"—that kind of rhetoric. Down in SNCC's Atlanta office, Sheila Michaels read the draft and shook her head. She rewrote the whole thing, making it less florid.

A few days before the march, John Lewis came to the March on Washington headquarters in Harlem. Excited about his latest draft, he showed it to Rachelle Horowitz, who loved it. He showed it to Bayard Rustin, who loved it. "Why not have Tom help make short, snappy, uncomplicated sentences?" Rustin said.

Lewis went to Tom Kahn, who liked it . . . *a lot* . . . but . . .

One of the movement's wordsmiths, Kahn could transform the blandest memo or press release. He had a knack for finding just the right phrase. He strived not just to inform, but provoke.

So he added this passage: "We will march through the South, through the heart of Dixie, the way Sherman did. We shall pursue our own 'scorched earth' policy and burn Jim Crow to the ground—nonviolently. We shall fragment the South into a thousand pieces and put them back together in the image of democracy."

No image angers the Old South more than that of William Tecumseh Sherman, the Civil War general who marched three hundred miles from Atlanta to the sea, burning every town along the way, destroying railroads and factories and silos, not just to destroy the Confederacy's economy, but also to its spirit and soul. The language scared the Catholics and the White House. They thought it was an incitement to riot.

But Lewis also emphasized nonviolence and love and reconciliation in his speech. "We must work for the community, love, peace, and true brotherhood," he said. In fact, no one in the movement spoke more earnestly about forgiveness. "He was so thoroughly Christian, and so fundamentalist Christian," said an old friend and mentor, a Baptist preacher named Will Campbell. "He would say, 'I didn't forgive you, Jesus forgave you long before we ever met.'"

As the controversy swirled, Rustin confronted Kahn. "How could you do this?" he asked. "Do you know what Sherman *did?*" He set Kahn straight about the Big Ten's rules. "There was an early agreement . . . that if the objective was to get the bill passed, that people could be critical of the bill and say they wanted additional things in it, but nobody was free to attack the bill as being useless." The attack on Congress also went too far. "You can't invite people to dinner and then insult them," Rustin said.

But nothing got settled that night. The crisis would continue into the afternoon.

THE JOHN LEWIS CRISIS ROBBED BAYARD RUSTIN of rest at exactly the moment he needed it most.

Rustin's face was puffy and lined. For weeks Rustin had slept little. He worked until the early hours of the morning, every day. He smoked too much, drank too much, and had to maintain his equanimity in the midst of a crossfire of demands and criticisms by segregationists, white moderates, mainstream civil rights leaders, and the growing ranks of young black radicals. And he looked pale and sallow.

Rustin's friends worried about his judgment in the days before the March on Washington. Some fretted about his decision to give $20,000 in march funds to a Socialist Party organization. Revelations of the gift could give fodder to critics who called the civil rights movement a pinko plot. Others worried about Rustin's drinking and carousing. When a Washington-based labor organizer named Ted Brown told King he hoped that Rustin "don't take a drink before the march," King agreed, chortling, "and grab one little brother, because he will grab one when he has a drink."

After years of controversy, Bayard Taylor Rustin lived for the day when he would coordinate a mass demonstration on the scale of the March on Washington. Since his college days, three decades before, Rustin had worked behind the scenes to organize people for civil rights, labor, and peace. Because of his three-strike background—former Communist, gay, and draft dodger—he could not play a public role in the movement.

Years before, W. E. B. Du Bois talked about the "twoness" of blacks in America: "One ever feels his twoness—an American, a Negro; two souls, two thoughts, two unreconciled strivings; two warring ideals in one dark body, whose dogged strength alone keeps it from being torn asunder." But if black America struggled with twoness, Rustin struggled with threeness, or fourness, or even moreness.

Bayard Rustin's manyness was palpable. Rustin could be formal and elegant, but he could also be rough, with his wrinkled linen suits and worn ties. He was tall and wiry—six-one, 190 pounds—but moved like an athlete. Brown-skinned with a Clark Gable mustache—and a shock of an Afro that reached upwards into a jagged flattop—Rustin was a kinetic force, always searching and moving. He lived on the road, but his apartment was rich and comfortable, filled with art from all over the world—centuries-old statues and paintings of Christ, Civil War–era lithographs and engravings, a Jacobean carved bed from the 1600s, Turkish rugs, and even columns from the old Penn Station. He could be formal, with an affected British accent, or he could talk like a street agitator.

Rustin came from West Chester, Pennsylvania, a Quaker town twenty-five miles southwest of Philadelphia. The son of a single mother, he did not know until he was eleven who was who in his own family. At that point, he learned that the couple he considered his parents, Janifer and Julia, were really *his mother's* parents; that the woman he considered his sister, Florence, was really his mother; and that his other "sisters" and "brothers" were really aunts and uncles.

Growing up in a Quaker community, Rustin embraced nonviolence, finding pacifism a compelling, consistent worldview: aggression begets aggression, love begets love, peace begets peace. Pacifism was close to absolute for Rustin. Morally, he did not believe that aggression and violence could build or repair anything. Violence spun out of control, breaking bodies and property and breeding resentment. But nonviolence could overcome even the most relentless violence.

"My activism did not spring from my being black. Rather, it is rooted fundamentally in my Quaker upbringing," Rustin said. "Those values were based on the concept of a single human family and the belief that all members of that family are equal. The racial injustice that was present in this country during my youth was a challenge to my belief in the oneness of the human family. It demanded my involvement in the struggle to achieve interracial democracy, but it is very likely that I would have been involved had I been a white person with the same philosophy." Rustin's grandmother gave him Quaker values, but he attended the African Methodist Episcopal church of his grandfather. That placed Rustin deep in the tradition of gospel music and emotional preaching.

The ever-dramatic Rustin adopted a British accent in high school, both to overcome stuttering and assert his own independence. By taking on a different persona, he cloaked his nervousness. The accent gave him courage —and authority. He used the accent to confront racist bullies. When other blacks were refused service on Route 40, the corridor in Delaware and Maryland notorious for its Jim Crow ways, Rustin stood over his tormenters and demanded service. Rustin also used this persona at protests. At one demonstration in Brooklyn, Rachelle Horowitz was taken away in handcuffs. Rustin turned toward the police. "*Officer,*" he said in his most dramatic British accent, "take those *handcuffs* off her *immediately!*" It worked. The cuffs came off.

"Very disarming," Horowitz said. "It's his all-handy weapon. Assert your authority. But he also talks like anybody—'Hi, baby, what you doing?'"

A natural performer—on the tennis court, football field, stage, concert hall—Rustin once sang with Josh White and Leadbelly. He performed on White's album *Chain Gang Songs*. He traveled tens of thousands of miles a year, speaking and organizing. He organized and agitated wherever he was—the local theater, school, or football field, churches, union halls, even jails.

Rustin first got involved in labor organizing in 1933. Expelled from both Wilberforce College and Cheyney, he moved to Harlem to live with his sister/aunt Bessie. Sitting at a park on 150th Street one day, he heard goons talking about a strike at Horn & Hardart, a chain of coin-operated self-service restaurants immortalized in Edward Hopper's painting *Automat*. They boasted about disrupting a labor picket line by throwing bricks at the restaurant and blaming the picketers. Rustin decided to join the picket line. Sure enough, someone threw a brick at the restaurant, and the police came and beat the demonstrators with clubs and carried them away to jail.

After spending a month volunteering for the 1941 March on Washington, Rustin worked full time for the Fellowship of Reconciliation (FOR), a global organization dedicated to pacifism and disarmament.

In 1942, Rustin joined James Farmer, George Houser, and Bernice Fisher in creating the Congress of Racial Equality. Like the NAACP, CORE was an integrated group dedicated to promoting civil rights. Unlike the NAACP, CORE was committed to nonviolent direct action. The organization would *confront* racism, physically—involving ordinary people in their own liberation. "Our power is in our ability to make things unworkable," he said. "The only weapon we have is our bodies and we need to tuck them in places so wheels don't turn."

CORE's boldest early experiment, the Journey of Reconciliation of 1947, tested recent court decisions that struck down segregation of all forms of interstate travel. Eight black men and eight white men—including Rustin—traveled together on buses through Virginia, North Carolina, Kentucky, and

Tennessee. The Freedom Riders were jailed several times. Rustin was sentenced to twenty-two days on a chain gang for violating North Carolina's Jim Crow laws.

As part of his creed of nonviolence, Rustin openly accepted physical attacks by others, believing his pacifism could change their hearts and minds. Serving time for refusing service in World War II, Rustin became a jailhouse activist, forcing racial integration of cells. But one white prisoner resented mixing with blacks. He attacked Rustin with a club, splintering the weapon, until he exhausted himself and could attack no more. Rustin took the blows with equanimity, protecting himself by crouching in a fetal position. A fellow prisoner later recalled: "Completely defeated and unnerved by the display of nonviolence, [Rustin's attacker] began shaking all over, and sat down."

Over the next decade Rustin became one of the most prominent pacifists in America. He was the "American Gandhi" in training, admired equally for his intellect and courage.

Then he crashed. In January of 1953, after a speaking engagement, Pasadena police arrested Rustin on a morals charge. Rustin never hid his homosexuality—his flamboyant escapades were well-known in the movement—but he was now publicly humiliated. A. J. Muste, his mentor at FOR, fired him. For six months, he wrestled with his conscience, concluding that excessive pride had led to his humiliation. He vowed to "sublimate" his urges.

The War Resisters League, seeing an opportunity to work with the most gifted pacifist around, hired him. It was like a ballclub getting a star slugger for a cut rate because of the star's past controversies. The WRL gave him permission to go to Montgomery and advise Martin Luther King, the young leader of the bus boycott. He also staged three marches on Washington—the 1957 Prayer Pilgrimage and the 1958 and 1959 Youth Marches for Integrated Schools.

By the time of the 1963 March on Washington, Rustin was both the most gifted and the most damaged organizer in the civil rights movement. Given a chance, he could use the hard-earned wisdom of his many controversies to make the March a success.

Rustin's greatest lesson in planning came from his youthful involvement with the Young Communist League, a quarter century before.

"The minute you get a blueprint, you tend to get ends and means separated," Rustin later said. "Because if you got a blueprint, then any means is good enough to get to it. But I reverse the process, nonviolent creative action now, take care of the rest as you go along."

Change has to come from countless people, in countless organizations, taking positive steps, every day. Sometimes they act separately, sometimes they create coalitions.

According to Rustin, "No movement which has a unified leadership is a strong movement. There need to be *tendencies*, there needs to be *accommodation*. Ultimately it's stronger. When the time comes, we do cooperate."

Rather than following a grand strategy, executed to perfection, Rustin now saw that real progress comes when people act right—with clear principles of nonviolence and equality—in a thousand different ways, every day.

"If you deal creatively and nonviolently with the problem which is before you, you are then setting the ground work for a hundred years from now, no matter what the objective situation is," he told Robert Penn Warren. "It's the same thing a psychologist says to a patient who comes in and talks about what he's going to be doing in two weeks . . . 'Now, wait a minute. Let us see what you intend to do tomorrow, when you get up.'"

THE FORMER STREET HUSTLER AND PIMP made himself at home in the lobby of the Statler Hilton Hotel.

Sitting off at the edge of the lobby, Malcolm X attracted a small cluster of people around him—reporters, civil rights workers, some people from the hotel. He sat erect, in his dark suit, arguing against the March on Washington. But he kept his eyes alert for people walking through the lobby.

"Hey, Nat Hentoff," Malcolm called out to the short, bearded reporter for the *Village Voice*, "you're part of this *farce* on Washington, too! You're part of the circus of Negroes! You're one of the clowns in the circus!"

Floyd McKissick walked over to embrace Malcolm. That afternoon, McKissick would take James Farmer's place and speak at the March on Washington. The CORE staffers recoiled. *How can you talk with him?* But McKissick owed his life to the Black Muslims. When the Ku Klux Klan threatened McKissick's house in Durham, North Carolina, a brigade from the Nation of Islam stood guard.

Courtland Cox, one of the March staffers in Harlem, smiled when he saw Malcolm. "He's denouncing us as clowns," he said, "but he's right there with the clown show."

The Nation of Islam was an all-black organization organized in Detroit in 1930. In 1958, Elijah Muhammad deemphasized the NOI's religious aspects and stressed an economic and social agenda, including programs for schooling and entrepreneurship. The goal was an independent black community—and, eventually, creation of a global coalition of people of color. In city after city, the Nation's strict standards of behavior—dress neatly, work hard, avoid drugs and liquor, care for family—rescued many a wayward slum dweller.

Elijah Muhammad had given out orders for all Black Muslims to boycott the March on Washington. The future of the black race, according to the frail sixty-five-year-old man wrapped in silk and sitting on a throne, lay not with the white people. The future lay in the creation of a separate homeland for blacks, either in territory ceded by the United States government or in Africa. It lay in getting away from the "white devil," killing him if necessary to establish a separate homeland.

Malcolm X, onetime street hustler, drug dealer, and pimp, was Muhammad's messenger. His commitment to Allah turned his life around, and now he was trying to spread the word.

Malcolm's russet, freckled skin and reddish hair, with a thin wisp of a goatee, stood out like a nail on a board—sharp, pointed, strong, cutting.

Bayard Rustin ignored the claims that Black Muslims would incite violence on the National Mall and invited Malcolm to join the mainstream movement. "If Mr. X and his followers appear in Washington on August 28, they will be treated no differently than any other participant," he said. "Similarly, we expect that they will abide by the same regulations which all other participants had accepted."

Everywhere civil rights activity took place—especially in big cities like New York, Chicago, and Washington—Malcolm stood on a street corner, wearing a severe black suit. His serrated voice cut the air with his attacks on the evils of the white race, naive Negro civil rights activists, Jewish landlords and businessmen, police, and mass media that ignored the Muslim movement.

"It is time to get a divorce," he shouted at a rally of four thousand in Chicago, "and we want a property settlement!"

"We don't preach hatred and violence," he said after moving to Washington that summer. "But we believe that if a four-legged or a two-legged dog attacks a Negro he should be killed."

"Real men don't put their children on the firing line," he said after the Children's Crusade in Birmingham, where police routed and jailed hundreds of teenagers.

On the TV program *The Negro and the American Promise*, Malcolm X predicted apocalypse.

"God is about to eliminate that particular race from this earth. Since they are due for elimination, we don't want to be with them. We are not trying to integrate with that which we know has come to the end of the rope."

Malcolm held his own version of the March on Washington—the Harlem Unity Rally—on August 10. He invited all the civil rights leaders. None accepted. But ten thousand people gathered, and Malcolm talked for more than two hours.

Malcolm explained that he had invited all the nation's black leaders to his rally. He called their names out, using "Doctor" in front of almost every one. "We invited all these so-called *Negro doctors* to give their analysis, their diagnosis of the ailments that our people are afflicted with," he said. "And after giving their diagnosis, offer their solutions . . . or give us some idea of what we can do to solve our problems, instead of always running to the white man."

All joking aside, Malcolm thanked the civil rights leaders for their polite letters. He eagerly shared a vision of blacks putting aside "minor" differences and described how self-help and entrepreneurship could wipe out the pathologies of the black community.

"If *capitalistic Kennedy* and *communistic Khrushchev* can find something in *common* . . . then it's time for the so-called Negro leaders to submerge our trivial minor differences in order to seek a common solution to a common problem by forming a united black front."

Then Malcolm X declared all whites enemies, charged that whites, especially Jews, conspired to enslave blacks through drugs and prostitution, and dismissed the tragedy of the Holocaust as nothing but Jews whining.

He spoke in a raspy voice. The longer he spoke, the more extreme he got. He mixed bitter humor with his attacks, looking for the lines that roused the crowd. When he got a reaction he paused and answered: *Yeahhhhh.* The more outrageous the lines, the greater the reaction—and then he ratcheted up the rhetoric.

Malcolm told his crowd not to trust the liberal allies of the civil rights movement.

"Don't *let* the white man fool you . . . Behind that smile is a *vicious heart.* Behind those teeth is an *animal-like beast* who doesn't have it within him to want for you what he wants for himself and his own kind. Don't *let* that man fool you."

Malcolm ridiculed the idea that racism was any less severe in the North than the South.

"And now the eyes of twenty million blacks can easily see that this *white fox* here in the North is even more *cruel* and *vicious* than the *white wolf* in the *South*. The Southern wolves always let you know where you stand. But these Northern *foxes* pose as white liberals, they pose as your *friend,* pose as your *benefactor,* pose as your *employer,* they pose as your *landlord,* they pose as the neighborhood *merchant,* they pose as your *lawyer* trying to help you. They infiltrate all your organizations, and in this manner, by *joining* you, they *strangle* your militant efforts toward freedom, toward justice, and toward equality."

Malcolm told the crowd to scorn Jews.

"You haven't got no time to cry no tears for no Jews. Cry tears for yourselves. . . . Why, they only killed six million Jews. . . . Uncle Sam killed one hundred million black people. *Yeahhhh!* . . . One hundred million black people were taken from Africa, and when the Civil War was over there weren't *six million* black people in America. . . . Where did they *go?* Where did they *disappear?* Why, that *dog* . . . he *butchered* them, he *mutilated* them. . . . Eighty million black people, *dead, murdered,* and these Jews have the audacity to run around here and want us to cry for them."

Malcolm predicted a race war when blacks started demanding jobs in all-white construction crews, service-industry staffs, and factories.

"Brothers and sisters, today here in America, [competition] for more of the white man's jobs, which are already scarce, can lead to nothing but *violence* and *bloodshed,* and it may even lead to a race war, a *bloody race war.*"

He sneered at mainstream black leaders.

"*That old* Uncle Tom–type Negro is *dead,* he's gone. *Tom is gone!* Our people have no more fear of *anyone,* they have no more fear of *anything.* We're not afraid to go to jail, we're not afraid to give our *very life itself.*"

He extolled physical violence.

"We'll give our life, *just like that.* But not only will we give it, we'll *take* the life of the one who tries to take our life. We believe in a fair exchange. We believe in an *eye* for an *eye,* and a *tooth* for a *tooth,* a *head* for a *head,* and a *life* for a *life.* That's justice. There's nothing wrong with that."

Now, eleven days later, Malcolm was in the Statler Hilton, reprising his street-corner attacks on whites, integration, and nonviolence.

"The Muslims who follow the honorable Elijah Muhammad won't have anything to do whatsoever with the march. No Muslim will be involved. Neither directly, nor indirectly . . . For all these Negro leaders to bring Negroes from all over the country and go down to a dead man's statue, a dead president's monument, who was supposed to have issued an emancipation proclamation one hundred years ago and if what he had issued had any authenticity or sincerity and had gotten the job done, this whole problem wouldn't exist now."

Ossie Davis, the master of ceremonies for the morning program at the Washington Monument, got a different perspective.

As they dressed in their room at the Statler, Ossie and his wife, Ruby Dee, heard a knock.

Malcolm X stood in the doorway.

What are you doing here? asked Ossie. *I thought the Honorable Elijah Muhammad banned members of the Nation of Islam from going to the march. I thought the march was a big fraud, a sad spectacle of house Negroes begging and beseeching the slave owner for favors.*

Malcolm was brief.

I want you to know that if you need help on anything, I am here to help. I will be discreet. I have told the proper people that I am available. If you need to find me, I'll tell you where to reach me. If there's violence and I can help, tell me. I'll do anything.

Ossie and Ruby thanked Malcolm.

He took the elevator back to the lobby of the Statler Hilton, where he had been holding court and would remain most of the day.

THE FBI ATTEMPTED TO EXPLOIT FEARS about violence and Communist infiltration of the civil rights movement—fears that were partly the result of J. Edgar Hoover's long campaign against the movement. FBI agents made last-minute calls to celebrities.

Do you know, the agents asked, *that many of the march's leaders are Communists? Do you know that Communists and other leftists could create chaos at the march? Do you know that it's not too late to pull out of the march? Stay away!*

The FBI planned to watch the march carefully. Agents would take positions along the edges of the reflecting pool, looking for any signs of trouble in the crowd. They would take pictures and notes for their reports to J. Edgar Hoover and his deputy, William Sullivan.

On August 23, William Sullivan sent Hoover a sixty-seven-page memo about Communist influence on the civil rights movement. "There has been an obvious failure of the Communist Party of the United States to appreciably infiltrate, influence, or control large numbers of American Negroes in this country," the memo said. "Time alone will tell."

Hoover sent the report back with a handwritten comment. "This memo reminds me vividly of those I received when Castro took over Cuba," he said. "You contended then that Castro and his cohorts were not Communists and not influenced by Communists. Time alone proved you wrong. I for one can't ignore the memos [about Levison and O'Dell] as having only an infinitesimal effect on the efforts to exploit the American Negro by the Communists." Jack O'Dell and Stanley Levison, aides to King, once had ties to the Communist Party, but Hoover contended they were still loyal to the Communists and used King to influence American politics.

Using material gained in wiretaps of others, FBI agents had followed King for years, and they wrote reams about what they saw and heard. When Stanley Levison emerged as King's closest adviser in 1961, J. Edgar Hoover warned Attorney General Robert Kennedy that King's ties to Levison and O'Dell fatally compromised the civil rights movement. Both Levison and O'Dell had extensive ties to the Communist Party. Even though both had severed those ties, Hoover remained suspicious. President Kennedy personally warned King to distance himself from both Levison and O'Dell.

King dropped Levison from his payroll but continued to seek his advice and support. This defiance angered Hoover. The government prepared a full-scale assault on King. Robert Kennedy approved wiretaps. Kennedy's assistant, Burke Marshall, said later, "I still don't know what other course we could have taken, I mean, if you accept the concept that there is a Soviet Communist apparatus and it is trying to interfere with things here—which you have to accept—and that there's a national security issue and the taps are justified."

Sullivan's memo endangered his relationship with Hoover—and his career. Hoover ridiculed Sullivan after that memo by quoting passages from the report, like "just infinitesimal!" or "I assumed CP functionary claims are all frivolous."

Sullivan panicked and reversed himself. From that point, he became the FBI's leading critic of King and his supposed ties to Communists.

By dawn on the day of the March on Washington, battle lines had formed for a full-scale war between King's movement and the FBI.

ON THE MORNING OF THE GREAT MARCH, Walter Fauntroy had reason to believe that the hatemongers would not have their way. Fauntroy knew that racists could provoke even the most mild-mannered blacks. But churches, fraternal organizations, schools—everyone, everywhere—had instructed blacks on how to respond. And Fauntroy saw their restraint work in his own neighborhood.

The week before the march, Nazis showed up on Fourteenth and T streets —right outside Fauntroy's church, which doubled as the local headquarters for the march—carrying banners and shouting slurs. Wearing swastikas on armbands and shouting for "Martin Lucifer Coon" to "go home," the Nazis did all they could to rile the blacks who lived in the neighborhood.

"I told them, when they saw these people, to just *laugh*," Fauntroy said. So they laughed.

But security planning for the march was dead serious.

For weeks, Bayard Rustin and Fauntroy met with officials from the federal government and the District of Columbia to prevent violence.

"We don't want to look at this thing with rose-colored glasses," Deputy Chief George Waldrot told Rustin weeks before at a meeting at the city's police headquarters. "In a demonstration, there are people who disagree. I hope your people will be as good as those June 14. Tell your people they must expect people who oppose you, as there were last time. So tell your people to ignore them."

On June 14, three thousand Washingtonians had rallied for civil rights. They walked, quietly, down Pennsylvania Avenue and gathered at the District municipal building and then the Justice Department. The only tension that day came when Attorney General Robert Kennedy emerged to praise the administration's record. Both the Black Muslims and the American Nazi Party protested the protesters, each calling for segregation of the races.

Plans for the March on Washington had sparked weeks of speculation about violence. "Tempers are bound to flare," a New York minister named Lee A. Belford said. "The great danger," a Washington police official said, "is the waiting, the sitting and stewing and sweating in the sun. Tempers and emotions are high enough to begin with. An isolated fistfight, maybe that's all it'll take." Russell Long, a segregationist senator from Georgia, admitted that "the South would just as soon it did get out of hand . . . [that] the whole thing broke out into riots, though I am not advocating this."

But Bayard Rustin promised that his marchers would not use violence.

"Violence has usually been caused by unorganized or unauthorized whites opposing the demonstration," Rustin said, and by "quite brutal police methods. If these factors can be controlled or avoided, there is no reason to anticipate violence."

The Detroit March for Freedom in June, which attracted at least a hundred thousand people, had taken place without incident, and the Detroit organizers took few security precautions. But tempers were now hotter, and the politicians in the nation's capital evoked more emotion. Still, blacks had shown an ability to avoid violence under the most trying circumstances, big and small.

Besides, Rustin said, he had been personally training Guardians in non-violent crowd control. "They will be identified with the distinctive armband which says 'Marshal,'" he said. "This is what we call our internal discipline committee."

The idea of private security forces made the Justice Department and D.C. police officials nervous.

"Remember that your marshals can't arrest those opposing people," Police Chief Howard Covell said.

Rustin challenged the Justice Department to protect buses coming from the South.

"The Justice Department must be just as vigilant as we are. Suppose Negroes from Mississippi are coming in a busload, and the buses are attacked and burned—say, the night before the march. Then the meeting [the march] will take place in an entirely different psychological atmosphere."

Could the Justice Department deploy FBI agents along the major highways to protect the buses? Could FBI or military forces escort the buses? Could they respond to attacks? Memories of Anniston—the Alabama town where hooligans firebombed the bus carrying the first Freedom Riders in 1961, and "people came out of a church, watching the bus burn like it was a festival"—still burned in Rustin's mind.

"No one in the Justice Department can take any preventive action," Arthur Caldwell of the Justice Department responded. "So if there is any thought that the FBI will police buses coming here, it will not be done."

"When the president of the United States is going to come in to New York, there are elaborate preparations to protect him," Rustin said. Couldn't the federal government—the Justice Department, maybe, or the Secret Service—make the same presumption of attacks against buses bearing demonstrators from the South? "It seems to me that Mr. Burke Marshall should be well aware of this," Rustin said, "and that he would not put the burden on us to handle this."

No, Caldwell said flatly. Specific laws gave the Secret Service responsibility for protecting the president. No such laws existed for protecting caravans of buses.

Walter Fauntroy stirred. "Can you, or *anyone here*, suggest a means by which protection might be secured?" he asked. "Is it at *all* possible that the National Guard or some enforcement agency might be approached?"

"I am in no position to suggest to you who you should approach," Caldwell answered. "If you feel that we should ask the FBI, go ahead and ask. I am just trying to be perfectly honest with you, because this is no time to mislead anyone."

Smallwood Williams, the bishop of the Bible Way Church, pushed the matter. "I think we should request that the FBI be alerted and make an investigation to see whether there were any plots or any likelihood of burning of buses. In their role of investigation, it is very important, *before* something happens . . . so that we can keep anything from happening, rather than after the fact."

Caldwell didn't budge.

"I have worked in law enforcement for thirty-five years," Caldwell said. "I can assure you that the function of preventing violence is left to the local police. That is not the function of anyone else."

State and local police, in the South, protecting blacks on their way to a civil rights demonstration? That did not sound promising.

Rustin had another idea. What about an escort for the buses once they approached Washington, for the sake of traffic control? We'll think about it, the police answered.

D.C. police then questioned Rustin and the other march organizers. Would the March on Washington rally along Pennsylvania Avenue? Picket the White House? Protest on Capitol Hill?

"How are you going to get a hundred thousand [near] the White House?" Waldrot asked. That street cannot accommodate more than a few thousand."

The march along Pennsylvania Avenue, Rustin said, would be staged to honor Medgar Evers and William Moore. It would be a solemn affair.

"Fine," Police Chief Howard Covell said, "but those parades can get out of control. Are you planning on carrying effigies or inflammatory signs?"

"The staff is proposing that all placards be designed by the central committee," Rustin said. "You can be sure they will be the kind of placards that will preserve order."

What would happen if the marchers, or outside agitators, got emotional and lost control?

"What we would do," Rustin answered, "is to intersperse the march, not with bands but with choirs, who would sing 'We Shall Overcome.'" That would overwhelm the troublemakers.

And what about Capitol Hill? The marchers planned to surround the Capitol building to make a symbolic statement.

"Two thousand Protestant, Catholic, and Jewish ministers and rabbis," Rustin said, "have requested the right to surround the Capitol at some point, standing in appropriate distances in meditation and prayer."

But any demonstration on Capitol Hill, Covell explained, would be illegal. "Mr. Rustin, you may not know our situation here, but the United States Capitol grounds are in a separate jurisdiction and anything pertaining to what [the marchers] would want, would have to be taken up with the authorities of the United States Capitol. That area is quite large. It's not that I'm saying that there would be any opposition. I do not know, but the Capitol . . . that's quite a big piece of ground."

The meetings in Washington resolved nothing. But they taught Bayard Rustin two things. First, no one could guarantee the safety of buses and trains—or even cars—coming to Washington. The police would probably offer escorts only for the sake of traffic control. Second, the idea of marching on the White House and Congress would not work. Rustin had to scrap it.

CAN A DEMONSTRATION CHANGE the way people think? Can a march persuade people to set aside old prejudices?

As the multitudes drove, took buses and trains, flew, walked, bicycled, and even roller-skated to Washington for the Great March, a linguistics professor at San Francisco State University named S. I. Hayakawa was on his way to a professional conference in Philadelphia to address that issue. He had concluded that nothing could turn back the civil rights revolution, and the reason was TV.

Prejudice—or any other form of ignorance—is really a form of infantilism, he said in his address. It originated "when each human being was too young and dependent to defend himself by using his intelligence." Before people had a chance to make up their own minds, they were poisoned. Rational arguments could not persuade someone with "a habitual confusion."

So what could break through that prejudicial environment? Television.

"The television set says, to white and Negro alike, always in the friendliest tones, 'You are an American. You are entitled to eat, drink, and wear what other Americans eat, drink, and wear. You must think about the same national and world problems other Americans think about. You are a member of our national community of Americans.' That is the meta-message that comes to us night and day from the friendly announcers."

TV messages did not *intend* to celebrate equality—they intended to sell Cokes, Winstons, and Fords. That TV characters were white, not black, didn't matter. What mattered was that blacks saw something besides the isolation and poverty of racism.

"It is deeply significant that young people are at the heart of the current racial demonstrations," Hayakawa planned to tell the conference. "Some editorials have said that the young are being exploited by Negro leaders to propagandize their demands. It still hasn't occurred to them that Negro leaders are not leading anyone. They are merely breathlessly trying to keep up with the revolutionary fervor of the young people."

Hayakawa's thesis was a mirror image of Gunnar Myrdal's argument in his landmark 1944 study *An American Dilemma*. Myrdal, a Nobel Prize–winning Swedish economist, argued that the terror against Southern blacks would end only when the nation could no longer ignore it. Only when segregation was exposed for what it was—a top-to-bottom system of subjugation, enforced by violence—could activists attack and dismantle it.

Hayakawa's twist on Myrdal's thesis was simple. Once blacks could see how the rest of the world lived, they would never again accept a legal system of violence and repression.

With the ideology of prejudice softened, the message of the March on Washington could be heard.

A KANSAS CITY MAN, in the days before the March on Washington, called the FBI with this message:

"King should have one hole between his eyes and I will put it there."

Noting that the threat originated from Missouri, by telephone, FBI officials told John Nolan of the Justice Department that the agency "plans no further action." Nolan agreed.

All summer, the death threats came in to the March on Washington headquarters. On a regular basis, the march office was cleared to search for bombs. Other civil rights organizations were also targeted.

On July 19, the NAACP received a postcard at its Chicago office that read:

ATTENTION!
  All NAACP members!
  If your head, Roy Wilkins, wants to live beyond Sat. 7/20 he had better leave the country. I worn [*sic*] you I make no empty threats! K.P.

Chicago's NAACP people called New York to tell Wilkins of the threat. Just two weeks before, the NAACP had completed a contentious national conference in Chicago, at which Mayor Richard Daley and the moderate Reverend Joseph Jackson were booed off the stage.

The FBI identified three suspects. "Two of these individuals reportedly have been involved in fights with Negroes," an FBI report stated laconically, "and the third was tried for murder and discharged." In interviews with FBI agents, the suspects denied threatening Wilkins. The FBI told Wilkins that it could not offer any protection; he would have to contact local officials wherever he went for police protection.

The *Los Angeles Times* reported getting this message, with a threat to bomb the *Times* building unless it was published in the newspaper:

Mr. President John F. Kennedy. A Nigger lover. I have a offer on your life two five zero zero zero dollars. To dispose you. But you have too many guards. Next offer is on Mr. Martin Luther King one zero zero zero zero. Next offer is Mr. Jimm A. Hood five zero zero zero. This is my work for money to kill. You know the majority rules minority. You don't give the rights to American Indian. Keep in concentration camps. The Niggers have some rights the whites have. Oll we want the Niggers stay away from whites places. If not be too many killings. I get my man if it takes a year. K.K.K.

Some threats were less direct:

You dirty Filthy Niggers have about broken the backs of white People with Taxes to take care of Niggers. . . .

If you Niggers are ever allowed to vote, we may as well put up Polling Places in all the Zoos so the Monkeys and Gorillas are allowed the same privilije. . . .

If One of you Filthy Niggers ever tried to live Next Door to me, I am quite sure that there would be a Nigger Funeral.

For more than a week, the march headquarters in New York and Washington got bomb threats on a daily basis. Volunteers gathered their materials and walked outdoors while police searched the sites. Nothing ever came of it.

The morning of the march, traffic controllers in New York grounded five airplanes because of bomb threats. An Eastern Airlines shuttle from New York, whose passengers included Mayor Robert Wagner, was forced to touch down in Philadelphia when a caller said there were explosives onboard. Seventy-nine passengers were quickly put on another plane and made it to the march on time.

Politicians and media fretted about the possibility of violence. They worried that outside agitators—racist groups like the American Nazi Party or the Ku Klux Klan—would wade into the crowd to start a fight. Carrying knives or guns, or just picking up rocks and bricks, they would attack blacks.

Talk of assassination was muted. Less than three months before, Medgar Evers had been assassinated in Jackson, Mississippi. But the possibility of shooting one of the speakers at the March on Washington seemed remote. After all, the last national political figure to be assassinated was Huey Long, in 1935.

PART 2

Into the Day

———

A HELICOPTER HOVERED OVER Washington, D.C., as dawn broke.

John McKelvey, the author of the *Washington Star*'s Rambler column, peered over the landscape of Washington with the pilot, Jim Schafer. A short and stocky man, Shafer had been flying above Washington for a decade.

The *Star*'s photographer Gene Abbott was there, too, with two small cameras around his neck, a leather case, a package of colored sponges, and a box of ping-pong balls.

Abbott's job was to get pictures of the traffic below and the crowds on the Mall and drop them onto the roof of the *Star* building in time for the afternoon editions of the paper. To judge the direction and strength of the breeze, he would drop the ping-pong balls. Then he could make allowances when he dropped the film, attached to the sponges to soften the landing.

At first, traffic was light. The copter hovered over the highways leading into Washington and spotted no traffic.

By eight or eight thirty they could see the long lines of buses, like pencils lined up from end to end, on Route 40 and the Capital Beltway (still under construction) from the north, and Route 29 and the Shirley Highway from the south.

They could see traffic cops—National Guardsmen—directing the buses in toward the Mall. They could see the areas along Independence Avenue and Constitution Avenue fill up.

At eight thirty the helicopter reached the *Star* building in Southeast Washington. The photographer decided he didn't need to use the ping-pong balls. The pilot put the helicopter at an angle and then the photographer dropped rolls of film. The afternoon editions of the *Star* would carry these images.

Also that morning, Eleanor Holmes flew into town.

Holmes, a staff member for the March on Washington, had volunteered to stay at the New York office on Tuesday night to take phone calls. Everyone else took a bus or train, but she got to fly. She caught the first plane out of La Guardia Airport.

The day was clear. As she leaned into the window, she saw the usual sights—Long Island, Philadelphia, Baltimore, the Chesapeake, and, finally, Washington.

The view of the capital surprises people flying into Washington for the first time. Imitating the broad boulevards of Paris, the streets provide clear views of the sides of the squat, sprawling white government buildings.

The Potomac River snakes around the city, giving the land the shape of a fat teardrop. Depending on how the plane angles into the city, passengers can see the two-thousand-acre greensward of Rock Creek Park . . . the Watergate building . . . the National Cathedral . . .

Approaching National Airport, the National Mall comes into view—looking almost like a barbell, with the Washington Monument and the Lincoln Memorial, surrounded by lawns, at the two ends, and the mile-long reflecting pool and lawn connecting the two.

Eleanor Holmes could see the Mall filling up. She saw the buses packed in along both sides, and more buses snaking toward the parking lots, like silver and yellow and white bullets. And she saw the throngs below, clustering near the Washington Monument; from a distance, they looked like ice-cream sprinkles thrown down on the ground. Then the Jefferson Memorial came into view, quickly, before the plane zoomed into the vast green approach to the airport.

BAYARD RUSTIN, WHO STAYED UP long after midnight, rose an hour before dawn broke at 6:33. He showered and got dressed—a dark blue suit, white oxford shirt, dark blue tie—and went to the lobby of the Statler Hilton Hotel to meet Tom Kahn, Rachelle Horowitz, and Courtland Cox.

The lobby buzzed that morning. People found the coffee shop and newsstand and talked about who was coming, who was speaking, who might disrupt the day. A bellboy saw Sammy Davis Jr., Diahann Carroll, and Sidney Poitier: "We haven't had this many people in a long time, famous people like this. . . . *Hello,* Mr. Davis!"

People greeted each other and talked about the group of CORE activists who hiked all week from Brooklyn. They talked about the celebrities who would perform that day—Odetta, Dylan and Baez, Mahalia Jackson, and Peter, Paul, and Mary. Insiders buzzed about the dispute between the

Catholic Church and John Lewis, the young leader of SNCC who had written a blistering attack on President John F. Kennedy.

It was already muggy and warm, but nothing like the paddy-wagon heat
of Mississippi.

The grounds of the National Mall were damp as the sun rose. The only
sounds were birdsong and hammers and staple guns echoing out of the
March on Washington tent. Workers for TV organizations—CBS, NBC,
ABC, Telstar—shouted instructions on the right side of the Lincoln Memorial's front steps.

A loose line of marchers—members of Virginia's NAACP—wobbled
along the eastern side of the reflecting pool and others clustered loosely on
the greensward between the Washington Monument's needle and the Doric
columns of Lincoln's shrine. Police began to assemble along the edges of the
Mall. Farther out, National Guardsmen in Jeeps deployed at the intersec-
tions of Washington's Parisian-style boulevards.

But the crowds had not arrived. "Nothing but grass," Courtland Cox
said.

"*Horowitz,*" Rustin said, his clipped tenor rising, "*where* are those buses
and trains you talked about?"

A week before, in New York, Rachelle Horowitz had shown Rustin a document listing all the buses coming to the march. The list tallied only 67,800
marchers. At the time, she was embarrassed to tell Rustin that she could not
assure him the crowd of 100,000 people that march leaders predicted. To this
eager young activist Rustin had chosen to run the march's transportation
operations, no one counted unless she had a record.

Rustin showed the list to Roy Wilkins of the NAACP.

"Hot *damn!*" Wilkins said. "Bayard, she didn't get *anyone* from Washington, D.C."

And others besides the uncounted Washington locals would show up at
the Mall. "*I know my people,*" said Wilkins. "She doesn't understand that in
the middle of the night someone's going to wake up, nudge her husband, and
say, 'Let's take the Greyhound to Washington.' All she has are the people
who have *signed up*. She has no idea how many other people are coming from
Virginia or Maryland, how many are driving."

Wilkins walked over and hugged Rachelle.

But now . . . where were they?

Rustin looked out over the Mall and saw no signs of the multitudes. He
could hear flags flapping in the early morning wind. A convoy of twenty
army trucks passed by, looking irrelevant.

Louis Martin, an adviser to President Kennedy, got in a car at the White

House to glide over to the Washington Monument. "The place is empty," he told the cabbie.

John Morsell, an NAACP staffer who had worked all summer at the March on Washington headquarters in New York, was getting dressed in his room when he heard a TV broadcast at about seven thirty: *Not many people seem to be showing up. It doesn't look as if it's going to be very much.* Morsell had "a sinking feeling." But he moved downstairs and got breakfast.

A few reporters saw Rustin's angular silhouette on the Mall, his assistants hovering around him. They rushed over. *Would the people come? Would they have a hundred thousand? More? Less? Suppose they got less than a hundred thousand, after weeks of predicting a hundred thousand? Would the march be a failure?*

Rustin pulled a sheet of paper from the inner pocket of his jacket. He pulled an ornate pocket watch out and flipped open the cover. He narrowed his eyes to peer at the piece of paper, then tilted his head to look at the face of the watch.

"*Gentlemen,*" he said, his voice rising to a first tenor pitch, in a familiar singsong, "we are *right* on schedule." Bayard used his British accent, which he affected when he was nervous: *sheh-zshule.*

He later showed the sheet of paper to Horowitz and Kahn. It was blank.

IN THE GREEN-AND-WHITE-STRIPED PARTY TENT, Rachelle Horowitz began her assignment as the March on Washington's transportation troubleshooter. She sat at the end of a long row of tables. The phone would ring and someone would report a stalled bus or traffic jam.

But after taking a few calls, she decided she could not tell the callers anything useful.

"Just hitch," she said. "Stop on the road, and when another bus comes by, try to get a ride." Then she left the tent.

March staffers worked at the forty-by-one-hundred-foot tent all night. Reporters demanded instant information: How many people were coming? How many blacks and how many whites? How many buses? Trains? How many lunches?

Miles of wires led in and out of the tent. Two video monitors were set up to transmit the day's events. More than a hundred media outlets ordered their own phone lines, and there were a dozen pay phones and a mobile trailer with more pay phones. The Coca-Cola Company sent in big coolers of drinks on ice.

A painting, leaning in the corner of the tent, told the story of the civil rights movement. Lincoln occupied the center of the painting, with the words "1863 emancipation." John Kennedy appeared in the lower right, with the words "1963 Armageddon." The words "The Day of the Yellow Dog" accompanied photos of police with dogs on leashes.

By eight in the morning, the tent whirred. Volunteers patched signs reading "We Demand FECP Law Now," covering "FECP" with "FEPC," which stood for Fair Employment Practices Commission.

More than a thousand reporters had credentials. Some sat at the tables, under bare bulbs, clacking away on portable typewriters. Some called in stories: *That's Rustin—R-U-S-T-I-N. . . . Police said they were ready for two hundred thousand—that's two-oh-oh-comma-oh-oh-oh.*

Reporters sat at long tables, opposite the politicians and celebrities. They leaned forward, shutting out the noise of hammers and shouting, buses and planes. Sammy Davis Jr., Odetta, Bob Dylan, Lena Horne, and Peter, Paul, and Mary sat for interviews. Senators Jacob Javits and Hubert Humphrey answered questions about the FEPC and filibusters, committee chairmen, and the president. Cops described logistics.

Filmmakers for the United States Information Agency shot hours of film for a documentary. Emphasizing the power of peaceful demonstrations, the film would be distributed worldwide as propaganda in the Cold War.

"Smile," the propagandists said. "This is going to *Africa.*"

Michael Thelwell, a SNCC worker, was nauseated by the activity in the tent. He watched white tourists stop by the tent like it was a museum exhibit.

"So it happened," Thelwell said later, "that Negro students from the South, some of whom still had unhealed bruises from the electric cattle prods which Southern police used to break up demonstrations, were recorded for the screens of the world portraying 'American Democracy at Work.'"

Volunteers shuttled back and forth from the tent on the Mall to radio station WUST, where volunteers in Washington had been preparing for the march for weeks. Student volunteers typed letters to associations listed in phone books. The march's press maven, Sy Posner, entertained reporters from all over the world. Organizers from New York set up shop until they could open the tent on the grounds of the National Mall. Most volunteers came and went. A few dedicated typists stayed all day.

"Everyone likes to turn out for the marches and demonstrations because they have a wonderful time and it's exciting with the police and everything," said one volunteer, who put in twelve hours a day. "But not too many like to do the drudgery work."

Workers piled up wooden sticks and the preprinted placards. A handful of volunteers—the three boys from Gadsden and some others who joined them for hours at a time—staple-gunned the placards and staffs and then stacked them into four-foot-high piles, ready to be taken by U-Haul to the tent the night before the march.

PLANNING FOR THE MARCH ON WASHINGTON had begun back in New York, when Bayard Rustin set up the March on Washington headquarters in Harlem. Rustin rented a building on West 130th Street and Lenox Avenue for $350 a month. Immediately, he raised a banner—NATIONAL HEADQUARTERS: MARCH ON WASHINGTON FOR JOBS AND FREEDOM: WED., AUG. 28TH—that stretched across the building.

That building had no real decor. It was just a run-down brownstone full of broken-down institutional furniture, typewriters, and hundreds of cardboard boxes of buttons and brochures. When local newspapers reported that pictures of John F. Kennedy and crucifixes lined the walls, someone went around and took them down.

"I simply don't know how they're going to do it," one Washington cop said. "We spend nearly a year planning for the inaugural parade. They're trying to pull off something much more complicated in [just] weeks." Another cop said: "It's just like they were getting ready for D-day in Normandy."

After a total of $146,917 had been raised—two-thirds from donations, the rest from the sale of souvenirs and tickets, and from concerts and other events—the march expenses totaled $133,229. The biggest expenses were printing leaflets and bulletins ($16,626), paying salaries and payroll taxes ($13,382), providing transportation for the marshals ($12,931), and printing buttons and pennants ($11,277). The Washington operation cost a total of $29,563, including $18,838 for sound equipment.

Bayard Rustin's first rule of management was to make lists of every conceivable task. If somebody thinks that something can *possibly* go wrong, come up with a specific solution, and put it on the list. Organizing anything —a massive march, a union picket, a training program, a newspaper— succeeds or fails because of details.

All day long, Rustin and his team crossed off completed tasks and added new tasks to the three- and four-page lists:

Briefing of Marshals
Sy does press release on cars to Negro press

Telephone for top command
Find out when office tent goes up
Wire Mahalia Jackson
Call Joe Rauh on insurance and inspection
Clarify with Washington police Rockwell's intentions
Small national office at the Statler

And there was more, much more. Most tasks were mundane. But these countless small actions made possible the orchestration of a historic event.

Always, egos had to be soothed. Politicians, writers, movie stars, singers, and financiers needed attention. Josephine Baker's manager, for example, wrote to Phil Randolph: "We trust that Miss Baker's appearance and participation in the 'March' will not go un-noticed and that proper and adequate accommodation at the 'March' will be accorded her." The Hollywood group sent a list of names for President Kennedy to meet regarding film and TV hiring practices, as if Bayard Rustin were a White House scheduler. Other notables—like Fred Shuttlesworth and James Baldwin—got upset when denied slots on the speaker lineup.

"All I can say is, thank God I don't have to deal with the Hollywood plane," Rachelle Horowitz said. Bayard Rustin gave that job to Ossie Davis. "He took care of prima-donna land," Horowitz said.

Senators Paul Douglas and Hubert Humphrey sent long letters fretting about the need for an ample supply of chemical toilets. "Without a good supply of toilets," Douglas warned in an August 8 letter, "some horrible things will inevitably happen which will bring discredit on the march and marchers . . . *I cannot exaggerate the need for a big supply of these.*" Everyone laughed about the "latrine letters." But Rustin added a line to his to-do list: *Chemical toilets—How many?*

Rustin's second rule of management was to assign trustworthy people to do these thousands of tasks. Rustin didn't care so much about training or even experience. He wanted brains and persistence. When he asked Rachelle Horowitz to organize the buses to get at least a hundred thousand people to Washington, she hesitated.

"Are you crazy? I don't know anything about transportation," she said. "I can't *drive.*"

"My dear, you're *compulsive,*" he said. "You won't lose a bus. You won't lose a person. Don't worry, you can do it, and I *want* you to do it."

So the compulsive Rachelle Horowitz got to work. She sat on the phone, calling bus companies and local organizers. She made a card for every bus that confirmed. She didn't book any buses—that was left to local organizers. They also put up the money and recruited marchers. But she explained how things worked and tracked progress.

When Rustin got a letter from someone like Mitchell Crane—a high school student in Rustin's hometown of West Chester who said he wanted to organize buses—he passed the note to Horowitz. Horowitz called Crane, told him what companies to call. And when Crane ran into trouble renting buses—however progressive the town's Quaker heritage, the owners of the bus companies did not approve of the march—he could always call on Horowitz for help.

Horowitz worked on the second floor with Joyce Ladner. The two women answered calls for each other. "Yes, this is Joyce," Rachelle would say, the Jewish woman from Brooklyn becoming a black woman from Mississippi to keep the operation moving briskly.

In the week before the march, Horowitz persuaded the Metropolitan Transit Authority to run subways on a rush-hour schedule after midnight, to make sure New Yorkers could get to their buses. And she got the bridge and tunnel authorities to pass out leaflets with march information at tollbooths.

Rustin always looked for ways to simplify operations. Giving staffers clear authority was one way. Another way was simplifying the march concept. Turning the march into a one-day event eliminated the need for overnight accommodations. Rustin also scrapped plans for marchers to meet congressional delegations all around Washington when police raised concerns about the chaos of getting them to the Mall from separate meeting places. When marchers from Delaware and Pennsylvania went ahead with plans to meet delegations, Tom Kahn panicked. "I suspect this is simply the top of an ugly iceberg," Kahn told Rustin. But Rustin was cool. Easier to let a couple groups do things their way.

Sometimes, Rustin just let ideas die. Ossie Davis wrote a skit for movie stars to perform. *Too complicated; forget it.* A company wanted to produce "NAACP freedom bells" for sale as a fund-raiser. *Too messy; forget it.* A student suggested outfitting blacks in Ole Miss T-shirts, a dig at "seggies" from Mississippi. *Don't involve us.* Only simple ideas requiring no work got the okay—like when a Hawaii songwriter donated five hundred orchid leis to major figures at the march.

The march office crackled from about ten each morning until two the next morning. Rustin operated in a small room, just off the dark and narrow hallway on the first floor. A sign saying "March Office One Floor Up" drew some visitors away from Rustin's office, but most knew he was there and burst in regularly.

One hundred or more often crammed into the building—there were usually at least forty or fifty. Typewriters clacked, phones rang, mimeograph machines thwacked, staff and volunteers murmured and shouted up and down the stairs. People smoked all day—wherever you went, you walked into a blue haze—and drank too. Blyden Jackson brought brown moonshine in Pepsi bottles.

A few volunteers came and went. Volunteers got assigned to senior organizers, but those organizers didn't always have the time to train or track their charges. One volunteer named John Williams, assigned to the march's press liaison, Sy Posner, drifted away after ten days. He concluded that he was not part of the civil rights "club"—"with the right kind of views, background, and aspiration"—and so got "shunted aside." But he wasn't bitter and he went to the march, getting close enough to watch Martin Luther King and other speakers up close.

Someone was clever enough to install the latest intercom system, but people forgot to use it. They yelled up and down the stairs, like parents calling teenagers to dinner.

"*Rachelle?*" Rustin would call up from his perch in the first floor's bullpen. "Rachelle, dear, I need . . ."

"Would you use the *intercom?*"

"Rachelle!"

"Use . . . the . . . *f*——. . . *intercom!*"

Relationships got inverted. Elliott Linzer, a shy, awkward seventeen-year-old high school student, supervised volunteers from the United Federation of Teachers. Higher-ups sometimes felt a need to assert their authority over easygoing volunteers. At one meeting, a volunteer chirped his thoughts and recommendations, only to get a rebuke. "You're doing the *Jimmy Higgins work*," the senior staffer said. Jimmy Higgins was the universal symbol of drudge work—typing and stuffing envelopes, fetching sandwiches, running to the post office, taking out trash—a term used both to honor the toiler and put him in his place. The comment stung.

But the Jimmy Higgins work mattered. Hundreds of thousands of leaflets, stacked in cardboard boxes, had to go to the right places. Details mattered. The March office sent out different versions of brochures for blacks and whites. "You're not going to get a whole bunch of whites to catch a bus at three in the morning to go to Harlem or Bed-Stuy," Elliott Linzer said, "but they *will* go to Forest Hills or Park Slope."

Every so often, a celebrity stopped by. Ossie Davis visited. So did Bob Dylan. Al Shanker of the American Federation of Teachers came by. John Lewis did too. Necks craned, Rustin or Cleve Robinson or Tom Kahn danced over to greet the visitor, and everyone got a five-minute break. And then . . .

"Come on, now, get back to work," Rustin called out in his matronly, high-pitched voice. "We're not having a *nigger fish fry*, you know!"

Rustin's manic joviality created a sense of urgency, even crisis. "He wanted us to live that couple of months as if every single day might be the last day of your life," said Norm Hill. "You had to accomplish as much as possible every day."

At the end of every workday, Rustin convened a staff meeting. Everyone was invited—and expected—to attend, from the heavies like Tom Kahn and Cleveland Robinson down to lowly interns like Peter Orris and Elliott Linzer.

Rustin let everyone else talk. Staffers reported on how many people had written requesting brochures and buttons. They reported on how many buses had been booked for Akron and Albany and New York. They raised questions about security arrangements or coordination with Walter Fauntroy's operation in Washington.

As others talked, Rustin doodled. As he scribbled notes and crossed out completed tasks, he drew squares and triangles that looked like mazes. Peter Orris, a brainy high school student, was convinced that the doodles helped Rustin think through the relationships between the many-layered tasks. He got Rustin to autograph one of his doodles.

Sometimes, like a herald from the past, Rustin suddenly interrupted the chatter with an old spiritual, his voice sweet and high pitched:

Sometimes I feel like a motherless child,
A long ways from home,
A true believer

Sometimes I feel like I'm almos' gone
Way up in the heab'nly lan'
True believer

Sometimes he sang alone. But he also called out songs everyone knew. Always the teacher, he told them where the song came from, what it meant. He talked to them, for example, about the syncopation in "Ezekiel Saw the Wheel" and the call-and-response patterns in "Swing Low." He sang the old spirituals with new words targeting Bull Connor, George Wallace, Ross Barnett, and Jim Clark, the most notorious symbols of segregation in the South.

As Harlem slept, the music of slaves and sharecroppers, sit-inners and picketers, gospel choirs and a capella college ensembles, filled the muggy night air.

IN THE WAR ROOM AT THE PENTAGON, a thirtysomething lawyer held power that only the president—or, in this administration, his brother—could dream of holding.

William Geoghegan was the assistant deputy attorney general. He reported to Nick Katzenbach. But Attorney General Robert Kennedy asked him to spend the day in the war room, overseeing generals. The group would monitor events by television and telephone. If any military action was needed, Geoghegan was to call Kennedy at the Justice Department.

"There were rumors and a lot of talk around the time there might be trouble," Geoghegan said. "Most of us felt it would be peaceful but also recognized that we had to prepare, and good preparation would reduce the chance of something bad happening."

In the weeks leading up to the march, Geoghegan and others developed a punch list of actions to take to make sure the march went off well. Toilets, food, cops, tourists, traffic—nothing was too small to matter. Bayard Rustin has his list, they had theirs.

Generals wearing a total of eighteen stars, including two four-star generals, sat in the war room. For this one day, Geoghegan—a private first class in World War II—could tell the generals whether they had the authority to act. "I could overrule them if I had to," he said. "They weren't supposed to undertake any initiative without conferring with the attorney general—and I was the one who made that connection."

The group sat at the giant conference table, talked, read reports, watched TV—mostly dead time. "What did you do in the war?" the generals asked Geoghegan. They discussed the ongoing civil rights conflicts. They had worked together during civil rights crises at Ole Miss and the University of Alabama.

Most of official Washington believed the March on Washington would not improve chances for passage of civil rights bills. Geoghegan disagreed.

"The pluses were all from the publicity," he said. "The speeches dwelled on what the Negro had been suffering all these years. [The march] conveyed that these people have been screwed for years and something had to be done. When you're working on the Hill, there were people you were never going to reach. But we had to get votes from the fence-sitters, particularly on the Republican side."

Over the course of the day, Geoghegan and the generals experienced "a certain sense of amazement that it was so peaceful, there were no incidents."

"When you see that crowd—and the biracial content of it—it was a huge success politically. I had to believe that it moved a lot of people and a lot of votes. It moved an awful lot of citizens who were very indifferent to realizing there's something that has to be done. It *had* to have a powerful impact."

ALL SUMMER LONG, THE MARCH GOT SOFTER as it was embraced by old establishment leaders like Roy Wilkins and Whitney Young, by John and Robert Kennedy, and the Catholic Church.

First, the march was switched from a two-day event to a one-day rally.

Then it was decreed that there would be no civil disobedience—no confrontations, no arrests, no sit-ins, no picketing. Then there were restrictions on what people could sing and the signs they could carry. Then the grand plans to bring unemployed workers to the march, and to give one of them a high-profile speaker's slot, got set aside.

Every time, Rustin came back to the march office and told his staffers at their daily meeting.

"Sellout!" they shouted, half angry and half amused to play the role of radicals.

"Now, *children...*" Bayard would say, his voice rising, smiling with weary eyes.

"What you have to understand," Rustin explained, "is that the march will succeed if it gets a hundred thousand people—or one hundred fifty thousand or two hundred thousand or more—to show up in Washington. It will be the biggest rally in history. It will show the black community united as never before—united also with whites from labor and the churches, from all over the country." The TV cameras would come—not just the Big Three networks, but also this new phenomenon of Telstar would transmit images all over the globe. For the first time, the whole world would watch, in Paris and Moscow, London and Beijing, Nairobi and Caracas. This was not some fifteen-minute evening news show. This was not some tape-delay presentation. This was the American freedom movement . . . *live and uncut.*

It's all about numbers, not ideology.

Grumbling, Tom Kahn and Rachelle Horowitz and Joyce Ladner and the others turned away and got back to work. They didn't have any choice. There were lists to type, cards to file, calls to make, buttons and brochures to mail, dollars to raise.

The journalist Louis Lomax charged that white philanthropists—chiefly Steven Currier, the head of the Taconic Foundation—had "defanged" the march with gifts to civil rights groups totaling $1 million. Currier initiated the gifts to tamp down the bitter competition for donations among the civil rights organizations.

"The Negro," Lomax said, "has long suffered from the myth of unity." When civil rights groups come together, they lose both bark and bite. Blacks, he said, should "master the art of deliberate disunity." He also attacked non-violence. "As a tactical maneuver, it's excellent. But the white power structure does not understand nor respect nonviolence as a total way of life. It's looked upon as a sign of weakness."

But different moments call for different tactics. A representative gathering of black America and its allies—a kind of civil rights congress, unprecedented in American history—would create a compelling vision of America after segregation.

"Bayard always knew he would have to trade in militancy for numbers," Norm Hill said. "Bayard had worked with Roy Wilkins and King before. He knew them. He probably let us put in militant actions [in the original plan] so he could trade it away. Four things mattered—numbers, the coalition, militancy of action, and militancy of words. He was willing to give up militant action for the other three."

Norm Hill traveled all over—Chicago, Cleveland, Detroit, Cincinnati, Louisville, Philadelphia, and Baltimore—to bring the masses to Washington. Every town had a Martin, a Malcolm, a Race Man, a Booker T. Washington. Somehow, they had to come together, united, for at least this one day. He had to find the one local leader who could organize all the others. Usually, it was someone from the NAACP—no organization could match the NAACP's network of local branches. Most of the NAACP members belonged to local churches, professional groups, and school boards. Sometimes Hill picked the local CORE leader. In St. Paul, the local organizer came from Phil Randolph's Brotherhood of Sleeping Car Porters. "If it's the chief's initiative, I'll fall in behind the chief," he told Hill.

Altogether, fifteen hundred local organizations helped to recruit, raise money, book buses, provide security, prepare food, and do the other work of the march. The churches brought as many as fifty thousand, and unions almost as many. New York, Philadelphia, Detroit, Chicago, and Washington sent the biggest contingents. As July turned to August, enthusiasm spread.

Sometimes it was too much. "Now if we let in any more sponsoring groups," Bayard Rustin said, "we're going to get some Communists; Maoists and the Trotskyites could give us trouble. If people want to march with us, they can march. But they're going to march on *our* terms."

Two weeks before the big day, new fears arose that whites—*whites!*—would dominate the march. In a conversation with Martin Luther King, Tom Kahn raised the issue. They decided to get march organizers to redouble the efforts in big cities with large black populations—in New York, Philadelphia, Baltimore, Washington—to get the black numbers up.

Washington organizers set a goal of fifty thousand marchers from the capital. Roy Wilkins said it couldn't be done. "We can't count on Washington turning out anybody," he said. "Those upper-middle-class Negroes down there are too comfortable and satisfied and they're not going to come." Early efforts to organize Washingtonians met with indifference. But local organizers sent out sound trucks and got ministers to exhort their flocks to march. And in the last two weeks, "the fever was building up," Sterling Tucker said.

On one matter, Rustin held the line against moderation. The Big Ten were divided about whether to invite President Kennedy to speak at the march. Rustin was against it. Inviting the president, he feared, would make it *his* march. It would no longer be a mass of activists demanding their rights, but instead a mass of people being *talked to* by the president.

Back in 1947, President Harry Truman spoke on civil rights at the Lincoln Memorial. Before ten thousand people at the closing session of the NAACP's annual convention, Truman declared that recent events at home and abroad—World War II and the Cold War—made clear the necessity of ensuring that all Americans enjoy basic rights. "When I say all Americans," he said, "I mean all Americans." Truman proposed legislation only to protect the rights of Guam and American Samoa. But he said "every man" deserved a guarantee of housing, education, medical care, a job, the right to vote, and a fair trial. "If this freedom is to be more than a *dream*," he said, "each man must be guaranteed equality of opportunity. The only limit to an American's achievement should be his ability, his industry, and his character." The next year, Dixiecrats bolted the Democratic Party and ran Strom Thurmond for president—the first crack in the allegiance of the South to the Democrats.

But now, Rustin feared that a presidential address would compromise the march.

During a break in one meeting in July, Rustin walked down to the men's room with Courtland Cox. Reaching into his back pocket, he took out a silver flask and took a swig of gin.

"Now, *how* am I going to stop this?" he said as he disappeared into the bathroom.

When he came out, a couple minutes later, he practically sang his solution.

"We'll say that we had heard from some Negroes that if Kennedy would come to speak, given their hostility, they would stone him."

So Roy Wilkins passed along the word to Kennedy's people that, in the interest of security, it would be better for the president to stay in the White House and receive the march leaders afterwards.

WHEN THE BUSES ROLLED INTO WASHINGTON, passengers peered out the window to see a city no one had ever really seen before.

"It was like coming into Rome, with all those marble buildings," said Jack Shattuck, who traveled from Maplewood, New Jersey.

If the city's grand boulevards looked imperial, some of its more modest streets looked afraid. The brick row houses looked empty. There was no traffic on the streets except march buses. Barbara Turner, a Washingtonian, looked out the bus window "feeling as though everyone in Washington had taken a holiday to the beach." She saw more cops than marchers. "The city looks scared," Elsa Rael, a marcher from New York, thought.

Washington police set up traffic barriers on New York Avenue in the early morning hours. The quicker police could establish order on the streets, the better. Some streets were blocked off, and others became major arteries. Rael's bus probably went down a street without much bus traffic.

Elliott Linzer traveled with the March on Washington staff on an old school bus donated by a church. Bomb threats delayed the departure from Harlem by two hours. Then, riding down the highways, the old bus exaggerated every bump on the highway, so no one slept.

But one of New York's leading radio personalities, Jean Shepherd of WOR, was giddy when he described his trip to the capital.

"We left Forty-seventh Street—rode on a bus with two hundred thousand other people, all riding on buses. We're going along . . . and you would see all these hands reaching out. After that it got so it was just normal. [Near] Delaware, we were skirting a railroad track—a train went past with eight, nine, ten cars, loaded to the gunnels, and . . . the crew at the front of the locomotive . . . and the whole train was waving at us."

As the buses blended together on the approach to Washington, and then coughed through Washington's streets, riders awoke and peered out the windows. Soon they would emerge from buses that had been filled with the cooped-up sounds and smells of long-distance travel—with fried and roasted chicken, pies, cakes, stale coffee, and sandwiches (the march organizers specifically called for PB&J and warned against any food with mayo). On one bus, marchers ate the sweet-potato pie of Betty Shabazz, wife of Malcolm X, who ran a bakery business in Queens.

Shepherd remembers a hearty welcome from Washington's neighborhoods: "[We were] riding along one of the main streets through the slums and here were hundreds of people on the steps—grandmothers, little old ladies, skinny kids, nuns, tough-looking guys who worked as garage mechanics . . . everywhere they're waving, we're happy you're here."

Getting off the bus, riders were stiff. One passenger looked down the aisle of the bus and saw all the men pulling ties on at the same time, as if choreographed. As they moved from the air-conditioned buses to the muggy Washington air, their glasses fogged.

At eight thirty, there were more reporters on the Mall than demonstrators. But by nine, the Mall started to fill. First 10,000, then 50,000, then 100,000 people laid out blankets and gathered in front of the Washington Monument. At one point, an additional 10,000 people came every ten or fifteen minutes. As the crowd swelled, the marchers felt it, physically—the sights, the sounds, the smells. By the middle of the afternoon, 2,173 buses had brought 110,000 marchers and the Mall held a throng of 250,000 or more. The *Washington Post* later analyzed a photograph with 1,038 people and determined that about 70 percent were black and the rest white.

A fifteen-year-old girl named Ericka Jenkins took the city bus from one of Washington's farthest ghettoes. She was amazed to see so many blacks in one place. Then amazed to see so many whites in one place. And finally amazed to see so many blacks and whites, together.

"I've never been so awestruck. They came every way—flatbed trucks with the wood floor that they used to carry tobacco, pickup trucks that were all dinged up, charter buses, school buses, station wagons, cars, motorcycles, bicycles, tricycles, and I could see people still coming in groups."

Her emotions welled up as she moved into the crowd.

"I saw people laughing and listening and standing very close to one another, almost in an embrace. Children of every size, pregnant women, elderly people who seemed tired but happy to be there, clothing that made me know that they struggled to make it day to day, made me know they worked in farms or offices or even nearby for the government. I didn't see teenagers alone; I saw groups of teenagers with teachers.

"White people [were] standing in wonder. Their eyes were open, they were *listening.* Openness and nothing on guard—I saw that in everybody. I was so happy to see that in the white people, that they could listen and take in and respect and believe in the words of a black person. I had never seen anything like that."

As the buses parked on both sides of the National Mall, most riders tumbled out toward the portable toilets and concession stands and then onto a patch of grass near the Washington Monument. One group of black teenagers with earnest faces marched in circles, singing almost defiantly, at twice the tempo of the classic gospel song, clapping rhythmically, ecstatically, in perfect unison:

> *May be the last time children I don't know*
> *May be the last time we stay together*
> *May be the last time I don't know*
> *I'm goin' home to meet my mother*

PART 3

Congregation

———

AS THE LEADERS OF THE MARCH ON WASHINGTON made the rounds on Capitol Hill—meeting behind closed doors to make the case for President Kennedy's bills—a black banker named Dunbar S. McLaurin approached the most important man in the congressional debate.

"I'm crippled for life because I've been told I'm inferior," McLaurin told Everett Dirksen.

But Dirksen opposed the most important provision of President John Kennedy's civil rights bill—the "public accommodations" provision, requiring private businesses to serve all willing customers, regardless of race.

Even though he was in the minority Republican Party, Dirksen would play a pivotal role in the civil rights debate on Capitol Hill. The Illinoisan was one of the "moderates" in the G.O.P. and he professed support for civil rights. His skills as a parliamentarian and as a coalition builder could give President Kennedy the votes he needed to pass a bill.

A heavyset, rumpled man, with a pile of silver hair atop his jowly face, Dirksen spoke the florid language of the world's greatest deliberative body but also conveyed an image of a shambling pol. But Dirksen never disguised the bottom line of politics—votes. He had to keep the support of the folks back home. Everything else paled into insignificance. And, he noted, he didn't get many black votes . . . so what was his incentive to support civil rights?

Concerns about the Constitution, Dirksen said, would not allow him to support the public accommodations provision. The federal courts, he said, had ruled that a public accommodations law would violate the property rights of private businesses. That settled the matter.

Dirksen was also concerned about states' rights. The Constitution gives the states all powers not specifically given the federal government. But of course, the New Deal long ago breached that wall. And as Senator Maurine Neuberger of Oregon pointed out, the federal government—with the support of avowed states-rights politicians in the South, and Everett Dirksen, too—specifically prohibited any discrimination against Mexican braceros. Under a 1951 law, Mexican citizens got federal protection for all public accommodations. American blacks, of course, did not.

The character lurking in all these conversation—and all debates about basic civil rights—was Mrs. Murphy.

Mrs. Murphy was the fictional owner of a small boardinghouse, where she also lived. Mrs. Murphy was not a bad person—she paid her taxes, went to church, cared for her grandchildren—but did not want to let rooms to blacks. Forcing her to rent to blacks was tantamount to making her live with strangers she did not like—a violation of her personal space.

No one knew, for sure, whether Dirksen believed this or not. Maybe he was being coy, waiting to see the trend of public opinion or watching the shifting coalitions on the Hill—or just figuring out his own approach to civil rights. Like Machiavelli's prince, wily legislators do not reveal their true sentiments or intentions, unless doing so brings them benefits.

Dunbar McLaurin was speaking about morality. Dirksen was speaking about politics. They might as well have been speaking Greek and Farsi to one another.

"Your position is based on narrow legalistic interpretation rather than a broad moral interpretation," McLaurin said. "I wish you could take your children on a trip and try to explain to them why you can't buy them ice cream. When times change we should abandon the old concepts."

Once, public accommodations for all, black and white, had been the law of the land. In 1875 Congress passed civil rights legislation with this language:

> All persons within the jurisdiction of the United States shall be entitled to the full and equal enjoyment of the accommodations, advantages, facilities, and privileges of inns, public conveyances on land or water, theaters and other places of public amusement; subject only to the conditions and limitations established by law, and applicable alike to citizens of every race and color, regardless of any previous condition of servitude.

But in 1883, the Supreme Court found that law unconstitutional, declaring that Congress does not have the power to govern the conduct of individuals.

Dirksen hewed to that 1883 line. Dunbar McLaurin's plea did not move him. "I didn't do a bit of good," McLaurin said. "What can I tell my kids?"

In fact, history offered little encouragement for passage of a meaningful civil rights bill. Besides the ill-fated 1875 law, Congress had passed only three civil rights bills since the Civil War. The Civil Rights Act of 1866, passed over President Andrew Johnson's veto, gave blacks the right to own property, make contracts, sue, and bear witness in court. The Civil Rights Act of 1957 established the Civil Rights Commission, with powers to investigate the issue broadly. The Civil Rights Act of 1960 enhanced the Justice Department's powers to enforce civil rights laws.

However cautious the 1957 and 1960 bills were, they offered a "crawl space" for the movement. Never before did the Justice Department have the authority to investigate Southern states for their police actions against minorities. "Without that law," said Bob Moses, SNCC's leading organizer in Mississippi, "the attorney general wouldn't have been able to do anything when sheriffs beat up protesters"—or when voting registrars abused their powers.

The bill that Dirksen and the rest of Congress were debating was introduced by President Kennedy on June 19.

Its most significant provision called for a ban on discrimination in public accommodations like restaurants, hotels, amusement parks, and stores. The humiliation of being refused service—"We don't serve Nigras here"—was universal and burned into every corner of black people's lives. Even extraordinary social and economic success could not guarantee a stool at a lunch counter or a bed in a hotel. That's the provision that Dirksen opposed.

On voting rights, the bill would ban literacy tests, allowing any citizen with a sixth-grade education to vote. For many Americans, the idea of testing voters still seemed reasonable. But in reality, testing for knowledge of civic issues was nothing less than a tool to suppress voting rolls. Registrars almost always rejected blacks and accepted whites.

The legislation also called for the use of referees for elections to make sure that blacks were not turned away or intimidated. What might happen when referees reported violations of voter rights was not stated. Presumably, the attorney general could initiate legal challenges if the people denied voting rights could not do so.

On education, Kennedy's legislation gave the attorney general the authority, for the first time, to initiate lawsuits in desegregation cases. The attorney general could exercise that authority—essentially, an end run around the legal requirements for litigants to have "standing" on an issue—only when black voters produced written complaints explaining that they could not bring legal action on their own.

To the disappointment of civil rights activists, the bill did not include a provision for a permanent Fair Employment Practices Commission. Franklin Roosevelt created the FEPC by executive order, as part of a deal to get Phil Randolph to cancel the 1941 march on Washington. The FEPC guaranteed blacks fairness in employment. But Congress never passed legislation endorsing the FEPC, so it lacked full authority to banish discrimination in the workplace. The FEPC was only as good as a president wanted it to be.

Originally, the March on Washington was to include a day of citizen lobbying on Capitol Hill, but March organizers had decided against bringing demonstrators to the Hill. Now, on the morning of the Great March, the Big Ten made the rounds on Capitol Hill. The group met first with Mike Mansfield, the majority leader of the Senate, for half an hour. Then they met Everett Dirksen and Charles Halleck, the minority leaders of the Senate and House, for forty minutes. Finally, they met with Speaker John McCormack and Majority Leader Carl Albert of the House.

Mansfield said he would prefer to get a bill from the House first, which would not be ready until October at the earliest. He didn't dwell on the possibility of a filibuster but hinted he might bring a House version of a civil rights bill directly to the floor of the Senate. He wanted to create a wholly new political environment that would wipe away any threat of a filibuster.

When the Big Ten came to see Dirksen and Halleck, the Republicans pledged their support. "The Republican attitude has always been friendly to civil rights," Halleck told Roy Wilkins.

Dirksen, of course, rejected the public accommodations provision but supported everything else in the bill. Dirksen said he would back an amendment calling for voluntary desegregation of accommodations. Civil rights activists rolled their eyes at the notion of a voluntary law. But the idea at least kept open the issue of public accommodations.

McCormack said the prospects looked good for fair employment and a provision for stronger federal intervention in civil rights cases. But he warned that Emanuel Celler was having a hard time getting a majority of his committee to support the FEPC and Title III.

A languor settled over Capitol Hill. The halls of Congress were quieter than on a day of recess. Members gathered in the cloakroom to watch the march on TV. Most staffers stayed home. The only real activity came on a bill to prevent a railroad strike by mandating arbitration between the railroads and unions. The House Rules Committee cleared legislation on civil defense and care for the mentally retarded. Arkansas senator William Fulbright held a secret meeting with Secretary of State Dean Rusk over the Kennedy administration's test-ban treaty.

WHEN BLACK LIMOUSINES TOOK THE BIG TEN from Capitol Hill to Constitution Avenue, Mathew Ahmann's emotions swelled at the sight of the marchers.

"To actually see them coming that way," he said, "they seem so much larger in the flesh than one could imagine."

But massing a crowd, and drawing a national TV audience for the March on Washington, would not produce success on Capitol Hill. The opinions of the masses, which are contradictory, get filtered through a complex process—in Congress, in the White House, in the lobbying on K Street, and in the media. Nothing just happens; things need to be *made* to happen.

Legislation passes when a majority of members of both chambers of Congress—a supermajority in the Senate, since bills cannot advance to a vote until two-thirds of the body agree—conclude that it is in their separate interests to vote for the bill.

Each House member's calculation of interest depends, primarily, on what his or her constituents think. On issues of little interest, representatives feel free to vote any way they like. On those issues of "low salience," they might listen to the pleadings of lobbyists for interested parties—say, automakers and tire companies on an interstate highway bill. When voters are indifferent to an issue, lawmakers are free to vote however they like.

When an issue is highly "salient"—when a lot of people care, for material or emotional reasons—House members need to pay close attention to constituents or risk getting kicked out of office.

So which constituents matter most?

After the census of 1960, the typical congressional district had a population of about 415,000. But only the people who vote—sometimes as little as 20 percent of all voting-aged citizens—really matter. In competitive districts, only the small percentage of undecided voters matter, since they can tip an election either way. In the majority of districts that are dominated by one of the two parties, only the tiny group of undecided voters in those low-participation nominating primaries or conventions really matters.

The same basic dynamic exists in the upper chamber. Senators care most about the voters who provide winning margins in primaries and elections. But to win a Senate seat requires a statewide campaign. Because they face election every six years, not every two years, senators do not feel as much pressure to follow their constituents' demands.

Because every state gets two senators, less populous states have proportionately more clout. In 1963, New York, the nation's biggest state, with almost 17 million people, had the same representation as Alaska, with 228,000 people. Voters from Alaska, then, carried about *seventy-four times* more weight than voters from New York. The senators from rural states, then, could hold the vast majority of the nation hostage.

That's even before the arcane rules and operations of the Congress come into play.

In both chambers, the real legislative action takes place in committees and subcommittees. Seniority determines committee assignments and chairmanships. The longer a legislator serves, the more important his or her committee assignments. It is easiest for senators from states with one-party rule—like those in the solidly Democratic South of the early 1960s—to hold their seats for extended periods, so they also hold most of the choice committee assignments.

The Senate Judiciary Committee was the province of James Eastland of Mississippi, a staunch segregationist. "Segregation is not discrimination," Eastland said after the *Brown v. Board of Education* decision. "It is the law of nature, it is the law of God, that every race has both the right and the duty to perpetuate itself." To move a civil rights bill out of Eastland's committee seemed an impossible dream.

The House Judiciary Committee fell under the rule of Emanuel Celler, a New Yorker and a supporter of civil rights. But if civil rights had a friend in the House Judiciary Committee, they had a sworn enemy in the House Rules Committee, which had to vote to approve all major legislation. That committee's chairman, Howard W. Smith of Virginia, opposed all civil rights measures. "The Southern people have never accepted the colored race as a race of people who had equal intelligence and education and social attainments as the whole people of the South," he said during consideration of the Civil Rights Act of 1957.

Can one small clique *really* hold up a major piece of legislation, no matter what others think? Yes, the tyranny of the minority has killed many a law. But unusual coalitions of progressives could upend an old pro like Judge Smith, as he liked to be called. A majority of the committee could defy Smith and report the bill out of committee. And so UAW leader Walter Reuther had an idea. Get Protestant leaders to pressure Republicans in their congressional districts. Republicans cannot defy their WASP constituencies.

"If the Rules Committee bottles up the civil right legislation and the church groups go to work in the area where the Republicans are the predominate political force," Reuther said, "I do not see how a Republican on the Rules Committee can stand up against a public pressure" for reporting legislation out of committee and allowing a floor vote.

Then there was the extraordinary power of a single senator to kill legislation. Under the filibuster rule, any senator could hold up a floor vote on any issue by simply talking on the floor of the Senate. That senator could read *War and Peace* or the New York telephone book, as long as he kept talking. To shut him up—to cut off debate and force a vote of the full body—required a "supermajority" of two-thirds of the Senate. But that was hard. Thirty-four senators representing about 12 million people could frustrate a group of sixty-six senators representing 168 million people, just by talking.

Because of the filibuster and the committee system, reformers often delete the most controversial provisions of their reforms—not because they lack a majority, but because they cannot get the two-thirds vote to cut off a filibuster, or the support of key committee chairs.

The champion of the filibuster, in fact, was Strom Thurmond of South Carolina. In 1957, Thurmond spoke for twenty-four hours to thwart a vote on civil rights legislation. Thurmond read the voting rights laws of all fifty states, the Declaration of Independence, and a history of Anglo-Saxon juries. Thurmond hoped that his marathon speaking session would rally Southerners against the civil rights bill pending in the Senate, but a coalition of two-thirds of Senators eventually rose up to stop the filibuster. The bill passed.

Miracles happen.

On one issue, the March on Washington could claim credit for the passage of controversial legislation. Soon after the Big Ten left Capitol Hill, both the House and Senate passed emergency legislation that directed an arbitrator to resolve the labor impasse between the nation's railroad companies and their unions.

At exactly the moment when Martin Luther King delivered his address, the House voted to accept the Senate's action establishing a seven-man arbitration board. Kennedy signed the railroad legislation at 6:15 p.m.

BONNIE PRINCE CHARLIE—CHARLIE GETER, the disc jockey from WDAS, Philadelphia's leading black radio station—was jubilant.

Getting off one of the thirteen buses sponsored by the station, Geter noticed the all-black military police directing traffic, moving bodies from the parking area to the Washington Monument.

"When you have black people who serve as special units, they take an extra pride," he said. "Those black police were *sharp*. Boots were spit-shined, helmet liners were chrome-plated, and they were directing traffic like, *precision*. Like *drill teams*. That really made my heart pound, made my eyes well up. They were doing everything, precision-wise, and they looked so great."

Philadelphia was one battleground in a broad new offensive in the civil rights war. The Northern Student Movement targeted ten cities in the North for organizing, and local organizers spread the movement to dozens more cities. In New York and Los Angeles, Muslims battled police in the streets. In New York, activists picketed construction sites for new hospitals in Harlem and Queens and took over the mayor's office, demanding that blacks get 25 percent of those jobs. Protesters in Elizabeth, New Jersey, linked arms and sat in front of a construction site for a new apartment complex, demanding fairness in hiring.

Segregated schools were also targeted in Northern cities. In Chicago, protesters rallied against the use of temporary trailers for schools in black neighborhoods. Protesters asked for the right to attend mostly white schools where there were open seats, rather than getting packed into the "Willis Wagons" (named after the school superintendent) in crowded black school grounds. Other protests took place in New York, Long Island, Boston, Cleveland, St. Louis, and other cities. Blacks were planning "stay-outs" of schools in Boston, Chicago, Detroit, New York, Oakland, and St. Louis.

Token efforts to integrate neighborhoods met with violence in Chicago and Philadelphia. But mobs were not the real cause of housing discrimination. Blacks and whites were kept apart by banking discrimination, realtor steering, restrictive covenants, and zoning. Only twenty-two of Chicago's 253 suburban towns had a hundred or more black residents. In California, blacks had access to fewer than 2 percent of all homes built since World War II. Housing discrimination was hard to confront. Settling into homes was not as easy as finding a stool at a lunch counter. Still, activists tried. In Bowie, Maryland, CORE picketed an all-white development.

In Philadelphia, things got . . . *rancid*. One week before the March on Washington, tenants in South Philly, ignored for years in their protests over slum conditions, dumped trash at the Laundromat owned by one slumlord and at the suburban home of another. More than 250 CORE activists gathered trash from all over the neighborhood—furniture, wasted appliances, garbage, even dead rats—and rode a caravan of trucks and cars to the dump-in sites. When police blocked access to a street, the protesters unloaded the trash and piled it at their feet.

Cecil Moore, the NAACP leader who led Philadelphia's protests, hung out most days at WDAS. He spoke more like a revolutionary than a member of Roy Wilkins's old-line organization. "My basic strength is those three hundred thousand lower-class guys," Moore said, "who are ready to mob, steal, and kill."

In civil rights battles across the country, the grim, square-shouldered cops usually battled the protesters. They hauled the pregnant women to the paddy wagons. They hacked away at the chains connecting protesters to bull-dozers and chain-link fences. They pulled the protesters out of the mayor's office. They were, almost without exception, white. Northern cops usually avoided the kind of meanness and racial venom found in Birmingham and Jackson. But not always.

But here in Washington, for one day, the cops looked friendly. So Charlie Geter skipped and smiled at the sight of black military officers, on duty to make everything *go right.*

WDAS, Philadelphia's premier black station, both stoked the fires of black resentment—mostly just by reporting black news—and cooled them off. On clear nights, WDAS signals covered parts of Pennsylvania, New Jersey, Delaware, and Maryland. Sometimes its signals reached as far as Nebraska.

The staff at WDAS was a royal court—Bonnie Prince Charlie (Geter), Sir Lancelot (George Johnson Jr.), the Gospel Queen (Louise Williams), the King of Blues (Kae Williams), Lord Fauntleroy (John Bandy), and the Bishop of Soul (Jimmy Bishop). The royal court dazzled listeners with rapid-fire banter: *This is your record-mixin', platter-pushin' papa, the blue-eyed soul brother, Bonnie Prince Charlie. . . .* Or: *Eee-tiddly-ock. This is the jock. And I'm back on the scene with the record machine, saying ooh-pop-a-doo, how do you do . . . ?*

WDAS played the full spectrum of music—jazz, R&B, gospel, soul, rock—and reported black news. A who's who of black music came to the station for interviews: Ray Charles, Louis Armstrong, B. B. King, Sam Cooke, Chuck Berry, Lou Rawls, and Count Basie. And also black leaders and intellectuals: Martin and Coretta King, Malcolm X, Adam Clayton Powell, Bayard Rustin, James Farmer, and Roy Wilkins.

The station issued blistering editorials. "President Kennedy has been a reluctant man surrounded by reluctant followers," one editorial said, while blacks faced "shotguns, blasts and bombings, physical and economic intimidation while peacefully demonstrating for rights which should have been theirs one hundred years ago."

The WDAS bus trips were jovial, rocking. The radio played. People packed sandwiches and coffee and sodas. Everyone buzzed about the enormity of the event. *A quarter of a million black people in one place! What would that be like?*

Booze could have been a big issue. Some brought beer in coolers. "But we kept that pretty much under control. We figured they'd have the liquor stores closed—not because of people drinking that day, but because if they didn't all those buses would have been filled with booze coming back." People all over the East Coast travel to D.C. for the cheap liquor and fill their trunks with fifths. Today was not the day for bargain booze.

The history gathered at the Mall made Geter's head swirl. Geter saw a lot of these people back at the station. But seeing them here, gathered in one place—as part of a mass, with everyone in black America—was different. And so he went prowling. He worked his way up to the platform at the Lincoln Memorial, caught glimpses of Martin Luther King and Phil Randolph, Roy Wilkins and Harry Belafonte, Mahalia Jackson and Andrew Young.

Geter used his press credentials to get up on the podium. He looked over the crowd and thought about Booker T. Washington, the Niagara Movement, and W. E. B. Du Bois.

"What a beautiful day this is," he exulted. "We've really come a long, long way."

BY THE TIME HARVEY JONES GOT TO UNION STATION, the place was jumping like it was 1945.

For years, Union Station had been a graveyard. Designed by Daniel Burnham to evoke the grandeur of global cities—Rome of Constantine, Paris of Baron von Haussmann, London of Queen Victoria—Union Station was now seedy and dilapidated. Traveling by train was an anachronism; Americans chose the convenience of cars and the speed of planes. Nationwide, the passenger miles traveled on trains declined from 96 billion to 20 billion between 1945 and 1960. The B&O and Pennsylvania railroads pondered selling or even giving away the station, or razing it to make room for office buildings. Cultural advocates debated turning the station into a performing arts center.

Early morning, and Union Station was quiet as usual. A few people sat on benches. Police lurked by the walls and doors. Newsboys and waiters at coffee shops craned their necks to see when the next train might come in. The dawn's light crept in, dust hanging in the air.

The first train for the March on Washington, the regularly scheduled Pennsylvania Railroad train from Boston, arrived at Union Station at 7:25 a.m. Then came the B&O train from Baltimore. Marchers carrying box lunches and signs stepped off the trains' steps.

The first official Freedom Train—cars specifically booked to bring people to the March—arrived from Pittsburgh at 8:02. Five hundred and thirty-five passengers got off thirteen cars and moved toward buses waiting outdoors.

Then trains came every five or ten minutes. At one point trains came into Union Station from five major trunks: Pennsylvania, B&O, C&O, Southern, and Atlantic Coastline. Ten thousand people moved through the station in twenty minutes. By noon, about forty special trains brought twenty thousand riders. People poured off the trains, onto the platforms, into the vast Beaux Arts rotunda, and out onto the streets outside. Seventy-five shuttle buses waited to ferry people to the Washington Monument.

People moved in continuous streams, flowing around each other, sometimes crossing paths, but always surging together toward the outdoors. When they bumped into each other, they uttered exaggerated *excuse me*'s and *my fault*'s and *no, my fault*'s.

Harvey Jones got off the train and heard a familiar folk song. He followed his ear until he stood before "three white folks," playing guitars and singing folk music. Peter, Paul, and Mary were singing the song that had hit number 2 on the Top Forty list that summer, Bob Dylan's "Blowin' in the Wind." Jones had never seen, in person, any music stars before. He marched with Martin Luther King and got to know all the civil rights notables—King, Medgar Evers, Roy Wilkins, Jim Farmer. But this was *different*. He decided to stay a few minutes and watch. When the song ended, he made a request—the folk trio's other big hit, "Puff the Magic Dragon."

Harvey Jones earned his trip by getting beaten up and jailed. He went to jail fifty or sixty times, in fact. He won this trip after picketing the *Charleston News and Courier*. Jones and other blacks in Charleston resented what they considered racist news coverage. Blacks were identified by race whenever there was an arrest; the paper never noted the race of whites in crime reports. Coverage of the protest demonstration was slanted, depicting peaceful, non-violent petitioners as raving rioters. The demonstrations started peacefully, but then a cop got hit with a brick. Cops scrambled around and grabbed sixty people—all of them black, more than the thirty-seven who were picketing—and threw them into police wagons.

The previous night, 150 supporters gathered in Charleston to give their marchers a proper sendoff. Crowds lined the road from Morris Street Baptist Church, the center of the city's movement. Special Train 792 pulled into the station on time at 10:45 p.m. Demonstrators on the train sang freedom songs, like "I Woke Up This Morning with My Mind Set on Freedom."

One of the train captains warned the crowd: "If you have any knives, please turn them in. If you get off the train with a knife, it *will be known to the authorities.* We have a way of finding out."

A white girl moved up and down the cars, swaying as she went, getting marchers to sign petitions, demanding the Justice Department drop the federal indictment against the Albany Nine.

A black girl shouted, "White folks, it's all over! In '63, we shall all be free." That was the slogan the NAACP had adopted a decade before, in anticipation of the centennial of the Emancipation Proclamation.

An old woman sang in one of the darkened cars: "What a friend we have in Jesus. We do not have everything we want because we do not carry everything to God in prayer."

Another rider on the Freedom Train, James Hauser, took the train for the 820-mile journey from St. Augustine, Florida, the nation's oldest city. The imposing forty-three-year-old laborer—six feet, two and a half inches, two hundred pounds—got off the train at 8:48 in the morning after an eighteen-hour trip.

"I lived in the North once, in Pittsburgh. Once my mother got out of the South, she refused to go back ever. I wouldn't have done it if the doctors didn't tell me to get out of the cold climate. It's harder to live in the South when you've been in the North and you know the rules."

Hauser wore a short-sleeved white shirt, a black-, white-, and gray-striped tie, red socks, black shoes, and a heavy charcoal wool suit. "It's the only suit I own," he said. "It's warm to wear today, but it's the only one I have. I came to Washington for freedom and better work, and coming here is an important thing. I know I've been held down in my work just because I'm a Negro."

Hauser had paid a steep price for demonstrating. "They warned us when I worked not to get involved in any race demonstrations. I did, on July 4, and I was laid off the next day. I was working for the Fairchild Corporation, stripping paint off airplanes. They have a big Air Force contract. I had a part-time job driving a school bus for the state. I lost that too. They told me they got someone else because they thought I had a full-time job picketing."

One of Harvey Jones's teachers on nonviolence was Martin Luther King. At a march downtown, a drunk threw a beer mug at him. When Jones tensed, King thrust himself in front of him. "If you don't think you can respond nonviolently, maybe you should leave the march," King said. "No, sir. I wasn't going after him." The drunk got no response from the crowd, grew bored, and left.

After the arrests at the *News and Courier,* Jones and the others refused to give their names and demanded to know the charges. Then they were herded out to the Hines Prison Farm, with hardened criminals. One day passed . . . two days . . . all the way to eleven days. Families came by to give fried chicken to the prisoners, but the jailers scarfed it down.

When Jones and the others finally got out of the prison yard, they went to a church meeting to tell their stories. Jones didn't know what to say, but he blurted out: "I have been in jail for eleven days, and I will go back for another eleven days to get my freedom." The packed church exploded with applause. And then the Reverend Benjamin Glover announced that Harvey Jones's courage in jail and eloquence at the meeting had earned him a free ticket on the Freedom Train.

As Harvey Jones and the other passengers moved outside, they saw Black Muslims selling *Muhammad Speaks*. Marchers passing by laughed at the futility of the Muslim effort. Washington Transit Authority buses filled up for the four-block trip to the Washington Monument. Some marchers frowned when they found out the shuttle service cost twenty-five cents, and decided to march to the National Mall.

Harvey Jones and the other travelers from the Deep South faced hostility when they paraded in front of newspaper offices and sat down at lunch counters. The demonstrators on the train from Cincinnati, on the border between North and South, faced the less lethal but more stubborn challenge of their own moral ambivalence.

In church services at Clifton United Methodist Church the Sunday before the March, the Reverend David Sageser urged his flock to go to Washington. But not without reservations.

"I must admit I dislike the thought of carrying placards, conducting demonstrations, or making a march on Washington," he preached on Sunday. "But I am growing desperate in my search for some way to identify with the Negro in his need. I have only to examine the example of Jesus Christ to know that he would not hesitate to make a public [display] of his allegiance, even though it meant public disorder. He did not simply write his congressman. He undertook to clear the money changers from the temple personally."

Sageser, a Kentucky native, struggled to overcome his own prejudices. He grew up, he said "a benevolent racist." But he kept himself open to new ideas and experiences and found himself involved in civil rights. He even had the courage to confront a bishop at a conference. But real growth took time.

"I remember with dismay," he said years later, "the first time I got involved, I wondered if I could shake the man's hand because it was black." But he knew racism was wrong, whatever his undercurrents of prejudice.

His congregation, affiliated with the University of Cincinnati, was a mix of students and older, conservative families. All but a few members were white. As Sageser struggled with his own prejudice, he wanted to avoid insulting parishioners who did not support civil rights. "Many members were reluctant," he said. "I was trying to protect my back against the accusation that I was a radical. I needed to continue in their good graces."

When they left from Cincinnati's C&O Railroad Station, "We all kissed our wives with unusual feeling because we heard Washington was closed and federal troops were all over," Sageser remembered. Concerned about violence, the organizers put two captains on each car to lecture passengers to turn the other cheek when bigots taunted them. After ten hours, they arrived at Track 24 in Union Station, at seven in the morning.

Traveling by train still seemed romantic. "The train is the movement, the movement of one person or people, from one place to another," one passenger told Studs Terkel. "It's dynamic, it's forceful, it always has a certain destination. It always reaches a certain point. And I hope this train is going to reach freedom."

HOLLYWOOD CELEBRITIES BUNDLED THEMSELVES into shuttle buses after arriving at National Airport. Two planes—organized by Ossie Davis, who would be the emcee of the first part of the march, held at the Washington Monument—brought the stars.

The leader of the group was Charlton Heston, the man who played Moses in *The Ten Commandments*. Actor Tony Curtis (*Some Like It Hot, Spartacus*) was there too, along with director Billy Wilder (*Double Indemnity, Sunset Boulevard*), actor Marlon Brando (*A Streetcar Named Desire, On the Waterfront*), singer Sammy Davis Jr. (*What Kind of Fool Am I?*), and actress Rita Moreno (*The King and I, West Side Story*).

Heston struggled to recruit women and TV stars to join the march. One planning memo warned that the poor representation of women was "playing into the hands of the segregationists." As part of the middlebrow medium, TV actors usually avoided controversy.

In their planning meetings back in L.A., they talked about leveraging their fame to get ordinary Americans to question their prejudices. "We know that motion picture personalities are to a great degree the style, fashion, and mores pace-setters of the impressionable masses in this country," one planning memo stated. "As someone in Torrance said: 'If integration is good enough for Marlon Brando, it's good enough for me.'"

So far, they had given their talents to fund-raisers and local campaigns, in both the North and South. Paul Newman and Brando went to Gadsden.

Dick Gregory protested in Chicago. Lena Horne and Harry Belafonte gave concerts to raise money.

On the drive from the airport, Joseph Mankiewicz, the director of *The Ghost and Mrs. Muir* and *Guys and Dolls*, suggested a boycott of film contractors that refused to give blacks equal rights. Marlon Brando immediately endorsed it.

"If every composer, every musician, every actor, *everyone* in our profession refused to allow his contributions to be displayed in any segregated place, it would be most effective."

Charlton Heston said he would call a meeting of fifty or more performers to develop a political strategy for integrated theaters. Hollywood stars had already started working behind the scenes for civil rights. Weeks before, representatives of eight film and TV guilds met with NAACP representatives to develop new standards for representation of blacks in movies and TV shows. The meeting led to the creation of a permanent committee to "implement the film industry's fair employment policy for casting Negroes and would further accurate representation of Negroes as they appear in American life."

Jackie Robinson, the man who broke baseball's color line in 1947, attended the march with his son. A lifelong Republican who supported a moderate approach to civil rights, Robinson endorsed direct action for the first time that summer. As a businessman—he served as spokesman for Chock Full o'Nuts—Robinson stressed the economic power of blacks.

"I think the boycott is going to come into being more and more because the Negro is recognizing their tremendous economic strength," he told the Educational Radio Network.

"We represent an income, more money than the whole of Canada. I think white businessmen are beginning to recognize it; the Negro now is beginning to recognize this tremendous strength. And we're going to use this strength to our best advantage. Businesses and industries that will work with us will get our cooperation; those who will not, then we're going to just go someplace else. It's as simple as that."

Burt Lancaster, wearing a dark suit and thin tie, his sweaty hair matted on his high forehead, later stood before the crowd at the Washington Monument. Lancaster had flown six thousand miles, from Paris. The star of *Elmer Gantry* and *The Birdman of Alcatraz* was working on a film called *The Train,* about members of the French Resistance smuggling out priceless art before the Nazis can steal it.

Lancaster announced that he had a petition with names of fifteen hundred Americans in Paris who supported civil rights. He unfurled the scroll, letting it tumble down the marble steps of the monument. Leaning to the side, pointing to the crowd, Lancaster read a statement avowing the support of Americans across the globe for civil rights.

As Lancaster talked, Dick Gregory moved around like the father of the bride at a wedding reception. That summer, Gregory led protests in Chicago and Gadsden, Alabama. Gregory insisted on spending time in jail instead of signing a recognizance bond. "I'd stay in jail fifty years before I'd sign up on a crime I didn't commit," he said. Chicago police, he said, are "drunk on hatred." He was released pending an October 10 hearing.

Gregory introduced people to a well-known Chicago prostitute known as Scarlet Mary. He told the story of how she came to the march. Back in Chicago, she approached Gregory, said she needed to see him alone. She told him she wanted help getting a job. He couldn't understand. She never had any problem with money. Why now?

"I want to go to the March on Washington," she said.

"Transportation, train fare, plane fare, that shouldn't be a problem for you."

"This is different," she said. "I want to go with clean money this time."

Later, Marvin Kalb interviewed Gregory on CBS.

"This is the first time in my life I've ever been hung up for words," he said. "It's probably the most beautiful thing in America I would ever want to see or be part of. As long as there's a man alive on the face of the earth, this day will always be remembered."

Later, Gregory chortled about news that a plane carrying Ku Klux Klansmen to Washington crashed. "Did you hear about the Grand Wizard's accident? Told him about burning those crosses on the plane!"

This is Dick Gregory, drunk on the moment.

"I *knew* there was not going to be no violence," he said. "I was so sure there wasn't going to be violence I brought my children. This is the first time in the history of the world that a bunch of Negroes have been invited anywhere and we didn't care to fight."

One of the growing legions of "firsts"—Carol Taylor, the first black ever to serve as an airplane stewardess—also celebrated.

Taylor's celebrity story began in 1957, when the New York State chapter of the Urban League began lobbying airlines to hire black pilots and stewardesses. A registered nurse, Taylor decided she wanted to do something new. "I had an interview [with TWA] and they said, 'We'll call you Thursday,'" she said. "I'm still waiting." She and two other black job seekers filed a complaint with the New York State Commission on Discrimination.

Seeing the PR potential, a regional carrier called Mohawk Airlines held a competition and interviewed eight hundred candidates for first black stewardess. "How would you respond if a passenger called you a nigger?" an interviewer asked Taylor. "I'm going to spill coffee on his lap," she thought to herself. "Can I help you, *sir?*" she cooed. She got the job and started flying on December 23, 1957.

She flew for six months, long enough to become the subject of newspaper and magazine articles, TV and radio spots. She spoke at conferences. And she started writing for the *Flamingo,* a London magazine. That's how, earlier that summer, she got credentials to a White House reception to mark the centenary of the Emancipation Celebration. When she met President Kennedy—"taller and thinner that I thought he was, ruddy face, and he took advantage of that charisma"—she considered how she might someday seduce him. Then she saw Jackie leave the party. "I guess there were too many black people in one room," she said.

Taylor sat next to a man carrying a cattle prod. He held it, looking at it from different angles. "Look at this sadistic weapon," he muttered. She looked closer. It was Marlon Brando. When he and Paul Newman went to Gadsden that summer to support civil rights demonstrations there, he came away with the electric device used to herd livestock, which police used to terrorize activists.

"Is that real?" she asked.

He glared back.

She looked over and saw Harry Belafonte and Sidney Poitier.

Since college, she had vowed to meet Belafonte one day. She prowled parties the night before the march, trying to find him. On the walk back to the hotel she met Malcolm X, who asked her to wait for him. She kept going, looking for Belafonte. She later regretted not talking with Malcolm. Now she had a chance to meet more stars. She introduced herself to Poitier, who introduced her to Belafonte. She sat between them as the festivities continued.

"Where have you *been* all my life?" Belafonte asked. "How can I get in touch with you?"

Ossie Davis, the emcee, came over.

"I'm here trying to organize this thing and you're causing a distraction. You were lucky enough to be admitted at the last minute."

"Don't bother about him," Belafonte said. "He's just a nervous Nellie."

Sammy Davis Jr., his hair tinged with red and a wisp of a goatee falling from his chin, approached Taylor, got on one knee, and kissed her hand.

"I'm just *loving* all this male pulchritude," she said.

She did not revere Martin Luther King, though.

"The white male media presents him as the peaceful black man, turning of the cheek," she said. "Me, being a roustabout, I am not too sanguine about the efficacy of someone turning the other cheek. Here you have the police force almost daily slaughtering black males. Malcolm said, When you pull a knife halfway out, don't tell me to thank you."

Finally, she stood up and played her role.

She got up at the podium and told the crowd to shout "Freedom!" again and again, loud enough "to be heard all over the world."

For the first time, everyone did something together. The march wasn't just a gathering of groups anymore. It was one group. And the shouts could be heard ten blocks away.

Watching the whole spectacle was Norman Thomas, the six-time Socialist Party candidate for president. He talked about the movement's history; it started with the Greensboro sit-ins, he said. And he marveled at the power of the masses to speak as one. He stood on the podium next to Rachelle Horowitz, the march's transportation planner.

"You know," he said, "it makes you believe in socialism again."

WHEN HANK THOMAS CONFRONTED A RACIST, he glared. A big man, lean and muscular—six feet, four inches tall, more than two hundred pounds—he stood over his adversary and stared right in his eyes. He did not yield until that adversary backed down. Only two times, in years of protesting, did anyone attack him.

"With my size, I would deliberately have the look on my face that says, 'If you mess with me, I'll crack your skull.' I looked directly at him. He's got to think, 'Is this guy really nonviolent? Maybe I'll pass this guy and get the next one.'"

That power of intimidation was just what the March on Washington needed for security. The mere presence of people like Hank Thomas could change the dynamics of an angry or restless crowd. Even though he was committed to nonviolence, he knew how to make his presence felt. He drew out the courage of his own people and exposed the cowardice of racists and punks.

And so, early in the morning, Thomas came to serve as one of the marshals of the march. He was part of a group trained in nonviolent crowd control the previous week. Julius Hobson showed a hundred volunteers how to deal with disorder.

"Those equipped with walkie-talkies and bullhorns will circulate through the crowd, trying to settle any altercation with friendly persuasion," Hobson said. "Those who are similarly equipped will patrol the fields of the march. I would not hesitate to call the police. All incidents will be radioed to me in a command booth. If it's bad, I'll report it."

So, holding white walkie-talkies the size of paperback books, Hobson's volunteers fanned out. They each got code names: Freedom, Equality, Justice, Jobs. They greeted each other: "This is Freedom Two to Equality One . . . Over . . ."

During that training, Julius Hobson emphasized the dangers posed by the FBI. Agent provocateurs would spread all over the Mall, looking for opportunities to start fights, Hobson said. The major task of the volunteer security guards, then, was to spot those agents and alert someone before any fights started.

No one knew it at the time, but Hobson was a paid informant for the FBI.

"I was surprised to be told that the FBI was doing this, because I still had this image of what the FBI was supposed to represent," Thomas said. "On the Freedom Rides, we knew the FBI was there, but they were just there to observe, and whenever they saw violence they did nothing. They were there looking for Communists. But to be told they would start something, that's something else."

Combined, more than six thousand security people—two thousand metropolitan police, two thousand National Guardsmen, and two thousand marshals trained—worked that day. Another four thousand marines and soldiers stood ready to move into the Mall from Fort Myer and Anacostia. And, of course, the soldiers at Fort Bragg would mobilize from Andrews. All but the marshals were armed, with guns and clubs and tear gas. No dogs, though. Dogs symbolized the tactics of Bull Connor. Police would keep dogs away from the Mall, but would use them if the march turned into a riot.

Before the military could act, President Kennedy would have to sign a special proclamation. The president would follow the same procedures he had used in Oxford and Tuscaloosa to integrate Ole Miss and the University of Alabama. First he authorized Secretary of Defense Robert McNamara to use troops, and then McNamara issued the necessary orders.

From the time he was a boy in St. Augustine, Hank Thomas protested the everyday indignities of segregation—refusing to leave a library, sitting in the front of the bus, drinking from the white water fountain. In those days, St. Augustine was a calmer, sleepier town, and the worst he got for his protests was dirty looks and quiet lectures on risk taking. When he got to Howard University in 1959, he eagerly joined protests in Virginia and Maryland.

He refused to sit in the back of the bus on trips home to Florida. Wherever he was, he used the Glare to avoid the kinds of beatings others got.

Thomas was the only Freedom Rider to take the whole journey—from Washington through Virginia and the Carolinas down to Georgia, then over to Alabama and Mississippi. He rode on the first bus, which mobs fire-bombed on Mother's Day in 1962, outside Anniston, Alabama. After the bus bombing, and the unrestrained attacks on the riders of the second bus in Birmingham, the Freedom Rides were called off. When students in Nashville decided to come to Alabama to finish the rides, Thomas came down from New York to finish the ride himself. As part of a deal the Kennedy administration struck with Mississippi governor Ross Barnett, police escorted the buses through Alabama and Mississippi—and then arrested all the riders in Jackson. Thomas served fifty-nine days in Parchman.

So Hank Thomas was plenty tough enough for anything that might happen at the March on Washington.

Conflict was most likely if a small knot of thugs—five or ten or fifteen of them—entered the crowd and started taunting the marchers or throwing bottles or rocks. Troublemakers could create a wedge and break up a line of marchers, trampling and beating people along the way. It happened all the time, in demonstrations in Danville, Plaquemine, Albany, Chapel Hill, Savannah.

The planning for nonviolent crowd control began with Bayard Rustin in New York. He recruited William Johnson, a retired police officer and the head of the Guardians, who in turn rallied more than a thousand active and retired cops.

The whole experience overwhelmed Johnson, who wrote an effusive letter to King on July 18: "The Rev. Martin Luther King, Jr., President John F. Kennedy, and God are walking hand-in-hand for the glory of the United States. . . . What with your foresight, insight, and faith in God—you knew 'This Day' had to come." Working for the march, he said, had "more significance than my years of military service—overseas with an army 'fighting for democracy' while spreading hate, distrust, and cancerous racial prejudice everywhere it encamped."

Rustin's first challenge was to disarm his men. A New York law required cops to carry guns twenty-four hours a day. Rustin worked out an arrangement with the police commissioner to let the volunteers leave their guns at home.

Rustin took the cops upstairs, to the third floor of the March on Washington headquarters in Harlem, and lectured them about the principles of nonviolence. He showed them maps of Washington, D.C., marked to indicate the bus routes, the parking lots, and the two avenues where marchers would walk. He talked about possible locations for troublemakers. The Nazis, for example, planned to meet at the Sylvan Theater, next to the Washington Monument, chant white-supremacist slogans, then move into the crowds of marchers.

Then Rustin took the Guardians out to the backyard for simulated conflict. He got some staffers and cops to stage mock disputes. He used the same kind of training that CORE and SNCC used to train new recruits. Some volunteers pretended to be marchers, and others pretended to be racist thugs—yelling and taunting, throwing things and kicking.

Then he told the Guardians to link arms and slowly move in to surround the aggressor. "Now you, here!" Rustin shouted. "You link arms and move in—*moooove* in. Press in—*more*! Do not swing, do not even *threaten* to hit anyone. Just move in! Move *in!*"

Hank Thomas, that fierce and lean man who put fear into the hearts of racist thugs whenever he demonstrated, never needed to link hands and *moooove* in. But he was prepared.

ON THE EDGE OF THE NATIONAL MALL, a minister from Farmville, Virginia, stood in the middle of three busloads of demonstrators, leading them in a rock version of "We Shall Overcome." A playful bopping beat replaced the long, mournful cadence of the civil rights anthem.

Goodwin Douglas was a young, hip minister who wore Bermuda shorts and T-shirts as he joined in protests against segregation and the shutdown of the county's schools. Douglas was the yin to the yang of Francis Griffin, the experienced minister who had coordinated protests by the Student Nonviolent Coordinating Committee against the closing of schools in their district, located in Prince Edward County.

The beginnings of the modern civil rights movement can be traced to any number of events—the founding of the NAACP in 1909, the U.S. entry into World War II, the postponed March on Washington of 1941, Jackie Robinson breaking baseball's color bar in 1947, the Journey of Reconciliation of 1947.

But one moment—the Supreme Court's 9–0 decision in *Brown v. Board of Education* in 1954, which rejected the doctrine that the races could be enrolled in separate schools as long as they had "equal" opportunity—transformed the politics of race in America. Segregation came under attack in every corner of American life—not just schools, but also buses and trains, department stores and eateries, theaters and playing fields, water fountains and bathrooms, parks and beaches, voting systems, hospitals and waiting rooms.

Brown originated when students in five school districts challenged the unequal conditions of segregated schools. The lead plaintiff was Linda Brown, a third-grade student in Topeka, Kansas. Prince Edward County, an agricultural community seventy miles southwest of Richmond, got involved when a girl there staged a dramatic walkout at the high school.

Most Virginia districts offered public education for whites from kindergarten through twelfth grade, but provided it to blacks only through the eighth grade. But in 1947, Farmville extended classes through the twelfth grade for blacks at Robert Moton High School. Then blacks flooded the district from other parts of the state. A school built for 180 students held 450 students by 1950.

In 1951, Barbara Johns, the daughter of a local minister, organized a boycott. When the protesters decided to sue Prince Edward County to get equal facilities, the NAACP agreed to take on the case—as long as they agreed to demand not just equal facilities, but full desegregation. So *Davis v. County School Board of Prince Edward County* got folded into *Brown*.

Throughout the 1950s most Southern states defied the Supreme Court's directive to desegregate "with all deliberate speed." In Virginia, communities avoided *Brown* by establishing "segregation academies," which, because they were private, did not need to comply with the ruling. Prince Edward County closed down its entire school system in 1959. Whites found opportunities in the new academies. Blacks simply went without any education at all.

Starting in 1962, the Reverend Griffin organized summer classes for blacks. The next summer, teachers and college students from New York—Queens College students and United Federation of Teachers members—came down to Prince Edward County to run "freedom schools" for children who, by this point, had been denied formal schooling for four years.

Some youngsters had never attended school and could not hold a pencil. Some ten-year-olds did not know the alphabet and did not understand numbers.

"But the worst was that they whispered when they spoke," said Marjorie Sulkes, one of the volunteers. "Their personalities were damaged."

They may have been damaged, but they were eager to learn. Some of those black children walked five miles over dirt roads to get to school. Others got up at five thirty to work the fields or do other jobs before school.

Over the summer, the group came together as a community. They held cookouts in backyards and sing-alongs in churches.

One day, a group of kids was jailed for demonstrating. Griffin worried about the conditions in jail. So he had volunteers print and distribute hundreds of flyers for a church meeting. The meeting's purpose, the flyer said, was to discuss adult education. Because of fear of retribution, Griffin knew he couldn't call a big crowd to protest the jailings.

With the church full, Griffin started preaching about adult education. Suddenly, seamlessly, he was talking about the kids in jail. He came down from pulpit and started marching down the aisle and out of the church. Everyone followed him. In minutes, hundreds were protesting in front of courthouse. The children were released unharmed.

That summer both ministers, Francis Griffin and Goodwin Douglas, worked with officials from the Justice Department to figure out how to open the public schools by the 1963–64 school year.

And when the Farmville volunteers arrived in Washington, they were too exhausted, physically and psychologically, to march.

After the rousing rounds of "We Shall Overcome," they lay in the glare of the August sun and passively took in the day's events. As they dozed, they wondered whether their summer had done any good, or was just another case of idealistic Northerners coming in to save the day and leaving before anything changed.

THE MUSIC WAS TOO CONTROLLED for Dorie Ladner. It was too white for Dick Gregory.

The music of protest went way back, to the antebellum and postbellum plantations, to the chain gangs and prisons, the factories and mines and union campaigns. When soldiers march to war, often they are sent off in song. Anthems like "The Battle Hymn of the Republic" overwhelm soldiers with patriotic fervor. Civil rights warriors used music for the same purposes.

As high school students in Palmers Crossing, Mississippi, Dorie and Joyce Ladner joined a local NAACP chapter and took trips to Jackson, where they met Medgar Evers. Then they went to college, first at Jackson State and then Tougaloo. They demonstrated everywhere, against the fiercest police and mob opposition. They landed in jail and sometimes feared for their lives.

Always, music gave them courage.

Dorie remembered when Fannie Lou Hamer got thrown off the plantation in Ruleville, Mississippi, where she had lived her whole adult life. Miss Hamer took a bus, with seventeen others, to Indianola to register to vote. The owner of the plantation where her husband worked warned against registering, an act of defiance. He told her she would have to leave if she insisted on registering—but her husband would be held in captivity to work off his debt. She left her home that very day. Ten days later, night riders shot into the home where she was staying.

Miss Hamer and her friends immediately started singing.

Oh, freedom,
Oh freedom,
ohhhhh, freedom over me
over me.
And before I'll be a slave,
I'll be buried in my grave.

"This *empowers* you," Dorie Ladner said. "At Medgar's funeral I sang, 'This little light of mine, I'm going to let it shine' *on North Capitol Street.* It was defiant. The music soothed the beast."

At every stage of the civil rights movement, singing provided emotional courage. Protesters would come back to the church, after beatings by mobs and cops . . . or gather to pray for murdered or disappeared activists . . . or find themselves isolated in rat-infested jails . . . or they would steel themselves to register voters or picket segregated stores. Despair edged dangerously toward violence. And then someone would start singing.

Music transformed the body—banished fear, created a vision of something better, brought people together as one. Music made the body move, and once the body was moving, it started marching.

"Without music, you don't have anything," said Dorie. "We were used to singing and getting everyone to join in. You can talk for only so long, but you need to sing or march to get people involved. If we were getting ready to go out for a protest march, we're going to start a song before we leave that door."

Ain't going to let nobody turn me around,
Turn me around,
Turn me around.
Ain't gonna let nobody turn me around.
Keep on a-walking, keep on a-talking.

Ain't gonna let no Sheriff Jones turn me around . . .
Ain't going to let no paddy wagon turn me around . . .
Ain't going to let no jails turn me around . . .

And on and on.

"If people start singing, people are going to start *marching.* And then nothing can stop you."

"How do you explain it?" said Robert Simpson, a high school student in Birmingham. "It was like a fire. It started out small. You start a fire, just fan it a little bit. Well, Birmingham was on fire. Once it got going it was no turning around. As that song sang, 'Ain't gonna let nobody turn me around.' All those things we sang about, we believed. If not, we would have just stopped, quit and said, 'That's it.'"

As they sang, they waved American flags at their segregationist tormenters—which was like waving a red cape at a bull. The American flag was a symbol of the Union, the hated force that defeated the Confederacy, took over Dixie during Reconstruction, issued *Brown,* and now tried to force-feed Southerners integrated schools and lunch counters and get blacks to register and vote. Activists loved using the symbol of America to arouse their self-styled patriot opponents.

Singing sometimes pacified the jailers too. "Sing that song for me, Miss Dorie! I want to hear that song again."

Now, to Dorie Ladner and her allies in the radical wing of the movement, the March on Washington was too scripted. "We Shall Overcome" was the official anthem of the march. When signers got up to perform, they didn't invite the crowd to join in. The crowd never joined in any of the courage-boosting song of the movement. At the march, music was something you listened to, not something that aroused the crowd.

White folk singers were the most visible figures at the march. People stepping off the train heard Peter, Paul, and Mary. As they walked across the Mall, they saw Bob Dylan. And up on the platform of the Washington Monument, they were joined by the ringing soprano of Joan Baez.

Dylan stood on the stage, a harmonica propped before his mouth and a guitar hanging off his shoulders, and played two recent compositions. He sang "When the Ship Comes In," which glimpses a future when "the sun will respect / every face on the deck." Dylan's voice—whining, wheezing, gravelly—belied the joy he foresaw, but suggested the retribution that enemies of freedom would face on their judgment day:

Then they'll raise their hands,
Sayin', "We'll meet all your demands,"
But we'll shout from the bow, "Your days are numbered."
And like Pharaoh's tribe,
They'll be drowned in the tide,
And like Goliath, they'll be conquered.

"Only a Pawn in Their Game" recalled the darkest day of the summer of 1963—the murder of Medgar Evers in Jackson. The song depicts Evers's killer as just a tool of the real hatemongers of the South, the politicians who use racism to further their own careers:

The deputy sheriffs, the soldiers, the governors get paid
And the marshals and cops get the same
But the poor white man's used in the hands of them all like a tool
He's taught in his school
From the start by the rule
That the laws are with him
To protect his white skin
To keep up his hate
So he never thinks straight
'Bout the shape that he's in
But it ain't him to blame
He's only a pawn in their game.

Bob Dylan sang for the movement all summer, on the back of a pickup in Mississippi and in the nightclubs of Greenwich Village. Sometimes he stayed at Rachelle Horowitz's one-bedroom apartment, where Dorie and Joyce Ladner lived that summer. When the three women came home at two in the morning, Dylan strummed his guitar in the living room. As they drifted off to sleep, Dylan strummed and sang.

Jonathan Takiff, a kid from suburban Philadelphia, went to the march wearing jeans and a work shirt, in the style of Bob Dylan. For Takiff, Dylan was the Mall's main attraction.

"For a lot of people, [it] took a lot of time to get past that voice," Takiff says. "He sounded angry and agitated, not pretty, and what he had to say was not pretty. It was intended to smack you over the head. He took a page out of the Woody Guthrie book."

In fact, Dylan's voice was an acquired taste. Earlier that month, a *Newsday* reviewer wrote: "This lad composes timely, spunky, folksy songs, all right—although I've watched Steve Allen make up instant lyrics just as clever. But Dylan is not a singer. He is a strident, nasal wailer. Someone else should have been drafted to do his tunes."

But Dylan had his biggest stage now on the Mall. Joan Baez harmonized for "When the Ship Comes In" and sang "Oh Freedom." Peter, Paul, and Mary sang "Blowin' in the Wind," their surprise Top Forty hit.

As those white folk stars sang, Dick Gregory covered his ears with his hands. "What was a white boy like Bob Dylan there for?" he asked. "Or who else? Joan Baez? To support the cause? Wonderful! Support the cause. March. Stand behind us, not in front of us."

Len Chandler joined the group to sing "Eyes on the Prize." A sprawling group of musicians—including the Freedom Singers, a quartet formed in 1962 to raise money for the Student Nonviolent Coordinating Committee— joined the group in singing the movement's anthem, "We Shall Overcome." Odetta sang the most soulful of civil rights folk songs, "Oh Freedom," and Josh White also performed.

The problem with all this—for Dorie Ladner and others who were so aroused by music during picketing and sit-ins, marches and demonstrations, church services and funerals, and in jailhouses—was that the March on Washington turned music into a passive spectator activity. It was a concert, a Newport festival, not a rousing call to action.

John Handy had another problem. A short black man with a shaved head and a boxer's build, wearing a black leather hat, Handy played sax with Charlie Mingus for a year and once jammed with Ella Fitzgerald. He played at Carnegie Hall and was a leading figure in the jazz craze of Greenwich Village. One reviewer said Handy "could have retired on the strength of his play[ing]" for Mingus's 1959 record *Better Git It in Your Soul.*

On the bus trip from San Francisco, Handy tried to avoid playing. "I'm here to go on the march," he said. A wide-eyed blond kid played "Study War No More" and "Blowin' in the Wind." Later, the whole bus filled with "We Shall Overcome." Finally, Handy agreed to play. "I've been listening to some bad singing," he said. "That's my inspiration to play." He played some jazz standards and civil rights songs.

Handy got involved with the movement when he lived in New York in the late 1950s. He took part in a sit-in at a Woolworth lunch counter in New York. When he moved to San Francisco, he joined CORE. In recent weeks, he had joined pickets at the Bank of America, an employer of eighteen thousand people but only twenty blacks.

Handy's motivation came from an incident in Texas when he was six years old. His stepfather was driving a pickup. "There was a place we weren't supposed to go through after sundown," he says. Three white men pulled up next to the pickup. "Pull over!" they shouted, again and again, nearly scraping the pickup.

"What they didn't know was that my people would fight to the death. They would have gotten us but they wouldn't have seen another day. My stepfather had a twelve-gauge shotgun right there. And he would have kicked the shit out of them. But we got out of town."

Now, standing on the lawn before the Washington Monument, he was angry when he realized that the greatest American contribution to the arts —a *black* contribution—was completely absent from the March on Washington.

Handy vowed to go back to San Francisco and create a jazz group dedicated to the civil rights movement.

ON THE EDGE OF THE TIDAL BASIN, a security officer approached a young Mississippian wearing a sandwich board. The protester's sign violated the sign policy of the March on Washington.

James Lee Pruitt's placard declared "Stop Criminal Prosecutions of Vote Workers in Mississippi" on one side and "We Must Have the Vote in Mississippi by 1964" on the other.

Pruitt was an eighteen-year-old student from Greenwood, Mississippi. Skinny, wearing overalls and a crisp gray-and-white-striped shirt, he wandered around the Mall looking lost.

"Has your sign been approved?" the marshal asked. "Did you make this yourself? All signs have to be approved."

"It's my sign," Pruitt said.

"Has it been approved?" the marshal asked.

A second marshal saw what was happening. "For God's sake, please leave the kid alone. He's all right."

"Rules are rules," said the first marshal. "Come with me."

In the weeks before the march, staffers back in Harlem drew up pages of lists of possible slogans for signs. Bayard Rustin took those lists to meetings of the Big Ten, who sat around a table, scratched out some slogans, edited others.

The march organizers did not want to leave the slogans open to chance. They wanted to avoid personal or crude declarations against President Kennedy or Congress—or even George Wallace or the Klan.

Jimmy Pruitt's was not the only handmade sign to appear. A group of black nationalist supporters carried unauthorized signs that read "Black Party, Yes; Democratic Party, No; Republican Party, No" and "Don't Talk Freedom, Act Freedom." Locked-out ILGWU workers from Philadelphia handed out bags that read: "Don't Buy Judy Bond Blouses."

One of Pruitt's companions from Mississippi called out: "Show them your papers, Jimmy."

After being ushered into the march tent, Jimmy Pruitt unfolded a piece of paper that told his story.

In June, James was arrested for participating in a civil rights march. He was sentenced to four months in jail and fined $300. He was first taken to the county penal farm and then transferred to Mississippi State penitentiary in Parchman. He was put into solitary confinement and all of his clothes were taken. And then the clothes were handed back to him. He and 13 other demonstrators were put in a 5 x 8 cell. Their bodies were greased. They were told that the grease was poison and not to get it in their mouths. They stacked themselves like cordwood in a small cell. They got two small meals a day. Then their rations were cut in half. Once they were put into the sweatbox, a 6 x 6 cell. After 12 hours James blacked out with a temperature of 106. Electric fans were turned on the naked men shivering in the cold. James was in jail a total of 52 days, 47 without any clothes.

The experience of James Pruitt was not unique in Mississippi that summer. Two years of steady organizing had once again aroused the segregationists. Protesters threatened to wash away the state's apartheid system.

Police and their allies in the Ku Klux Klan and White Citizens Councils staged waves of attacks, sometimes using dogs. Police also arrested activists attempting to register voters and picket local businesses. Jailed activists were abused and starved. Employers, landlords, banks, and insurance companies all punished blacks who attempted to register to vote or otherwise worked for civil rights.

The Greenwood Citizens Council burned six black businesses in an attack on the SNCC office. Jackson mobs swarmed all over sit-inners at Woolworth and bombed a house near Medgar Evers's home, before Byron De La Beckwith murdered Evers. In Clarksdale, NAACP leader Aaron Henry's home was firebombed. Black Greenville voters were arrested for playing ball at a park. A gas bomb broke up a voter registration meeting in Itta Bena. The mayor of Ruleville beat a fourteen-year-old.

Even when blacks found allies, they could not depend on them. The Kennedy Justice Department issued an injunction against interference with efforts to register by Greenwood's blacks—but then withdrew the injunction.

In June, someone machine-gunned a car carrying Bob Moses and Jimmy Travis outside Greenwood. Travis was hit in the neck as he drove the car. As Travis cried out, Moses managed to glide over into the driver's seat and prevent the car from veering off the road. At first, "everyone was terrified"— fearful of helping civil rights workers—so Moses could not get help. Finally Travis was admitted to a hospital. No one was ever arrested for the attack.

After reading Jimmy Pruitt's note, the March on Washington security official folded the paper and gave it back.

"Let Mr. Pruitt march with his signs," he said.

So the March on Washington offered Jimmy Pruitt a day's reprieve. The next day, he would be back in Mississippi, demonstrating and sitting in and registering voters, and risking his life.

NOT FAR FROM JIMMY PRUITT, Harold Reape carried another unauthorized sign, reading: "I Face Life Imprisonment in Monroe, N.C., for Fighting Racism."

Back where the buses were parked, marchers from Ohio and North Carolina passed out handbills to protest the extradition of a woman named Mae Mallory on charges of kidnapping. Reape and Mallory were part of a group of four activists in the North Carolina town of Monroe who were indicted for kidnapping. They protested that they had actually protected the couple who claimed to be kidnapped. Caught in the middle of a race riot, the couple found refuge in the home of a fiery rights leader named Robert Williams.

That story had begun two years and a day earlier.

Robert Williams—who directed the Monroe branch of the NAACP until Roy Wilkins expelled him for advocating the use of violence—invited the Freedom Riders to come to town in August 1961.

For years, Williams claimed that blacks could defeat the terror of the town's racist system only by arming themselves for self-defense. As evidence, Williams cited episodes when blacks armed themselves to fight off white mobs. Williams and his posse protected the home of Albert Perry, an NAACP official, from an impending attack by the Ku Klux Klan. Williams saved his own life when, surrounded by a mob on a highway, he threatened to shoot.

"I do not advocate violence for its own sake or for the sake of reprisals against whites," Williams said. "Nor am I against the passive resistance advocated by Reverend Martin Luther King and others. My only difference with Dr. King is that I believe in flexibility in the freedom struggle. . . . Massive civil disobedience is a powerful weapon under civilized conditions where the law safeguards the citizens' rights of peaceful demonstrations. . . . But where there is a breakdown of the law, the individual citizen has a right to protect his person, his family, his home, and his property."

In June 1961, Robert Williams led hundreds of blacks in protests against the city's all-white swimming pool. As protesters massed at the pool, police and their allies in the Ku Klux Klan gathered 2,500 people. A familiar chant began: "Get the niggers! Get the niggers!" Williams called local police and the Justice Department, but no one responded. He got out waving a gun. The protests against the whites-only pool continued for weeks, but the pool remained open only to whites.

Criticized for his advocacy of violence for self-defense, Williams asked a group of Freedom Riders to show how nonviolent strategy might work. "If they could show me any gains won from the racists by nonviolent methods," Williams said, "I too would become a pacifist."

Seventeen Freedom Riders came to town, and the city responded by enacting draconian anti-picketing ordinances—controlling the content of signs, demanding that counterdemonstrations accompany all protests.

After six days of protests, on August 27, 1961, the local police chief rallied members of a group called the Minute Men—a racist mob—to confront the demonstrators. Thousands gathered in the town square, surrounded the protesters, and began beating them. Jim Forman's head was split with the butt of a shotgun. Some of the protesters started to fight back. Twenty protesters were arrested for "inciting to riot." Violence spun out of control.

Early that evening a white couple named Charles and Mabel Stegall drove into the riotous area downtown. Days earlier, they were spotted with a pro-segregation sign on their car. Surrounded by angry blacks, the Stegalls feared for their lives. Robert Williams saw the danger of a black mob killing a white couple and acted to protect them.

"I saw the circle closing in around the Stegalls," Williams said. "I knew that if just one person lost control of himself the Stegalls would be killed." Williams brought them into his house for a few hours. After the mob dispersed, the couple left his house and then left town.

During the melee, the police called Williams and hinted that he might be lynched. He fled town for New York. There he planned to mount a PR campaign to publicize the atrocities in Monroe. But before he could settle in, he learned that he and four others—Mae Mallory, Harold Reape, Richard Crowder, and John Lowry—had been indicted for kidnapping.

Williams fled to Cuba, leaving his codefendants behind. Mae Mallory made her way to Cleveland. Reape, Crowder, and Lowry were jailed for weeks before being released on bail. They awaited trial.

At the time of the March on Washington, North Carolina officials sought Mallory's extradition so she could be tried for kidnapping in Monroe.

So a group from Cleveland circulated pamphlets at the March on Washington. A pamphlet with the headline SAVE MAE MALLORY FROM THE NORTH CAROLINA LYNCH MOB appealed for Mallory to be left alone in Ohio. Mae Mallory, the piece said, is a "courageous and militant black mother who has been fighting extradition to racist ruled North Carolina. She was unjustly jailed for over a year in Cleveland, Ohio, without trial in a trumped-charge of kidnapping. This charge arose out of a KKK-racist attack in Monroe in August 1961." The pamphlet asked that recipients write Ohio governor James Rhodes to demand that she not be returned to North Carolina.

The unfinished story already had a subplot.

When Robert Williams fled to Havana, Cubans greeted him like a hero. He broadcast *Radio Free Dixie*, a mix of black-power politics and music, and wrote a memoir, *Negroes with Guns*. Williams's small-*d* democratic rhetoric began to irritate Cuban dictator Fidel Castro and his broadcast signal was reduced. Eventually, he would leave Cuba.

That summer, Williams persuaded Chinese dictator Mao Tse-tung to issue a statement congratulating the March on Washington organizers. In a cable to the March Committee, Mao called the Kennedy administration "the chief culprit for the ruthless persecution of Negroes, champion of racial discrimination, and main source of policy of oppression and aggression throughout the world."

That statement would be just one more brush fire that the March on Washington would have to address.

"THE AUDIENCE IS SO OBVIOUSLY ONE-SIDED," the CBS anchorman Roger Mudd said, that he had to shift to Capitol Hill to find proponents of segregation and states' rights. So he asked Robert Pierpoint to interview Senator Spessard Holland of Florida.

Since learning he would anchor the live coverage, Mudd had been nervous. He feared making mistakes, having feeds from producers fail, getting names wrong—and, worst-case scenario, having to manage coverage of a race riot. "I never did this before," he said. He got to the Mall early and promptly went into the box shrubs and threw up.

As a congressional correspondent, he knew civil rights legislation faced a tough course no matter how well the march went off. He wanted to inform his listeners that one glorious day could not trump the old ways of Congress or segregation. So he sought out the skeptics.

"I don't think anything Congress does will be the result of this march," Holland said. "I can't predict because I don't know [that] it's going to come off.... I don't think it'll influence anything. Why should it? This is not vox populi at all. It's the views of a very divided minority."

Senator Strom Thurmond of South Carolina stood waiting for an interview. Thurmond broke from the Democratic Party in 1948 when it adopted a pro–civil rights platform; that year, he ran for president on the States' Rights Party, getting 1 million votes, winning Alabama, Louisiana, Mississippi, and South Carolina and thirty-nine electoral votes.

Nothing anyone could say would shake Thurmond of his belief that separating the races was better for both, that whites were inherently superior.

So Robert Pierpoint asked Thurmond his opinion about the March on Washington. Did Senator Thurmond think the march would enhance the prospects for passage of President Kennedy's civil rights legislation?

Thurmond, thin as a pole, with just some fuzz left for hair, stood erect as he listened to Pierpoint's question. "No, I *do not*," he said. "Negroes have as many rights in this country as other people. They're better fed, they're better housed, and they enjoy as many benefits as other people. They have every opportunity here. They have more opportunity here than in any other nation in the world.

"I don't know of any place where they have as good housing, as many refrigerators, as good automobiles, dishwashers, and washing machines, as here in the United States. I feel that they ought to be proud that they have the opportunity to live in a land of freedom, and where they have accomplished as much as they have accomplished."

For weeks, Thurmond had tried to discredit the March on Washington. Fortified with files from the FBI, Thurmond waited for just the right time to launch a public attack on Bayard Rustin. On August 13, Thurmond attacked.

Standing in the well of the Senate, Thurmond argued that Rustin's background showed the moral depravity of the March on Washington.

"Many people across the country," Thurmond said, "are not satisfied with the Attorney General office's decision to whitewash the question of Communist influence or involvement in these Negro demonstrations which have been turning into race riots in various cities in this country."

Then he turned to the character of Bayard Rustin. "In 1958," he said,

"Rustin saw fit to travel to the Soviet Union and meet with the butchers of the Hungarian freedom fighters to participate in a communist propaganda show called nonviolent action committee against nuclear weapons."

Thurmond claimed Communists dominated the March on Washington. For evidence he pointed to Carl Braden, a labor activist and newspaperman who in 1954 purchased a suburban home in a Louisville suburb for a black couple. After escalating violence against the couple by their white neighbors, the home was dynamited, and a related investigation of Braden for alleged Communist Party ties resulted in his conviction for sedition and sentencing to fifteen years in jail. The U.S. Supreme Court, finding the use of sedition laws capricious, released him after eight months. "Except for the action of the Supreme Court, Carl Braden would today be in jail where he belongs instead of being field secretary for the Southern Conference Educational Fund, associated with Reverend Martin Luther King, and causing racial strife and agitation throughout the South."

Thurmond also dredged up Rustin's arrest in Pasadena and his refusal to serve in World War II. Thurmond put Rustin's police record into the *Congressional Record*. The package included an article from the *Los Angeles Times* and the booking slip from the arrest.

Rustin waited in fear for the response to the attack. Back in 1960, Martin Luther King had dumped Rustin when Congressman Adam Clayton Powell threatened to "expose" the two as homosexual partners. Would such smear tactics still work? Did it matter that Rustin took his pacifism seriously, that he was willing to accept punishment for refusing service in the war? Was it still a career breaker that he was attracted to other men? Did it matter that his pacifism once drew him, like countless other leftist activists, to Communism?

Phil Randolph called a press conference as soon as he returned to New York from a labor conference.

"I speak for the combined Negro leadership in voicing my complete confidence in Bayard Rustin's character. I am dismayed that there are in this country men who, wrapping themselves in the mantle of Christian morality, would mutilate the most elementary conceptions of human decency, privacy, and humility in order to persecute other men."

A reporter asked whether Rustin would resign.

"Why, heavens no," Randolph said. "He's Mr. March himself!"

When the news of Randolph's statements filtered back to the office, Tom Kahn, Rachelle Horowitz, and Norm Hill broke out in big smiles.

"It was a sense of exuberance, excitement," Hill said later. "It was like all those fears were bottled up, and just like that they were gone. It was one of the happiest moments any of us had. We just felt so good for Bayard."

Thurmond made two tactical mistakes. First, he waited too long. By the time he spoke, two weeks before the march, plans for the demonstration had generated excitement across the country—and the unwavering commitment of conservative blacks like Roy Wilkins and Whitney Young, as well as President Kennedy. Second, Thurmond's sweeping attack looked desperate, even pathetic. The FBI fed him folders stuffed with clippings and reports from agents, but Thurmond couldn't create a coherent line of attack.

Thurmond's attack united civil rights activists. "I'm sure there were some homophobes in the movement," Eleanor Holmes said, "but you knew how to behave when Strom Thurmond attacked."

AS BLACKS DEMONSTRATED FOR EQUAL RIGHTS, forty states were considering three constitutional amendments that would remove—maybe forever—the possibility of national legislation for civil rights.

The first amendment proposal would eviscerate a Supreme Court decision that enshrined equal voting rights for the first time in American history.

In 1962, in *Baker v. Carr,* the U.S. Supreme Court affirmed the ideal of equal representation for the first time. The case arose when a Memphis man named Charles Baker sued to force the state to redraw district lines. Tennessee had not redistricted since 1901. The population of Shelby County, ten times greater than that of many rural districts, got only one-tenth the representation of smaller areas. Baker claimed that Tennessee's electoral system violated his right to "equal protection of the law" under the Fourteenth Amendment.

The Supreme Court agreed, ordering states to create districts with roughly equal populations. *Baker* was destined to be a landmark case, giving the notion of "one man, one vote" the highest status as a principle of democracy.

But now, forty states were considering an amendment to revoke this basic principle of equality. Thirteen states already approved the amendment.

Another constitutional amendment would give states the right to amend the Constitution without any federal involvement. The founding fathers required Congress or a national convention to approve constitutional amendments, by a two-thirds vote, before the states ratified them. This proposed amendment would bypass the need for any national action on revisions to the Constitution.

A third amendment would create a Court of the Union, giving state chief justices authority to review U.S. Supreme Court decisions. The bedrock principle of the American system—Article VI of the Constitution, which declares the Constitution, federal laws, and U.S. treaties the "supreme law of the land"—would be abrogated.

Mischief making extended beyond the constitutional amendment process.

Governors George Wallace of Alabama and Ross Barnett of Mississippi, for example, led a movement to subvert the Electoral College selection of the president. Traditionally, the candidate who wins the popular vote of a state wins all that state's electoral votes. But Wallace and Barnett encouraged Southern states to vote for uncommitted electors. By withholding their votes, these electors could prevent either party from winning an election. That, in turn, would send the election to the House of Representatives. In the House, representatives from the South could hold the balance of power in presidential elections.

Ross Barnett, meanwhile, proposed massive relocation of blacks. In 1963, 60 percent of all blacks lived in the South. Barnett wanted to move most of them out of the region, so that all states would have 10 percent black populations. "This race problem is a problem of numbers," he said at a meeting of the Southern Governors Conference in White Sulphur Springs, West Virginia. This is a "workable solution to equalize the population."

These efforts to rewrite the Constitution and change the rules of electoral contests were slowly moving toward adoption. And so building a new national consensus for civil rights, and carving it into law, was a race against time.

JEROME SMITH WAS PART OF A GROUP of fifty black workers from the Mississippi Delta who got the biggest, most sustained applause of anyone on the National Mall. As the group walked together, in denim overalls and T-shirts, people cheered. Everyone in the movement knew the horrors of Mississippi.

Smith was a lean twenty-three-year-old man from Jackson; his dark face bore the scars of abuse and his eyes were tired. But he looked eagerly for people who could draw public attention to the violence of the segregationist South.

When Smith spotted Paul Newman, he walked over. He apologized for not seeing Newman when the actor had traveled south to voice support for the civil rights movement.

"There was a warrant out for my arrest," Smith explained.

And then he challenged Newman to do more for the movement.

"I think the country misses a lot when a person of your caliber isn't exposed to the *real* trouble—the *real* problem," he said.

"It doesn't take a general in the front trenches to fight the war," Newman said.

"But if you got slapped in the face it would be noticed," Smith said. "It would give us faith."

Since he was ten years old, Jerome Smith had challenged his elders. In 1950, Smith picked up a "race screen" on a New Orleans bus and threw it to the floor. Race screens were slats that could be slid into grooves on the aisle sides of seats up and down the bus. One side read "Whites Only," the other "Colored Only." Only whites had the right to move the screen, to force blacks to move out of seats they wanted. The bus driver threw him off the bus.

"I was crying, and this old women, an old black woman, told the driver and some of the white people, 'Please don't call the police. I'm going to take this boy home and see that his grandmother bust his behind. This boy gives too much trouble.' And when I got off the bus with this old lady, she took me to the back side of the Autolec store and she grabbed me and hugged me and kissed me and said she was proud of me."

Jerome Smith grew into one of the thousands of young people willing to risk all for civil rights. He was one of the Freedom Riders in 1961 and took his place in demonstrations across the country.

But in the spring of 1963—on Friday, May 24—Jerome Smith made his greatest contribution to the civil rights movement. He spoke directly, bluntly, crudely, to the attorney general of the United States. This blunt talk angered the attorney general. But it also changed him.

James Baldwin set up a meeting. A who's who of black culture—performers Lena Horne and Harry Belafonte, sociologist Kenneth Clark, playwright Lorraine Hansberry, King adviser and attorney Clarence Jones, and the Urban League's Edwin Berry—went to Kennedy's Upper East Side apartment to talk about the race crisis in the United States.

Baldwin had become a major intellectual figure associated with race in America after a decade-long exile in Paris. A small man—five feet, six inches, barely 130 pounds—he spoke with anguish about how generations of racism had twisted the soul of black America. He lamented the despair he saw in his old neighborhood in Harlem. He grew angry at the temporizing of politicians, academics, and journalists. And yet—despite his own decision to leave the United States—Baldwin refused to embrace the separatist ethos of Malcolm X. Somehow, blacks and whites had to live together in America.

In all his years in the States, Baldwin had struggled to understand his own alienation. "It was in Paris when I realized what my problem was," he told the *New York Post*. "I was ashamed of being a Negro. I finally realized that I would remain what I was to the end of my time and lost my shame. I awoke from my nightmare." The whole race problem, Baldwin argued, required the same kind of rebirth nationwide. But he feared that such a rebirth would not occur. Black communities from Harlem to Watts were committing slow suicide with violence, drug and alcohol abuse, and alienation from school and jobs.

"There is drift and danger today," he said. "Despair is a sin ... It is too expensive and too futile to hate. It is like poisoning yourself."

But while rejecting hatred, Baldwin also chafed at the colonial mentality of white liberals. "The role of the white liberal in my fight is the role of the missionaries, of 'I'm trying to help you, you poor black thing, you,'" he said. "The thing is, we're not the trouble. *You are.* I'd like to suggest that white people turn this around and ask what white people can do to *help themselves.* No white liberal knows what Ray Charles is singing about. So how can you help me? Work with yourself!"

And that is why Baldwin set up the meeting with Robert Kennedy—to show the attorney general this alternate reality that he could not know growing up in the affluent family of a financier, ambassador, and kingmaker.

Robert Kennedy welcomed the group with a recitation of the administration's record on civil rights. *This administration has more Negroes than any previous administration. . . . The Justice Department has three Negro lawyers and twenty-nine clerical staff. . . . Burke Marshall is working down in the Southern states. . . . The Justice Department has filed twenty-nine suits to force state and local officials to register blacks to vote—and won about half of them. . . .*

Baldwin thanked the attorney general for the meeting, then said he wanted to hear how young people, the movement's foot soldiers, were feeling. He asked Jerome Smith to talk. Smith sat on the floor, at Kennedy's feet, in the living room. A circle of chairs formed around the attorney general. A few people stood on the edges of the room.

"Mr. Attorney General," Smith said, "you make me want to *puke.* I don't care what you think, and I don't care what your brother thinks either."

The room stilled. Kennedy, his face red and his muscles tightening, looked around for someone to admonish the young man. No one did.

Smith said he didn't really feel like a citizen of the United States. If he was drafted to go to war in Cuba, Smith said, he wouldn't go. How can you expect me to fight for democracy down there, he asked, when the administration doesn't fight for democracy in the South? Smith talked about the police beatings, how FBI agents watched the violence but refused to intervene. They just stood on the side, watching the mayhem, taking notes.

Not fight for the United States? Robert Kennedy was shocked. Again he scanned the room for support.

"Even though the rest of us were more genteel, everyone backed up Jerome's concept that things had gotten to the point that ordinary Negroes could have the shit kicked out of them," said Henry Morgenthau, a television producer in Boston who was one of the onlookers lined up against the wall.

The meeting lasted three hours. After the meeting, Kennedy was shaken. So was James Baldwin, who left with Kenneth Clark to film an interview for educational television. "Kenneth, I need a drink," he said. "Can't we stop at the nearest bar?" Clark said no and hustled Baldwin into a cab.

In the TV interview, Baldwin was ashen, disoriented. He had had no idea, before now, just how aloof the Kennedys were. He thought the administration's caution came from ruthless political calculation. But now it seemed that the pampered sons of old Joe Kennedy just had no idea—*no understanding at all*—about race in America.

The secret meeting was immediately leaked to the press. Within weeks, the velocity of the civil rights movement would lead President John F. Kennedy to give the most aggressive presidential address in history on race, which was quickly followed with the most comprehensive legislation in modern history.

THE KENNEDYS HAD BEEN WARNED ALL YEAR—in fact, their entire time in the White House—about the growing anger among blacks. On May 13, Louis Martin wrote a memo to Bobby Kennedy to alert him about plans for the March on Washington.

"Events in Birmingham in the last few days," Martin wrote, "have seemed to electrify Negro concern over civil rights all across the country. As this is written, demonstrations and marches are underway or being planned in a number of major cities, including Chicago.

"The accelerated tempo of Negro restiveness and the rivalry of some leaders for top billing, coupled with the resistance of segregationists, may soon create the most critical state of race relations this country has seen since the Civil War."

Sooner or later, he warned, the black community would come together for a massive march on the capital.

Republicans, Louis Martin reported, were gleeful that a Democratic president was being forced to make a firm commitment on civil rights. No matter what Democrats did, they would alienate a major constituency. If they embraced civil rights, they would alienate their base in the South. If they hesitated on civil rights, they will alienate the black community—which was responsible for their narrow margin of victory in the 1960 election.

The administration, Martin said, needed to "seize the initiative." How? Legislation? Executive orders?

"The most dramatic and constructive project that seems feasible immediately is the extension of the Negro-white dialogue . . . through a White House Conference. Negro leaders and representatives of the Southern white power structure, including state and local government leaders, can meet, at the call of the president."

On May 20, President Kennedy discussed civil rights with his leading domestic policy advisers. Attorney General Robert Kennedy was there, along with Larry O'Brien, Burke Marshall, Ted Sorensen, Lee White, and Kenny O'Donnell.

The president asked about the comedian Dick Gregory. Earlier that month, Birmingham police had arrested Gregory and 850 others after a protest march. Gregory stayed in jail three days before getting released on bail. When he got out, he complained about mistreatment by jailers. He said he was "whipped by five policemen using billy clubs, hammers, and sawed-off pool sticks." Calling his jailing "the most miserable experience of my entire life," Gregory said he "was hit all over, including about the face."

But Robert Kennedy insisted that Dick Gregory was a moderate who was as concerned as anyone about the radicalization of the black community.

"He says Negroes get mad for no reason at all. He said they want to fight. They want to fight with white people. He says it's true in Chicago. He thinks that's going to be a big problem area—it's going to be the Northern cities. They're just antagonistic and they're mad. You might run a picture with a white boy being chased by a Negro with a knife and they get mad at that because they say that shows the papers are against them and the white people are against them.

"They're awful tough to deal with now," Bobby Kennedy said. "He [Gregory] says, you can't have a moderate Negro anymore. They can't be moderate, because their competitors are not moderate. Everybody's going to be a little bit more extreme than the other one."

The president wondered aloud: "Don't they realize the necessity of maintaining support in the white community?"

Bobby remarked: "Like one of them said, yesterday I read in the paper, 'We've got them scared. Now let's make them run.'"

That was Adam Clayton Powell, the New York congressman who had used his church in Harlem to build a black political machine.

The conversation continued. They talked about Powell's popularity, his exploitation of black mistrust of white America. Then they returned to Robert Kennedy's conversation with Dick Gregory.

"He said he was sitting in a bar where the Negro underworld of Chicago hangs out. Ordinarily if they hear a police car come down the street they all run. And a police captain walked in and a couple of the gentlemen told him to get the hell out. They didn't want to see him. He said that's what the riot in Chicago was all about. It's because the Negroes are not just antagonistic and mad . . . they're going to be mad at *everything.* You can't talk to them," said Bobby.

"My friends all say the Negro maids and servants are getting antagonistic. She said you don't know how they're sassing me back in my house."

Larry O'Brien, chuckling, wondered about Malcolm X's image in the black community.

Robert Kennedy quoted Dick Gregory: "He's nothing!"

The president talked about his encounters with black audiences. "We got a damn good hand in Nashville from the Negroes," he said.

Burke Marshall reported on the unrest ripping across the country. Even minor incidents become flashpoints—like when police raided a craps game in St. Louis. "It turned into a riot," Bob Kennedy said.

The president told the group about his recent conversations with Alabama governor George Wallace and Senator George Smathers of Florida. He asked them why Southerners couldn't just take down signs for segregated facilities. Blacks didn't necessarily want to use public facilities, he told Smathers, but they just didn't want to be told they couldn't. Why couldn't the segregationists loosen their grip on separate public facilities? If they didn't, "the Negroes are going to push this thing too far."

Public accommodations, Burke Marshall argued, were the most emotional issue to blacks. "This business of going in and eating at a lunch counter . . . is [the] one thing that makes all Negroes, regardless of age, maddest," he said.

Robert Kennedy didn't understand.

"They can stand at the lunch counters," he said. "They don't have to eat there. They can pee before they come into the store or the supermarket."

But however uncomprehending the attorney general could be, he still pushed for legislation on public accommodations, voting rights, and school desegregation. He also raised the possibility of meeting with Martin Luther King and other civil rights leaders, though his brother was wary.

"I think we ought to have some of the other meetings before we have in the King group," the president said. "Otherwise the meetings will look like they got me to do it. . . . The trouble with King is, everybody thinks he's our boy anyway. So everything he does, everybody thinks we stuck him in there. So we ought to have him well surrounded."

The 1964 election was the specter haunting the White House. Kennedy owed his narrow victory in 1960 to the black vote. Cities with big black populations like New York, Chicago, Philadelphia, Detroit, Baltimore, Cleveland, and St. Louis gave Kennedy big majorities that offset weaknesses in rural and suburban areas. But Kennedy also won six states of the old Confederacy (and five of eleven electoral votes in Alabama).

But for all practical purposes, maneuvering to save the Southern vote ended when Kennedy gave his June 11 televised speech on race:

> The heart of the question is whether all Americans are to be afforded equal rights and equal opportunities, whether we are going to treat our fellow Americans as we want to be treated. If an American, because his skin is dark, cannot eat lunch in a restaurant open to the public, if he cannot send his children to the best public school available, if he cannot vote for the public officials who will represent him, if, in short, he cannot enjoy the full and free life which all of us want, then who among us would be content to have the color of his skin changed and stand in his place? Who among us would then be content with the counsels of patience and delay?
>
> One hundred years of delay have passed since President Lincoln freed the slaves, yet their heirs, their grandsons, are not fully free. They are not yet freed from the bonds of injustice. They are not yet freed from social and economic oppression. And this Nation, for all its hopes and all its boasts, will not be fully free until all its citizens are free. . . .
>
> We face, therefore, a moral crisis as a country and a people. It cannot be met by repressive police action. It cannot be left to increased demonstrations in the streets. It cannot be quieted by token moves or talk. It is a time to act in the Congress, in your State and local legislative body and,

above all, in all of our daily lives. It is not enough to pin the blame on others, to say this is a problem of one section of the country or another, or deplore the facts that we face. A great change is at hand, and our task, our obligation, is to make that revolution, that change, peaceful and constructive for all. Those who do nothing are inviting shame, as well as violence. Those who act boldly are recognizing right, as well as reality.

That speech changed everything. Kennedy now stood firmly on the side of the movement. Events forced Kennedy's hand. "They got scared," said one politician. "All at once they saw a national situation out of control. You know as well as I that we could have martial law in one hundred cities all over the country."

For weeks, Martin Luther King and his advisers debated whether to make President Kennedy or Congress the movement's target. King resented Kennedy's hesitance to embrace civil rights. But when the president proposed the most important civil rights bill since Reconstruction, King was jubilant. "He was really great," King told Stanley Levison. Congress should be the target of protests.

Two days after submitting his bill, Kennedy hosted the leaders of the March on Washington and gamely asked them to call off the march. Protest in the streets, he said, could only serve to anger Congress and hurt the bill.

"Mr. President, they're already in the streets," Phil Randolph said.

And so rather that resisting the march, President Kennedy embraced it. He recruited unions, Catholics, and foundations. He ordered the Justice Department to help—and keep tabs on the organizers. He approved the use of the military to respond to any disturbance. And he agreed, tentatively, to greet the march leaders when the day was done.

A TYPICAL WASHINGTON RESIDENT—that's what reporter Al Hulsen went searching for early on the morning of the March on Washington. And at nine thirty, he found one. Simon Cloonan was wandering around on the Ellipse, the circular greensward between the White House and the Washington Monument. He wasn't there to march. He was there because he was curious.

Radio listeners could not see him, but could imagine who he was from his voice.

He sounded like an agreeable man—maybe a factory or construction worker, he spoke in the mixed patois of New York and the mid-Atlantic states. He had moved to the Washington area from New York twenty-five years before. He spoke with a rough accent, raspy, rounded with exaggerated vowels. He said *justy-fied* for "justified" and *qually-fied* for "qualified."

Simon Cloonan contained all the contradictions of race in Washington, D.C., on this muggy August day.

HULSEN: How do you feel about this march today?
CLOONAN: The way I feel about it, I think it's absolutely justified.
I think that they should get their freedom and their liberties and public accommodations and jobs and things like *that*. But at the same time . . .

I'm for it, but . . .

President John F. Kennedy famously remarked that Washington was a city of "Northern charm and Southern efficiency." That split personality found expression in race relations.

Washington lay on the cusp of north and south. Once an Indian cross-roads, then a dormant swamp, Washington offered little economic or cultural life before the New Deal. But with the growth of government—filling the city with monuments, universities, hospitals, agencies, and lobbying organiza-tions—Washington became more cosmopolitan. A dashing young president brought Nobel laureates, poets, and composers to the White House, the Na-tional Gallery of Art displayed the *Mona Lisa,* and civic leaders planned a new performing arts center.

But old attitudes persisted. A reporter for the *San Francisco Chronicle* in-terviewed cabbies and found fear and loathing of the civil rights movement and the upcoming March on Washington.

"I don't want any damned nigger throwing a brick through my window," one burly driver said.

"All hell is going to break loose," an older driver predicted.

"They couldn't pay me enough money to drive in the city when all them niggers are here," a younger driver said.

"There's going to be real trouble and blood spilled," a fortysomething driver said.

CLOONAN: I think there's a lot of Communism mixed up in this. Some of these white people are not truly at heart for the colored people. They are here for a *purpose*.
HULSEN: And what do you believe is that purpose?

CLOONAN: I think that purpose is absolutely Communism. I can see it around here—the looks of 'em, their actions, and things like that. Now, some of these white people are down here *truly* trying to help them, but others are not. I think they're just after their own purpose, to mix Communism in with this thing, and I think that's bad. I think what they should have done when they came down here, and white people offered to go, they should have selected the people that they wanted to come with them, people that are really Americans and for an American cause. I think this is all an American cause, but I don't like to see this Communism mixed up in it.

Planners feared that black Washingtonians would not go to the March. Other cities—New York, Chicago, Detroit, and Atlanta—filled streets and buses for demonstrations. But the people of Washington—the only major city in the United States with a majority black population—seemed aloof. More than in any other city, blacks had found a foothold in the nation's capital. Fifty-five thousand worked in the federal government and another 12,300 in city government.

By some basic measures, Washington outperformed other cities in both North and South. Ten years before, Washington had formally desegregated its public accommodations, and a year later desegregated its schools. The city had a thriving black middle class, with many blacks forging careers in the civil service. Blacks in other cities lacked industries to make their own, the way previous immigrants took over police departments and schools, waterfronts and factories, garment districts and construction sites.

The weekend before the march, a half dozen sound trucks moved through Washington's black neighborhoods, exhorting all to go to the march. Preachers told their flocks to go to the march. And local TV and radio coverage hyped the event.

HULSEN: Do you have any definite evidence that there are Communists here?

CLOONAN: I don't have any definite evidence but you can generally pick 'em out.

HULSEN: How can you do that, sir?

CLOONAN: Well, by their looks, by their actions, and things like that. Take some of these girls that fall all over these colored fellows. I don't believe they're down here because they want to help 'em. I think they're actually mixed up in this Communist movement that's gone on in the country. And I'm afraid of it, I'm afraid of it.

The fear of blacks and whites having sex with each other lay at the center of segregationist fears about civil rights. The logic went like this: Miscegenation is contrary to God's plan and the future stability of America. When the two races are allowed to interact on anything but a formal basis, there is a danger that at least some will develop romantic relations . . . and have sex. When that happens, the races will no longer be "pure."

Senator Paul Douglas, who supported civil rights, predicted integration would produce a single "coffee-colored race." That's just what the segregationists feared. Whites would lose their superiority to "mongrelization."

Intermarriage was still illegal in twenty-one states, ten of them in the South. Louisiana banned marriage to "others of colored blood." Kentucky specified "mulattos." Other states banned marriages to Malays, Mongolians, Indians, Hindus, and mestizos.

But blacks and whites had always had sexual relations with each other. Slave owners forced themselves on slaves, plantation owners forced themselves on sharecroppers, and heads of households forced themselves on maids. Mr. Segregation himself, Strom Thurmond, had sexual relations with at least one black woman. He fathered a child with his teenaged maid back in 1925, when he was twenty-two years old. Privately he acknowledged his paternity; publicly he remained an ardent foe of race mixing.

HULSEN: Do you think it's a very serious or a very large element?
CLOONAN: Of Communists?
HULSEN: Yes.
CLOONAN: Well, so far I wouldn't say that I've seen too many, but I think
    there is a pretty good element in it because there's always people who
    are agitating. Just like this Rockwell gang is agitating for the Nazis.
    So I think the same damn thing happens for the Communists. But
    I think, taking it as a whole, I think they're full-heartedly for their
    movement. I think they should get their rights.

After sex, Communism formed the other great objection to the civil rights movement.

Was the March on Washington an event run by Communists in cahoots with Moscow, as Arkansas attorney general Bruce Bennett and every other arch-segregationist charged?

"It pains me to think that every good idea in America has to be credited to the Communist," said L. C. Bates, the publisher of a Little Rock newspaper. "If Mr. Bennett was informed about Communist doctrine, he would clearly understand that the practice of racial equality in these United States of America would serve the Communist no purpose."

Over the years, leftists of all types—Communists and socialists, fat-and-happy unionists and syndicalists, Trotskyites and Shachtmanites—joined the civil rights crusade. But it was a fragmented, noisy, cross-talking coalition. Some focused on labor exploitation, others on global revolution; some focused on urban issues, others on rural; some worked within the system, others disdained it. They lacked the discipline or means to take over the civil rights movement.

Talk of Communism was so common it became perfunctory. A New York television reporter named Gabe Pressman came by the march headquarters one day looking for a story. "I guess the best angle would be whether the Communists and Black Muslims are trying to take over the march," he said. "That's new. Well, not really new, but it may get a steamy answer."

If Simon Cloonan wanted a moderating influence, the churches supplied it. As soon as President Kennedy realized that the Great March was inevitable, he mobilized his network to recruit *respectable* marchers. That meant old-fashioned unions—and old-fashioned churches. And that meant working the capital's own backyard, long indifferent to political protest.

All over Washington, churches organized efforts to get their flocks to the march. They wanted blacks, local blacks, to show their faces. They wanted the march to be an authentic rally for civil rights—a *moderate* rally for rights. Bible Way Church, led by Bishop Smallwood Williams, held an all-night vigil. More than one hundred churches announced special services or vigils.

HULSEN: Mr. Cloonan, what do you think this march will achieve?
CLOONAN: Well, it all depends. If it's peaceful and quiet, I think they'll get most of what they're after. I don't think they'll get public accommodations through the South, but I think it'll help 'em a lot. If they're peaceful and quiet, if there's nothing happens, if there's no fights. My wife was afraid for me to come down today. She thought I'd get into an argument [chuckles], but I'm not going to argue with anybody.

And well might Mrs. Cloonan have worried. Whatever progress Washington had made, the city was consumed by sensational reports of crime in the daily newspapers. Washington ranked first among cities for aggravated crime among cities with a population of 500,000 to 1 million. In the last two decades, per capita crime had increased by 57 percent. Crime got bad enough to scare the criminals. A liquor-store robber said he preferred working in daylight because the city streets were too dangerous at night.

The 1962 Thanksgiving Day football game exposed the city's raw racial tensions. Fifty thousand fans packed the city's new stadium to watch St. John's High School, almost all white, defeat Eastern High School, almost all black, by a score of 20–7. After the game, black youths ganged up on whites inside and outside the stadium. After hours of fighting, about five hundred were injured.

> CLOONAN: I have been in favor of it, I believe every man is put on this earth for a purpose. I don't think that we're any better than the next fella, whether he's colored or whether he's a Japanese or a Chinaman or what the devil he is. He's a *human being*. We could have all been colored, we could have all been *snakes* as far as that goes. God is the only one that has created all of this.
>
> So I don't think that they should be held back. I think they should get jobs, providing they're *qualified*. I don't think a fella that's a *laborer* should go to work and demand a job as an *engineer*. I think he should be *qualified*. I think they should start a program where they train a lot of these people, where they take fellas in as apprenticeships.

The gap between the *qually-fied* workers and the lumpen proletariat, of course, was Phil Randolph's original motivation for organizing the March on Washington. Even as they slowly gained civil rights, in some places anyway, blacks found themselves outside the economic mainstream. In Washington, as the black middle class proudly filled the federal government's massive marble buildings, poor and working-class blacks labored in menial jobs and lived in houses without plumbing.

But on this day, no one did much work in Washington. Less than half of all government workers showed up for work. Southern congressmen told their secretaries to stay home because of the possibility of riots. In most District and federal agencies, fewer than half of all employees went to work.

Traffic at the Washington Monument declined by at least a third. The monument had gotten 3,351 visitors by five o'clock, about 2,000 fewer than on a normal day. Many took the elevator ride up and found the view from 555 feet in the air so compelling that they stayed. At one, a bomb threat forced police to evacuate the needle and refund the tourists' dimes. A few blocks away, only 1,612 people took a White House tour, down from the usual crowd of 10,000. Even the company town's premier private business—lobbying—declared a holiday.

Stores did little business. Garfinkel's had a single customer on its main floor. Hotel lobbies sat empty. A ten-cent shuttle bus for shoppers drove around town empty. Jewelers, florists, travel agencies, realty offices, optometrists, and luggage stores closed. Washington's board of trade reported that business was down 80 percent.

The city's liquor stores closed, by order of the District Commission. The Liquor Dealers Association complained that stores would lose $1 million in sales. "They don't close the bars for an American Legion convention or the Elks convention," the owner of one liquor store said.

Even prisoners took the day off. The District's jails let 4,600 inmates, 70 percent of them black, watch the live coverage of the march on TV. A prison official called their behavior "gentlemanly."

Police guarded banks across the city, wary of a silent spree of robberies while police and National Guardsmen watched over the march. They left to patrol the streets at two. The bridges leading into Washington—the Theodore Roosevelt Bridge and the Arlington Memorial Bridge—were closed for the day.

CLOONAN: The unions should recognize the fact that this is a growing population, they're gonna get larger, we have 54 percent here in Washington of colored and you *can't* hold a gang like *that* down. They're either gonna do that [hold apprenticeships] or they're gonna get into rackets, they're gonna get into robbery, which they have already done, and things like that.

So they should start a program where they train 'em, provide 'em with jobs. There should be jobs for all, white or colored or anybody. Don't you think so?

The migration of Southern blacks to Northern cities made Washington America's first majority-black big city. As much as 60 percent of the city's population was black. And a committee of segregationists in Congress ruled that population.

Washington became two cities, one affluent and the other poor. Black schools had poor facilities, outdated books, and less money for teachers. Blacks were excluded from most jobs and housing. Police gained a reputation for brutality. The welfare system's "man in the house" rule denied benefits to women living with a man—which, predictably, broke up families. And even if public accommodations were legally integrated, the city's neighborhoods and schools were either black or white.

The Washington contingent at the march won permission to promote the cause of home rule on the Mall.

From 1802 to 1812, Washington was ruled by a mayor appointed by the president and a city council elected by the people. Starting in 1812, the elected council selected the mayor. From 1812 to 1872, voters elected both mayor and council. But racists recoiled when freed slaves flocked to the capital. By 1878, democracy ended in the capital. The district was ruled by a three-member commission appointed by the president and a congressional committee dominated by Southern racists.

At the end of the day, marchers would sign "pledge cards," expressing their commitment to civil rights. Years later, Walter Fauntroy used the names and addresses he collected to write to these marchers, asking them to deluge Congress with letters demanding home rule for Washington—ultimately leading to home rule for the capital city.

Always, Washington expressed ambivalence about its place in the American system and civil rights movement.

The black janitor at WUST, where March on Washington volunteers worked, did not support the march. He said he planned to stay in bed. Race was a problem in America, he agreed, but "prayer is the answer." Civil rights were going to be attained without the march. He feared that two groups—American Nazis and Black Muslims—would disrupt the march. Everyone was at a breaking point. Any stray incident could spark violence.

"I don't want to see bloodshed," he said.

LENA HORNE APPROACHED the podium at the Washington Monument, just after eleven in the morning. Out on the National Mall, a fifteen-year-old girl stood on a mound of dirt and waited to hear her voice.

Horne wore a beige cotton shirt and blouse, with a yellow chiffon scarf and a blue NAACP hat. As she peered out from her cat glasses, her copper skin gleamed in the afternoon sun.

For years, Horne struggled to define herself. Producers, directors, press agents, and reporters publicly debated what she should be. As a light-skinned black, the product of a mixed marriage, she enjoyed great "crossover appeal."

But crossing over was hard. Horne moved between black and white worlds, never totally part of either one. She won worldwide fame with her rendition of "Stormy Weather" in the 1943 musical. Tellingly, theater posters depicted her as both white and black.

Finally, introduced by emcee Ossie Davis, she leaned on the podium and shouted:

"Freee-*eeeee*-dommmmmm!"

The word took about four or five seconds for Lena Horne to call out, but it carried and charged the air for longer. The sound was as sinuous as Horne herself, but also rough, as it rang out across the Mall.

She spoke only one word—she felt too ill to say more—but people would be talking about Horne's "performance" for years to come.

When Ossie Davis realized that Horne would say just that one word, he paraphrased Nina Simone's famous introduction to "Mississippi Goddam": "You can be sure she means every word of it."

Far, far from the podium, that word changed the life of a girl from the most segregated section of the capital city. A tall, slender black girl named Ericka Jenkins stood alone on a mound of dirt. Just hearing the word echoing over the Mall changed her.

Ericka heard Lena Horne sing out "Freedom!" and she could feel the word landing inside her. People nearby writhed in joy. She stood on her dirt mound and let the word become part of her. And Ericka wept.

"That word landed where that hurt lived, very deep inside," she said. "I felt it in my heart and in my belly. It was like a meeting, a moment of joy and the transcendence of suffering. Where there had been tension, before I got on the bus, the busyness in my body *settled*. I became so peaceful. People were crying."

At a young age, Ericka Jenkins was already confronting the injuries of racism.

She lived with her parents and brother and sister on Fifty-fifth Street and East Capitol Street, not far from the Maryland border. The Washington side was almost all black, the Maryland side almost all white. When she ventured across the line, to buy soda or chips at a convenience store, she got spat on and called *nigger*. Her parents took drives through the city's poor and rich neighborhoods. Some black neighborhoods lacked basic plumbing and people slept outside in cars, even when there was snow all around, while in wealthy neighborhoods she saw people "dressed in beautiful coats and hats and smiling."

In the summer of 1963, everyone was talking about the March on Washington, in school and in the streets and on the radio and TV.

"Mama, I'm going to the march."

"No you're not. Something will happen."

"Mama, you taught us to respect and support our people."

"I didn't mean *you.*"

So that morning Ericka took the bus to the Washington Monument. She found herself a mound of dirt where she could stand all day and watch Martin Luther King and Roy Wilkins and John Lewis.

And when Lena Horne's voice wafted over the crowd, Ericka made a vow.

It wasn't just Lena Horne's call of freedom. It was also this mixed assembly—she had never seen whites standing alongside blacks like this. She was amazed to see priests in collars, black men in dark suits and younger men in overalls, Chinese and Native Americans, women in print dresses—all with an openness in their faces, in their eyes. The muscles were relaxed. All the tension was gone, for a moment.

Ericka Jenkins vowed to commit herself to civil rights, and to education. It was like what her mother told her about preachers getting a "calling"—"when you know deep in your heart you're meant to do something."

Ericka made a vow to go to college, do something for children, and fight racism . . . no matter where it took her.

A TRIM MAN WEARING A TIE AND BLAZER and puffing a corncob pipe—not wearing his usual armband with a swastika—gathered his followers on the east side of the Lincoln Memorial just after six o'clock in the morning. He looked more like a Brown graduate, which he was, than a brownshirt. Burt Lancaster could have played him in a movie.

"My men will aid the police in suppressing the mob," he announced, standing with three bodyguards and seventy-three followers.

After police led the Nazis to a section of the Mall near Fourteenth and Fifteenth Streets, two hundred Washington police and National Guard MPs surrounded the group. They created an empty zone, with a radius of fifty feet, around the group.

Washington police captain Thomas Herlihy told the pipe-puffing Nazi that he lacked a permit for a demonstration. If he or anyone in his group spoke, police would arrest them for parading without a permit.

George Lincoln Rockwell, the leader of the American Nazi Party, spent the summer touring the small cities of the South—especially the areas surrounding Washington—to recruit counterdemonstrators. He spoke to as many 2,000 people in some towns. Working with a mailing list of

13,000, Rockwell vowed to bring 10,000 white supremacists to disrupt the March.

Rockwell's flyers described the March on Washington like this:

When such an unspeakable, vast, storming ocean of half-ape African savages—300,000 of them—marches on your Capitol, white man, you will be whipped ... unless you do something about it. ... If there ever was a time to fight, it is now. But where is our fight? Martin Luther King is stomping Virginia, inciting the blacks to a mass uprising on August 28. His terrifying black sea of chanting, sweating, filthy, hate-crazed niggers —drunk with their growing power—will become America's master on that day.

Rockwell said he "wouldn't shed a tear" if there was violence at the march. "Furthermore," he said, "I would love to see Marlon Brando and his crowd of actors trampled to death by their coon friends."

But rallying the racists proved hard work, even in the meanest precincts of the old Confederacy. Even the city of Danville, Virginia, which had just beaten and jailed hundreds of civil rights protesters, turned against Rockwell. The city granted Rockwell a permit to rally in the city, then abruptly withdrew it. The city manager, T. E. Temple, said Rockwell failed to pay the rental fee before the filing deadline. Rockwell said he would hold a rally anywhere, even a garbage dump, but Temple would not allow it.

Ten days before the march, Police Chief Robert Murray tried to convince Rockwell to stay away. Rockwell said no. So Murray prepared for the worst. He passed out photographs of known Nazis and told his officers to arrest anyone doing anything that did not look marchlike. "They need no permit to walk to the Capitol or to carry signs and picket as long as they stay on the sidewalks and observe traffic signs," Deputy Howard Covell said. "But they will not be allowed to mass in a parade." Washington police had arrested Rockwell before. He was once ejected from a congressional hearing for carrying a placard—in that case, a swastika lapel pin.

Now, waiting inside that circle of cops—hoping that more Nazis would arrive, wondering whether to risk arrest by speaking without a permit— Rockwell and his troops posed for snapshots. Rockwell had ordered his storm troopers to leave behind their brown uniforms and armbands with swastikas, since the police had banned any kind of symbolic clothing or banner. Wearing civvies, the Nazis looked up at the camera. They looked like classmates at a tenth-year college reunion.

"People all over Virginia said they would be here," said Rockwell. "I had twelve thousand pledges from people who said they'd show up. Where the hell are they? I'm ashamed of our race.

"We have nothing but shame. You know why? Because our people are cowards. They're yellow. Our cause is almost ridiculous."

Laughter from the audience.

"*We* are ridiculous. I don't think the liberals are a bunch of Communists as I used to. At least they have guts and are willing to die for their cause. That's what the conservatives need."

Rockwell's efforts to arouse the extremist right, said a rival named William Pattison, were failing because he hadn't learned the lessons of the civil rights movement. "Organization is the very criteria of success and those who procrastinate more or less miss the boat . . . In California it is legal to have rifle clubs. It is legal to have a drill team. It is legal to have a military society. When all three groups suddenly are brought together, what would that be?" Pattison proposed creating public spectacles to arouse public sympathy. "Some little old lady reads about how the Nazis did something for charity and thinks, 'They're not so bad.'"

Other segregationists vowed to raise hell at the March on Washington. Robert M. Shelton, the Imperial Grand Wizard and Grand Dragon of the Ku Klux Klan, was flying to the march when his private plane crashed. Traveling in dense fog near Walhalla, South Carolina, the plane dropped from eleven thousand to four thousand feet. So he did not get to the march.

The American Council of Christian Churches, which opposed civil rights legislation and the march, sought an audience with President Kennedy but got rebuffed. Carl McIntyre, a radio preacher who called for his followers to carry a sign reading "Kill a Commie For Christ's Sake," vowed to bring a hundred thousand pieces of literature to the march. But no McIntyre flyers were to be found that day.

Another group, called the Prospects, also promised to stage a counter-demonstration. The Citizens' Council of Jackson and Madison County, Tennessee, announced plans to drop a hundred thousand pamphlets entitled "Abraham Lincoln Opposed Integration" on the Mall. No one saw the Prospects or the pamphlets.

Finally, just after eleven, Rockwell's deputy commander, Karl Allen, began to speak. After Allen said a few words, Captain Herlihy warned him to stop or face arrest. He began again, and police warned him again. On his third try, he said: "We are here to protest by as peaceful means as possible the occupation of Washington by forces deadly to the welfare of our country." Herlihy then arrested him for making a speech without a permit.

Police took Allen to the emergency quarters of the General Sessions

Court—with the possibility of mass arrests, D.C. officials saw the need for a fast-track tribunal to process cases—and took mug shots and fingerprints. After a brief trial that afternoon, Allen was convicted of speaking without a permit and fined fifty dollars.

"Most people must be showing their approval by staying away," Allen told a reporter from the Educational Radio Network. The march, he said, was "instituted by communist-inspired people. Martin Luther King, for one, has a pinkish background. Other March leaders are members of the Young Communist League. . . . This is the first stage of the communist revolution in America." Allen also said he resented that "a group of people can take control of Washington for their own purposes."

As Allen spoke, Rockwell and his troops walked, in single file, over the Fourteenth Street Bridge into Arlington, Virginia.

A HULKING FIGURE—OVER SIX feet and 190 pounds, with a balding head— walked to the Mall and watched the crowds pour through the streets. And he the felt the guilt of a Catholic who knows that he and his church have failed to meet their basic Christian duty to love thy neighbor.

Ned O'Gorman came to bear witness. He watched the marchers, by the thousands, march, sing, and clap. He saw young people singing in harmony, chanting slogans. He observed old people stand by and watch the swelling protest.

These people should despise me, he told himself, *but they don't.*

He wondered what they wanted. All his life, O'Gorman assumed that black people wanted the same things as whites. He assumed blacks wanted to be more like whites in every way—not just eating with whites at lunch counters and going to school with whites, but embracing the whole white lifestyle. But now he wondered . . . What black would want to give up his blackness?

Color blindness, he decided, is blindness. Marching down Constitution Avenue and Independence Avenue, O'Gorman saw the real future. Black and white walked side by side, sometimes hand in hand. Suddenly, he realized that when they gained their rights, blacks could not, *should* not, just blend in with white society.

"To know the Negro as my brother, I must know him as a Negro, love him as a Negro, wish him well as a Negro, as I would know the Chinese or the Indian as my brother. The genius of the Negro upturned my imagination. When we marched together we did not march as white men and black men but as men, unique, solitary, somehow alike, very different, but ultimately men, ultimately good, joined by the spirit and by our divine origin. It was all very mysterious. It still is."

Earlier that day, as he looked out the window of his Penn Central train from New York, O'Gorman considered himself "a moral sluggard, a hypocrite who sat by for twelve adult years, silent, self-deluded, and blind, making no change in my life."

"I had never known what it means to be despised, to be avoided as the Negro had in his own country. What then was I to think about these men and women who increased their courage the more they were attacked; who, as they reached the last extremes of humiliation, renewed themselves with each defeat?"

After arriving in Washington, O'Gorman called Catholic churches. *You sending a group to the march?* Most showed no interest. Some were rude. One priest said that since he was obese he should not risk his health by marching.

Some Catholics marched. President Kennedy got his political helpers to mobilize priests and nuns, filling the Mall with collars and habits.

"For the first time in their lives the priesthood was suddenly out in the open, out of the waxed old parlors, the sanctuary, the confessional," O'Gorman said. "The world had made a demand on it, on the Church, that could not be answered by referring to a communiqué from the Chancery, dogma, prudence, politics, or Rome."

For O'Gorman, maybe the most liberating idea of this march was that people did not need to melt together in love. Earlier that day an old black woman took one look at a beatnik and shook her head. "White trash," she muttered. Maybe that was okay. Maybe you didn't need love *everywhere.* Failed revolutions—Russian, French, now African—demanded equality and fraternity. When they didn't get it, they exploded or melted into corruption. This was quieter, more modest, maybe more *possible.*

"They did not need to speak to one another; there was no attempt at friendship. They simply needed to march together, to go toward something together. For years they had gone different ways, now they went toward the same place."

JACK TAKAYANAGI ALSO WENT TO WASHINGTON to bear witness. The pastor of the South Congregational Church in Utica, New York, Takayanagi brought four boys from his church's youth fellowship program. He drove his blue and white 1957 Studebaker all night and arrived as dawn broke, just as police were putting up road barriers. He got inside the cordoned-off area, close to the Washington Monument.

As soon as they got to the monument, Takayanagi's boys decided to take a nap. When they lay down, the Mall was empty. A few buses rumbled toward the city. TV crews worked on their camera setup, volunteers staple-gunned signs, and a few people ambled around the Mall. But all was quiet. When they woke up a few hours later, the place was alive.

Like blacks—but not like them, too—Takayanagi had struggled his whole life against racism.

"It made me also feel that this is addressing my own concern," he said. "It wasn't just African Americans or Native Americans or Asians, but this is a problem that was all of ours. This problem involved a far greater number of people than just blacks."

Five feet, six inches with a medium build and short black hair, Takayanagi was a second-generation Japanese American. His parents moved to California in 1913 from Japan. "The West Coast was supposed to be the land of prosperity," he said. "The plan was to make a lot of money and go home. But they discovered they had to make a living, so they stayed." The Takayanagis settled in San Jose and worked on farms.

Then came Pearl Harbor, December 7, 1941. The following spring, the U.S. government posted official "exclusion orders" ordering people of Japanese ancestry to leave their homes and live in internment camps. The government gathered 125,000 people, up and down the Pacific coast. Seventy percent were native-born Americans; the rest had moved from Japan over the past few decades. The quarantine applied without any consideration of background, profession, or even connections. If your family came from Japan, you had to leave home.

Official statements claimed the camps' purpose was to "protect" Japanese from attacks. To be sure, Japanese Americans faced ugly slurs and attacks from their Caucasian neighbors. But General John DeWitt explained the real logic: "Along the vital Pacific coast over 112,000 potential enemies, of Japanese extraction, are at large today. There are indications that these are organized and ready for concerted action at a favorable opportunity. The very fact that no sabotage has taken place to date is a disturbing and confirming indication that such action will be taken."

Jack Takayanagi was studying art in downtown Los Angeles when he found out that he would be forced to live in a camp. A poster on a telephone pole declared the area a war zone. All people of Japanese ancestry had to leave, bringing only what they could carry. So families piled duffel bags onto trucks and climbed onto buses. They learned their destinations only when they got there.

Jack and his parents went to Manzanar, a one-square-mile camp in the desert, about one hundred miles east of Fresno. More than ten thousand people lived in the camp. Each block had a mess hall and a common latrine and recreation hall. Guard towers with snipers and high walls topped by barbed wire circled the camp. Inmates farmed or worked in kitchens or yards. Children went to school.

Jack's brother Harry lived in Riverside, so he went to a different camp, in Poston, Arizona.

Prisoners had three ways to get out—enroll in a reputable school, join the military, or work as a sugar-beet farmer in Idaho.

At the time of his family's incarceration, two of Jack's brothers, John and George, were fighting for the United States in Italy. They were, in fact, part of the most decorated unit in the history of the United States Army, the 442nd Infantry, under General Mark Clark. By the end of the war, eight thousand men from the unit had been decorated. When the men of the 442nd came home, they paraded down Constitution Avenue in front of ten thousand cheering spectators. President Harry Truman honored the unit in a ceremony on the White House lawn.

"While my brothers were fighting in Italy we were being concentrated in this country," Takayanagi said. "The only other country that did this was Germany."

But no one had any choice. "*Shikataganai,*" they said, meaning, "it cannot be helped." So they endured.

Jack left Manzanar in 1943 when he enrolled in Drake University in Iowa. Jack found work for Harry, a polio victim, with a watchmaker in Des Moines. After he settled there, his brother sent for his parents. They found a job for his father at a nursery, then for his mother as a housekeeper.

After graduating from Drake in 1946 and from he Colgate Rochester Seminary in 1950, Takayanagi sought positions in both Baptist and Congregational parishes. The Baptists said no because he was Japanese. "We don't think you'd be at home here," he remembers one saying. "We're not ready for this yet," he remembers another saying. But Congregational churches welcomed him. "They were broadminded, big-hearted," he said.

He finally settled into a position with the South Congregational Church in Utica. The church worked to improve the quality of slum housing, which meant dealing with absentee landlords. They also worked on school desegregation. In the late 1950s, Takayanagi and other like-minded souls petitioned the city council to create a civil rights commission. They eventually won. "It helped to raise the consciousness of the city that these problems did exist. Yes, we have a problem."

When Jack Takayanagi and his group woke up after their nap by the Washington Monument, they all felt like Rip Van Winkle. The place was transformed. Joan Baez and Peter, Paul, and Mary were singing. The green lawn of the Mall was filled. The sun was hot.

Jack Takayanagi didn't see any Asians on the Mall that day.

But, he said, "this was my march too."

THE BIG TEN LINGERED ON CAPITOL HILL, talking about filibusters and committee bottlenecks. When someone noticed the leaders were late for their own march, they hustled out of the meeting with Speaker John Mc-Cormick and Majority Leader Carl Albert.

Thousands of marchers, meanwhile, moved from the Washington Monument to Constitution Avenue, waiting for the leaders to come from Capitol Hill. They stood around, chatted. "We're going to wake up Lincoln—tell him to get up and stop dragging his feet." They craned their necks to spy the limousines carrying Martin Luther King and Roy Wilkins and the others. Irritation competed with eagerness to see these famous men arrive.

The March on Washington staffers—Bayard Rustin, Norm Hill, Rachelle Horowitz, Cleveland Robinson—did all they could to hold the people back.

"My first impulse was to try and stop it and wait for the leaders," Rustin later said, "but I figured I was going to get run over, I'd better get the hell out of there, and I left."

Loudspeakers echoed commands, but no one listened.

Some marchers started singing. The NAACP youth were especially excited, bringing themselves to higher and higher peaks with their clapping and chanting and singing.

"F-R-E-E-D-O-M spells freedom," they sang, to the tune of "Eyes on the Prize." People stood and watched, grateful for the entertainment while waiting for the march leaders.

Finally, a group of several thousand marchers broke away and started walking up Constitution Avenue. They sang "We Shall Overcome" and "Freedom!" Before long, as many as thirty thousand marchers started without their leaders. They wanted a spot in front of the Lincoln Memorial. (Rustin had already arranged for fifteen thousand of his own people to fill in that space. "One must always secure the front of one's platform," he said.)

Then three black limousines deposited the Big Ten—the civil rights, religious, and labor leaders who had organized the march—on Constitution Avenue. Rustin and Hill and the others cut the line in two, creating a gap of about thirty or forty feet between the two segments. The leaders took their places at the head of the second group.

As in Hollywood, the cameras started rolling once the lead players arrived. A photographer stood in that open forty-foot band of space as the leaders got ready to march. He raised his arms to get their attention.

Now the march leaders—Floyd McKissick and Martin Luther King, Cleveland Robinson and Joachim Prinz and Carson Blake, Whitney Young and Roy Wilkins, Phil Randolph and Walter Reuther—linked arms.

"This is the king of all marches!" Wilkins exulted.

A group of women led the march down Independence Avenue: Daisy Bates, the spiritual leader and protector of the Little Rock Nine . . . Gloria Richardson, the tough woman who led the youth movement against terror in Cambridge, Maryland . . . Rosa Parks, the face of the Montgomery bus boycott, which inaugurated the modern civil rights movement and brought Martin Luther King to prominence . . . Casey Hayden, the student leader who pushed the male-dominated movement to embrace women.

Prefab signs bobbed behind the leaders, proclaiming, "We Demand Decent Housing Now," "Gradually Isn't Fast Enough," "We Demand an End to Bias Now," "We Demand Voting Rights Now."

Farther back, people carried more colorful signs. One read: "Horses Have Their Own Television Shows. Dogs Have Their Own Television Shows. Why Can't Negroes Have Their Own Shows?" Another: "No Matter How You Polish It, Segregation Is Dirty, Rotten Evil." From a nine-year-old from Plaquemine, Louisiana: "My Name Is Charlie Jones, Mr. Kennedy, And I Can't Wait."

NED O'GORMAN LOOKED OUT ON THE MARCHERS and saw "a suddenly stirred-up village and moving woodland, an alerted fortress, a pilgrimage." *Birnam Wood remove to Dunsinane.*

At first, the march looked like fans spilling out of a Washington Senators game, not a mass demonstration. But by noon, as a marcher named Edward Morgan wrote in his diary, "suddenly the March is like a flash flood. Constitution Avenue is awash with a human river, signs for freedom now bobbing like sailboats above the marchers' heads."

"This," thought Rita Schwerner, "is a *movement*." After hundreds of separate campaigns, everyone came together for the first time. "There are people from all over who want the same thing. There is something quite remarkable about seeing all these people in the same place."

Helen Fineman came to march from New Haven, where she worked as an editor of the Benjamin Franklin papers at Yale. She quoted Franklin to express her own emotions. "I was not ashamed of the suffusion of a few drops of moisture on my cheeks," Franklin said when he came home from England in 1726. Franklin's last public act, Fineman proudly noted, was to sign a petition to Congress to abolish slavery.

Some treated the march as a funeral procession. A group from Alabama carried a coffin with a sign draped down the side reading: "Jim Crow Die-hards. The Filibuster Is But Death Rattles. Rev. Martin Luther King, Officiating." Another group moved a coffin draped in a Confederate flag.

At some points, marchers moved silently, the only sounds the pad-pad-pad of feet underneath and the whispering of friends and family. At other points, the march was a parade, with rhythmic singing and chanting. Chanting started softly, then gained power after the shy ones joined in. Walking backward, a black man shouted: "Jamesey Crow!" Meekly, the crowd responded: "Must go!" Then: "Jamesey *Crow!*" and with more force: "Must *go!*"

A group of eighty-two people from Wilmington, North Carolina, dressed in black jackets and hoods, strolled down Constitution Avenue, mocking the segregationist senator from South Carolina with a variation of "Oh Freedom":

No more Sam Ervin
No more Sam Ervin over me
And before I'll be a slave
I'll be buried in my grave
And go home to my Lord and be free.

Some marchers sang the old dirges, like "John Brown's Body," an old Civil War marching number set to the tune of "Battle Hymn of the Republic":

John Brown's body lies a-mouldering in the grave.
His soul's marching on!

Toby Stein, a writer and editor who spent her childhood playing with her brother Sol and their neighbor Jimmy Baldwin, first resisted singing. *Can they really mean it, about overcoming?* "I listened, as I never had before when I had heard them over television, to the words of the songs," she later explained. "And they were so—simply—true. I couldn't very well *not* join in with my half-dead-frog voice."

The march alternated between noisy and quiet. Sometimes, it just took a hammy ringleader to start the crowd. Other times, marchers moved quietly until they saw the booms of camera microphones. Then they snapped to order, called out slogans, sang songs, moved with purpose.

Bob Forsberg, a minister from New Haven, passed a crippled old black man, bent over, unable to move. In that old body, Forsberg decided, he "saw the Lord."

"I'm too old to march, but I'm praying with you," the old man called. "This is your day, young folks. You keep marching and keep fighting 'cause you just got to be free. The Lord will make it so, but you got to keep on marching."

Ledger Smith, a twenty-seven-year-old truck driver, roller-skated seven hundred miles to the march. He held up his skates before the crowd. "I let my legs do most of the talking," he said. Smith took two pairs of skates on the ten-day journey but used only one. The NAACP arranged hotel and food stops along the way. When he arrived at twelve thirty the day before the march, he was twenty pounds lighter.

An eighty-two-year-old man named Jay Hardo rode a silver bicycle five hundred miles, from Dayton, Ohio. He got off his bike and walked down Constitution Avenue.

A dozen CORE activists, who walked 225 miles from Brooklyn, rippled down the street. All summer, they protested at the construction site for the Downstate Medical Center, demanding that one-quarter of all building jobs go to blacks and Puerto Ricans. On a Brooklyn street corner, Malcolm X derided their efforts but they kept going—all the way down to Washington.

Outside the Navy Building, two white workers watched the spectacle.

"Well, I don't know. I'm one of the people who think they already have their rights."

"I think they should have their freedom and equal rights."

"But don't push the South. That's all I say. Take it easy."

The Reverend Frank Dukes marched with a group from Alabama. He wore a sandwich board reading DUKES FOR GOVERNOR. He handed out papers describing an organization he was trying to promote.

"Speech! Speech!" people called out.

"What are your plans for '68?"

"What's your platform, Governor?"

"When are you going to delouse the Congress, Governor?"

Dukes smiled and moved with exaggerated rhythm.

A white cop, a Bull Connor double, approached him. "Governor, would you step up on the sidewalk?" The levity of the moment lost, Dukes paused and then agreed. Then he brightened. "And when I'm elected," he said, "I'm going to make you *chief of police.*" The crowd roared, called for him to come back. He handed out leaflets. "Don't throw them away," he said. "I want to hear from you."

Two people standing nearby could not get into the spirit. "He'll never make it," one said. "It's the only funny thing I've seen all day," said the other.

It took three hours—from eleven thirty until two thirty—for a quarter million people to walk four-fifths of a mile. The march moved in segments, with groups walking thirty abreast taking about a half hour or so to make the journey.

Earlier that morning, the Reverend Duncan Howlett, minister of All Souls Church, had conducted a special service and then led 1,500 Unitarians down Sixteenth Street, toward the Mall. Looking down at the river of humanity on Constitution Avenue, he felt a rush of anxiety disappear, replaced by a wave of joy.

"You don't understand the euphoria until you first grasp the anxiety that existed throughout American society and in Washington over the gathering of a quarter of a million people on this explosive issue," he said. "I don't think anyone was under an illusion that this represented a permanent state of affairs. This was simply an incredible demonstration of what might be. If you had asked me that day if this was where we were, I would have said, 'No. Tomorrow we will go back to work.'"

Celebrities bypassed the main avenues, walking between a double human chain of District policemen and National Guardsmen. Fans finally spotted celebrities using a set of stairs in the rear of the Lincoln Memorial. They rushed toward Hubert Humphrey, Burt Lancaster, and James Baldwin. Cheers and whoops rose up from the crowd.

B. M. Phillips of the *Afro-American* counted 1,200 steps from the Washington Monument to the Lincoln Memorial. So by the time the march was complete, people lifted their feet and put them down again as many as half a billion times.

As marchers approached the Lincoln Memorial, the organist could not find sheet music for "We Shall Overcome." She had music for "The Battle Hymn of the Republic," so she played that. Finally, a minister sketched out a simple score and the movement's anthem quavered over the Mall.

Norman Mailer watched the marchers proceed down the great boulevards. All summer, he had watched with alarm as the civil rights revolution veered toward violence in New York and Chicago, Philadelphia and Jackson, Danville and Cambridge. He wrote about the march for his column in *Esquire*:

> The Negro had already demonstrated to the collective psyche of America that they have the greatest potential for violence of any political body in our American world; now, on this afternoon, they chose to show that they also possess the finest capacity for order and discipline in the nation. Could one dream of bringing together 200,000 whites steaming with bitterness and a hot heart of injustice on a hot summer day with no riot breaking forth? Impossible. A deep blues went out from Washington in these hours: a revolutionary force existed in the land; it could move with violence, and it could move with discipline.
>
> No invasion of Congress, no sit-down in the halls could have crossed the message so far into the 50 million or 100 million Americans who are neither for nor against the revolution. Indeed a violent demonstration could have alienated them. The Capitol building is one of the altars of the Republic—a sit-down inside Congress on that day would've made Governor Wallace a candidate for president and a new party. To the average American it would have been equal to stomping on the flag. A revolution withers if it is afraid of creating outrage, but it is killed in ambush if it accepts and attacks each and every possibility for outrage presented to it.

Maybe, as the Young Jacobins complained, Phil Randolph and the other march organizers lost their nerve when they agreed to control their masses. Maybe President Kennedy and his allies—the Catholics, the foundations, the media moguls—co-opted the march. But maybe, by allowing others to play a role, the March on Washington created the grandest image of dissent the nation had ever seen.

Maybe, then, the march organizers co-opted the co-opters.

AS DEMONSTRATORS BROKE OFF from the March on Washington to carry their message to the White House, President John F. Kennedy met his foreign policy advisers at noon to discuss the crisis in Vietnam.

All morning, White House workers drifted onto the White House porch. They saw hundreds of demonstrators walking along Pennsylvania Avenue carrying signs, singing songs, and chanting slogans. In the distance, they could see the Ellipse and the Washington Monument.

"Shout loud enough so the president can hear you!" one demonstrator called out, not knowing that Kennedy was meeting in a room on the opposite side of the White House, by the Rose Garden.

In the Cabinet Room of the White House, President Kennedy struggled with one of the indirect consequences of the civil rights movement—the rise of a populist movement in South Vietnam. Martin Luther King had inspired Buddhist activists in Vietnam. A wave of Buddhist protests, in turn, had undermined America's allies in Saigon. That, in turn, was leading the United States deeper and deeper into Vietnam—ultimately with disastrous consequences for the civil rights movement in the United States. But that's getting ahead of the story.

The Buddhist crisis began on May 8, when Diem's government broke up a celebration of Vesak, the Buddha's birthday (his 2,527th). When three thousand people gathered at a radio station to hear a special program on loudspeakers, five armored cars moved through the area and fired on the crowd, killing one woman and eight children. Using King's strategy of protest, Tri Quang rallied Buddhists to fight the government. Just as the lunch-counter sit-ins spread within weeks in 1961, or campaigns in both the North and South exploded after Birmingham in 1963, the Buddhist movement spread quickly across South Vietnam.

Disorder in South Vietnam, eerily, tracked events of the American civil rights movement.

On June 11—the same day that President Kennedy delivered a major speech on civil rights—a monk named Quang Duc burned himself to death to protest Diem's refusal to acknowledge Buddhists' basic rights. Surrounded by a group of three hundred chanting saffron-robed priests and nuns, Quang Duc, sat in a lotus position as others doused him with gas. He then lit a match. The flame leapt and sucked oxygen out of the air, making a *whoosh* sound. The monks sobbed as his body shriveled and blackened. The smell of burning flesh filled the air.

Protests spread and American diplomats pressed Diem to conciliate with Buddhists. But Diem rejected the pleas. Diem claimed that Communists had initiated the rebellion. Then he blamed Americans. When another monk died from self-immolation on August 16, Madame Ngo Dinh Nhu, Vietnam's de facto first lady, declared: "Let them burn, and we shall clap our hands."

The Buddhist crisis led to this meeting of President Kennedy's foreign policy team. The players filled every seat of a hexagonal oak conference table, surrounded by cases jammed full of books, with model sailboats on the top shelf. The topic of the day was whether to support the plans of South Vietnam's dissident generals to stage a coup d'état against President Ngo Dinh Diem.

General Maxwell Taylor warned the group that South Vietnam could collapse at any time, with or without Diem. What was the scenario for losing the war? Would the U.S. military get helicopters to the embassy to ferry four thousand Americans to the airport and out of South Vietnam?

Should the administration support the coup? The group swerved back and forth between yes and no, with an occasional maybe.

Yes: Henry Cabot Lodge, as U.S. ambassador to South Vietnam, had worked secretly with the dissident generals. Now he argued that South Vietnam had no chance to defeat the Vietcong if Diem remained in power. In a nation 70 percent Buddhist, Diem's Catholic kleptocracy controlled the government, media, universities, and industry.

No: Maxwell Taylor estimated that Diem's forces outnumbered the rebels two to one. Maybe Diem *could* survive, if he reached out to the Buddhists.

Maybe: Defense Secretary Robert McNamara warned against getting pushed into supporting the coup. If the United States backed the coup, it had to succeed.

Yes: President Kennedy leaned toward the coup. The new ambassador, Henry Cabot Lodge, supported the coup. So did General Paul Harkins.

No: Roger Hilsman, the new ambassador to South Vietnam, hesitated. He supported the coup but warned against abandoning Diem. America's reputation, he said, would suffer if the United States forced Diem out.

Yes, but: Bundy said the United States shouldn't worry about breaking promises. After all, Diem broke promises, too. America didn't owe him anything. The only question was whether South Vietnam could win the war with Diem as president.

Maybe: Treasury Secretary Douglas Dillon hesitated. The United States, he warned, would get the blame if the coup failed . . . so it was vital to make sure the coup succeeded.

Yes: Then the president made a fateful move. He ordered the Pentagon to build up the coup forces.

It looked like the coup was a go. It was like another moment when Kennedy seized someone else's agenda, the Bay of Pigs invasion. People moved forward, despite doubts. Absent an order to halt and turn around, the coup *would* happen.

The greatest concern seemed to be keeping American fingerprints off the coup. But was that even possible? Just recently, Diem complained that he had gotten a telegram from someone in California warning him that the United States was plotting a coup with South Vietnamese generals. No one in the room knew who could have sent that telegram. But Diem knew something was happening. The plot already had American fingerprints.

Attorney General Robert Kennedy, spoke for the first time.

What would happen, he asked, if Diem foiled the coup? Would the United States disavow its support for the generals? Redouble its support for Diem? Or pull back from Diem? Could the U.S. government put more pressure on Diem to acknowledge the Buddhists' cause? Or would Diem become even more arrogant?

The yes–no game resumed.

As the meeting concluded, it looked like the group—including the president—supported a coup. But overthrowing America's ally in South Vietnam and handing control over to a group of dissident generals could be messy. Someone had to think about *that*.

President Kennedy adjourned the meeting, saying he wanted to meet again at six o'clock, after meeting with Martin Luther King and the other leaders of the March on Washington.

PART 4

Dream

—————

JAMES FORMAN OF THE STUDENT NONVIOLENT COORDINATING COMMITTEE banged away on a portable typewriter on his lap, in the janitors' closet underneath Daniel Chester French's marble statue of Abraham Lincoln.

The afternoon program of the March on Washington was fast approaching. And Archbishop Patrick O'Boyle was still staying away. O'Boyle was supposed to deliver the invocation, but he would not come to the Lincoln Memorial unless John Lewis deleted objectionable passages from his speech.

So Bayard Rustin and the other march organizers stalled. They added some music to the program. And they asked Fred Shuttlesworth to speak.

When the Big Ten arrived at the Lincoln Memorial, a message from the White House greeted them: "The archbishop isn't going to wait anymore."

Originally, the Big Ten planned to resolve the Lewis crisis—which had begun the previous night, when O'Boyle threatened to pull all Catholics out of the march—after their morning meetings on Capitol Hill. They would take limousines to the Washington Monument, where they would eat box lunches and fix Lewis's speech. But the group stayed late on the Hill, started marching late, and did not have time for lunch.

Walter Reuther of the UAW called O'Boyle at his Mayflower suite to beg for more time.

"I have got the statement ready," the archbishop said. "I have got the thirteen bishops. We have all agreed upon it, so I won't be there to give the invocation, so this public announcement will be made . . . that the Catholics are dissociating ourselves."

"You have been very patient, your Excellency," Reuther said, "but I would like thirty more minutes."

Reuther took a hard line in the debate with the other members of the Big Ten.

"Look," he said. "We have got a decision to make real quick, and there is no use debating it because we haven't got time . . . If John Lewis feels strongly that he wants to make this speech, he can go someplace else and make it, but he has no right to make it here because if he tries to make it he destroys the integrity of our coalition and he drives people out of the coalition who agree to the principles . . . This is just *immoral* and he has no right to do it, and I *demand* a vote right now because I have got to call the archbishop."

Roy Wilkins joined Reuther's attack.

"I just don't understand why you SNCC people always want to be different. You're double-crossing the people who gathered to support this bill." As he spoke, he poked Lewis in the chest.

"Mr. Wilkins, you don't understand," Lewis said, poking back. "I'm not just speaking for myself. I'm speaking for my colleagues in SNCC, and for the people in the Delta and in the Black Belt. You haven't *been* there, Mr. Wilkins. You don't understand."

Reuther demanded that the Big Ten vote to either force Lewis to revise his speech or drop Lewis from the afternoon program. "Poll the committee," Reuther told A. Philip Randolph. Nine members of the Big Ten agreed to revise the speech to satisfy O'Boyle. Lewis did not vote.

Under the verdict of the Big Ten, Lewis had to honor the March on Washington's support for the president's civil rights bill and rally all factions of the civil rights movement.

Then the Big Ten appointed a subcommittee—Randolph, Martin Luther King, and Carson Blake—to resolve the crisis. They went to an anteroom under the Lincoln statue and called O'Boyle.

"Your Excellency, I think we have solved your problem and ours too," Reuther said. "We have set up this subcommittee. If they agree the speech complies, then John Lewis will make the speech. If they agree it doesn't, he will be denied the floor."

Randolph and Blake got on the phone and said they agreed to the arrangement. "Whatever you do is fine with me," O'Boyle told Blake—the first time anyone remembered a Catholic cleric using a Protestant as a proxy for church policy.

As Jim Forman typed, Lewis pleaded: "Just don't change too much." Lewis stood behind Forman's shoulder. In less than an hour, Lewis was supposed to give his speech. Now, other people were debating what he could say.

Others leaned over Forman, the most prolific writer among the Young Jacobins of the civil rights movement. Forman's wife, Mildred, Tom Kahn, Courtland Cox, and Cleveland Sellers suggested phrases. Bayard Rustin and Phil Randolph stood nearby. At different times, Walter Reuther and Martin Luther King looked in.

John Lewis had become the leader of SNCC only that summer. He was the public face of SNCC, but Jim Forman was its intellectual and spiritual leader. Forman was the one at the center of the protests and debates and maneuvering. He was the one who went to many of the March on Washington meetings. He was the one keeping records. But now John Lewis was becoming more visible.

Everyone near Forman offered advice. Carson Blake and Walter Reuther complained about the words *masses* and *revolution*. Randolph disagreed. "I use that word [*revolution*] all the time," he said.

Lewis felt the pull from the other direction, too. The SNCC people told him not to compromise. They wanted a speech that called attention to the violence and horror of the South. Why should Lewis or the Snickers go soft on Kennedy? Just days before, his administration had indicted protesters in Albany, Georgia, on specious charges of perjury. Not far away, in Americus, four civil rights workers faced the death penalty for participating in demonstrations.

Lewis argued that the speech expressed sentiments of the whole youth movement. King and Randolph agreed. Randolph said that Lewis should be able to say what he wanted to say, but he might change some specific words.

Rachelle Horowitz thought she knew why John Lewis was so upset. Part of the reason, to be sure, was anger over censorship. But just as important, Horowitz thought, was the fact that Lewis had a speech impediment. He feared that he might not be able to deliver, smoothly, a complete rewrite of the speech. One of Lewis's first friends in Nashville, the Reverend Will Campbell, winced at his struggle to speak clearly. "John couldn't speak an *English sentence*," he said. "He couldn't speak much of anything. But he was the *toughest* of any of them."

A few nights before the march, Lewis went to Rachelle Horowitz's apartment to practice the speech. Rachelle was drifting off to sleep as Lewis shouted out: *We march today for jobs and freedom, but we have nothing to be proud of. . . .* Lewis had worked hard to say the words just right—learning how to pause at the right spots, glide from sentence to sentence, and modulate his voice. Now they were changing the speech—subverting his careful preparation.

The Snickers who assembled on the apron just in front of the Lincoln Memorial grew angry as they heard rumors of censorship. For the first time, free speech became a major part of activist politics. The particular points of dispute almost didn't matter. The nudging of words and phrases would leave Lewis's message intact. But still . . .

"We were on the front lines and we were the ones being shot at," said Dorie Ladner. "I didn't see anything wrong with the speech. Who the hell was he [O'Boyle] to tell us what to say? It wasn't that we were going to tear down the White House." She paused, wondering aloud about O'Boyle's motives. "He may have been sympathetic with the South."

The elders of the civil rights movement made direct pleas to Lewis.

"If it's a choice between you and O'Boyle," Randolph told Lewis, "it's you."

"John, I think I know you," Martin Luther King said. "This is not you."

Phil Randolph made a personal appeal. "Young man, I've waited twenty-two years for this," he said in a weary baritone. "Would you young men accommodate an old man? I've worked all my life for this."

Lewis looked at Randolph, fifty years his senior, who had done more than anyone to bring mass demonstrations into the civil rights movement and who single-handedly created the black labor movement.

Lewis agreed to the changes.

Then the White House sent Secret Service cars to the Mayflower to pick up the Catholic leaders. The flock in black entered through the back entrance to the Lincoln Memorial. "I never saw a bishop look so good in my life," Reuther later said.

Fred Shuttlesworth, the fiery preacher from Birmingham, stalled for time during the crisis. Upset that he hadn't gotten a prime-time speaking slot, he still reveled in the moment that became his.

"We didn't come to *molest* nor to *cajole*, we came to be *peaceful* and *loving* and *law abiding* because we are a *law-abiding people*," Shuttlesworth cried, moving to his own rhythm. "We came because we love our country. We came because our country *needs us* and we need our country. We came to serve notice that if our country wants peace and tranquility and quiet, they might as well just free the Negro because until the Negro is freed nobody else *will* be free."

He went on like that for a while. And then, knowing his time was short:

"We're going to *march*. We're going to *walk* together, we're going to *stand* together, we're going to *sing* together, we're going to *stay* together, we're going to *moan* together, we're going to *groan* together, and after a while we'll have *freedom*! Freedom! Freedom now!"

Josephine Baker, who had flown in from Paris the night before and wore her Free French uniform, took the stage after Shuttlesworth. She was speaking to the crowd, soaking up the love, when Rustin interrupted her.

"I want you to know this is the happiest day of my life," she told the crowd.

Rustin nudged her. "Madam," he said, "you will have to stop now. We are beginning this march."

"I'm going to finish this," she whispered back.

"You are going to have to stop *now*," he snapped. "I don't care who you are. We are *beginning* this march."

No one had ever whisked Josephine Baker off the stage. She fumed.

The John Lewis controversy was over. The show was about to begin.

"WE ARE NOT A MOB."

In the weeks leading up to August 28, Asa Philip Randolph basked in his celebrity as the visionary of the March on Washington for Jobs and Freedom. *Life* magazine put him on its cover with Bayard Rustin. Reporters culled old newspaper clips describing Randolph's planned 1941 march and his eight-year effort to organize Pullman railroad porters. Randolph could be connected to every civil rights and labor figure of that century, from the now-exiled W. E. B. Du Bois to the young John Lewis.

Standing at the Lincoln Memorial before a swelling throng—175,000, 200,000, 250,000, more—he described just why the march was necessary to both blacks and the American political system.

"We are not an organization or a group of organizations," he said. "We are not a mob. We are the advance guard of a massive moral revolution for jobs and freedom. The revolution reverberates throughout the land, touching every city, every town, every village where blacks are segregated, oppressed, and exploited."

His idea of civil rights always included whites as well as blacks. Back in 1941 he planned an all-black march, but only to assert the black's mass voice for the first time and avoid charges of Communism. But always, Randolph insisted that blacks must figure out how to operate in a white society.

"This civil rights demonstration is not confined to the Negro; nor is it confined to civil rights; for our white allies knew that they cannot be free while we are not. And we know that we have no future in which six million black and white people are unemployed, and millions more live in poverty."

Always—even as a seventy-two-year-old who moved slowly and could not take on the organizing tasks he once had—Randolph expressed the urgency of youth.

"Those who deplore our militancy, who exhort patience in the name of a false peace, are in fact supporting segregation and exploitation. They would have social peace at the expense of social and racial justice. They are more concerned with easing racial tensions than enforcing racial democracy."

When Randolph created his own national organization, the Negro American Labor Council, in 1959, he hoped to merge the two great concerns of blacks in America—racial discrimination and economic isolation. But other labor leaders, like the AFL-CIO's George Meany, resented Randolph's bid for influence. "Who appointed you as the guardian of Negro members in America?" Meany snapped at Randolph in a famous clash in 1959.

Encounters like that persuaded Randolph, if he needed persuading, that blacks could never count on the decency of whites to win civil rights. No ruler ever yields power voluntarily. Power—and rights—must be *seized.*

"And so we have taken our struggle into the streets, as the labor movement took its struggle into the streets, as Jesus Christ led the multitudes through the streets of Judea. The plain and simple fact is that until we went into the streets the federal government was indifferent to our demands.

"Not until the streets and jails of Birmingham were filled did Congress begin to think about civil rights legislation. It was not until thousands demonstrated in the South that lunch counters and other public accommodations were integrated. It was not until the freedom riders were brutalized in Alabama that the 1964 Supreme Court decision banning discrimination in interstate travel was enforced, and it was not until construction sites . were picketed in the North that Negro workers were hired."

Randolph envisioned the March on Washington—from the 1940s onward—as a permanent movement. He dreamed of a time when progressive forces could mobilize thousands of have-nots and have-littles to put pressure on their government. He always called his creation the March on Washington *Movement.* If a filibuster paralyzed Congress, he wanted to send the masses to Capitol Hill. If old-line labor unions excluded blacks, he wanted to mobilize his people to confront the labor barons and their goons.

"We here today," he said, "are only the first wave. When we leave, it will be to carry the civil rights revolution home with us into every nook and cranny of the land, and we shall return again and again to Washington in very growing numbers until total freedom is ours."

After Randolph spoke, upwards of a hundred congressmen filed to the front steps of the Lincoln Memorial. They paused as they passed the cameramen, headphones around their heads and windbreakers fluttering in the breeze. People waved American flags.

Then people standing on the Memorial's apron spotted the congressmen, and marchers called out to their own congressmen. Then the chants merged together: "Pass the bill! Pass the bill! *Pass the bill!*"

ONSTAGE, THE WOMEN OF THE MOVEMENT sat together—Rosa Parks, Diane Nash Bevel, Rose Lee, Gloria Richardson, Daisy Bates—ready to take a bow.

Bow was about all they would do once the official program began. The Big Ten, all men, scheduled no women to give formal speeches. At the appointed moment, these "heroines" of the movement would stand and acknowledge the crowd. Then Daisy Bates—who helped the Little Rock Nine to brave the shouts, spitting, threats, and punches of white mobs when they desegregated Central High School in 1957—would read some scripted words. Finally, Phil Randolph, the master of ceremonies, rose "to give awards" to acknowledge "the great role that the Negro women have played in the cause of freedom." And he asked Daisy Bates to say a few words.

The life of Daisy Bates encompassed all the extremes of the black experience—and the twisted mentality about men and women that lay at the heart of segregation.

Soon after Bates was born, in 1914, three white men raped and murdered her mother. Her father left Daisy in the care of another couple. Her adoptive father experienced racist abuse himself. Dressed for Daisy's mother's funeral, he was called a "dressed-up ape" by white hoodlums who painted a red stripe down the suit. As she grew up, Daisy watched her Daddy, Olee Smith, absorb constant torment.

As a child, Daisy Bates was full of rage. But her father told her:

Hate can destroy you, Daisy. Don't hate white people because they're white. If you hate, make it count for something. Hate the humiliations we're living under in the South. Hate the discrimination that eats away at the soul of every black man and woman. Hate the insults hurled at us by white scum—and then try to do something about it, or your hate won't spell a thing.

And so she did something. She joined the NAACP, started an independent newspaper, and rallied support for the nine black children who integrated Central High School in Little Rock. For that, she was honored at the March on Washington.

Now Daisy Bates wore a pillbox hat and a sleeveless beige dress, with big costume jewelry and earrings. She spoke words that John Morsell of the NAACP had written earlier that day.

"Mr. Randolph, the women of this country pledge to you, Mr. Randolph, to Martin Luther King, to Roy Wilkins, and all of you fighting for civil liberties, that we will join hands with you, as women of this country . . .

"We will *kneel* in, we will *sit* in until we can eat at any counter in the *United States*. We will walk until we are free, until we can walk to any school and take our children to any school in the United States. We will *sit* in and we will *kneel* in and we will *lie* in if necessary, until we can vote. This we pledge you, the women of America."

And that was all.

For days, the battle over women speakers raged behind the scenes. The morning of the march, Anna Arnold Hedgeman confronted staffers of the march organizers. When she entered the lobby of the Statler Hilton, she saw Rachelle Horowitz.

Hedgeman walked up to Horowitz.

"What are you going to do about *the women?* You are betraying the cause of women if you go along with this."

Anna Hedgeman was the doyenne of the movement. Inspired by a talk by W. E. B. Du Bois, she became a teacher at Rust College in Mississippi. She later became executive secretary of the Fair Employment Practices Committee, the entity that President Franklin Roosevelt created to get Philip Randolph to cancel the 1941 March on Washington. Hedgeman also served as a dean at Howard University. She sat on every conceivable board in the civil rights movement.

Eleanor Holmes walked by. "Philip Randolph represents *me*," she said, and then she walked away.

Hedgeman could not stand the betrayal of a black sister. She started calling after her.

"You too have betrayed me—*and all womanhood!*"

Hedgeman also scorned the woman given the most visible role in the March on Washington. Hedgeman considered Mahalia Jackson, the gospel singer picked by Martin Luther King to sing "I Been 'Buked and I Been Scorned," to be crude, unkempt, too large, and ungainly.

For weeks, Hedgeman, Dorothy Height, and younger activists like Casey Hayden and Pauli Murray tried to get women at least one major speaking role on the program. They called, wrote, and directly confronted Phil Randolph and Bayard Rustin.

Women played some of the most important roles in the movement. Everyone knows about Rosa Parks refusing to yield her bus seat in Montgomery. But other women drove the movement forward. Ella Baker helped to teach Martin Luther King, back during the Montgomery boycott, and helped create SNCC. Fannie Lou Hamer built the Mississippi movement. Gloria Richardson led the Cambridge movement. As the old movement adage held, the women organize while men lead.

Dorothy Height led a small delegation of women to the Utopia House to lobby Rustin to put women on the program. But Rustin resisted. "Well, we have women," Height remembers him saying. "There are women members of the NAACP, we have all the denominations of the churches, our congregations are filled with women. The labor unions—we have Walter Reuther, he represents all these. We have Eugene Carson Blake, the National Council of Churches—well, the churches have so many women."

"Yes, that's why we want a woman to speak."

"But women's voices will be represented."

"Nobody can speak for us but us. How can we be marching for freedom and jobs and not have a woman speak?"

Looking back, Height theorized that young people got a speaking part because of their radicalism. "They knew that the women were not going to turn over the Lincoln Memorial, but the students might."

Hedgeman suggested inviting Myrlie Evers, Medgar's widow, to speak. Or if the march organizers wanted to give young people a voice, what about Diane Nash Bevel? *Who* Randolph and Rustin chose didn't matter, as long as at least one woman got a speaking role.

Rustin answered that picking one woman would anger the others. He talked about "the difficulty of finding a single woman to speak without causing serious problems vis-à-vis other women and women's groups." *Women get jealous of other women.*

Hedgeman and other women also protested Phil Randolph's decision to speak at the National Press Club the week before the March on Washington. The Press Club did not allow women to sit on the main floor during events. They were seated in the balcony, cut off from the event's give-and-take.

"The time has come to say to you quite frankly, Mr. Randolph, that 'tokenism' is as offensive when applied to women as when applied to Negroes and that I have not devoted the greater part of my adult life to the implementation of human rights to condone any policy which is not inclusive," Pauli Murray wrote to Randolph. "You are doubtless aware that the great abolitionist, William Lloyd Garrison, and Charles Redmond, a Negro delegate, refused to be seated at the World Anti-Slavery Convention in London in 1840 when they learned that women delegates from America would be excluded."

The battles over the National Press Club and over who would speak at the March split women in the movement.

Maida Springer was bringing a Guinean labor delegation to the march. She offered to let Pauli Murray use her apartment while she figured out what to do. Murray turned Springer's living room and foyer into a headquarters for the cause. She talked about picketing the National Press Club.

"You will join us, if it comes to that, won't you?" Murray asked Springer.

"No, I will not join you in a picket line to picket A. Philip Randolph a week before the March on Washington."

Angry, Murray cleared her materials out of the apartment and left.

When Randolph got to the National Press Club, he objected to women's exclusion from the event. For the first time, the club invited women down from the balcony to the main floor for Randolph's speech.

Those skirmishes—early signs of a gender split in the civil rights movement—were forgotten for the time being. Now, as the women sat down, the chant rose again from the front of the Lincoln Memorial: "Pass the bill! Pass the bill! Pass the bill!"

ALSO ABSENT FROM THE PROGRAM was a representative of the poor.

Early drafts of the March on Washington program listed "Unemployed Worker" as one of the keynote speakers. The early transportation plans included busloads and trainloads of the poor and unemployed. The hope was to bring at least ten thousand people from the plantations and ghettos of the South.

But the march became ever more middle class. In July, "Unemployed Worker" got crossed off the list of speakers. The logic that applied for women—someone else will speak *for* them, so there's no reason for them to speak for themselves—applied to the poor.

Courtland Cox, a Howard University student who worked at march headquarters all summer, was distressed at the undercurrent of class bias among the Big Ten.

"There was always a sense that this is a civil discussion between *educated people,*" he said about the civil rights movement. "The *underbrush,* with their broken English, they would not fit in. It was all right to speak *for* them, but we shouldn't allow them to speak for themselves. . . . I was so pissed. These were the people engaged in the demonstrations and people who were supposed to represent them felt it would be better to not have them there."

Rallying poor and unemployed workers also clashed with the everyday demands of organizing in tough states like Mississippi, Alabama, and Louisiana. Jane Stembridge, a civil rights worker in Mississippi, told Tom Kahn that the Delta would not send a Freedom Train "due to lack of funds."

"This is very bad," she said. "These sharecroppers and jobless Delta folk should really lead the parade!"

Labor unions and churches often paid the bus fare of people too poor to pay their own way. When activists expressed an interest, local leaders sometimes found some help. Wyatt Tee Walker, Martin Luther King's top aide, said ten thousand sharecroppers were coming to the march. Bayard Rustin once estimated that about half of all buses set aside five or six seats for unemployed workers and the poor. But the process was haphazard, not a concerted effort to bring the dispossessed to Washington.

Cox wrote to Stokely Carmichael to express his frustration: "You remember the old saying in Harlem that says, I feel for you brother, but I can't reach you? This seems to be exactly the case with our brothers down here. . . . You know, good buddy, that when Billie Holiday said 'Mama (NAACP) may have and Papa may have (SCLC), but God bless the child (the sharecropper) that got its own,' she wasn't funning."

"WE COME LATE, LATE WE COME," Eugene Carson Blake, pale but dapper in his bowtie, told the throng at the March on Washington.

The crowd stirred—baked in the sun, tired from a night or more of travel, no place for anyone but for a few hundred VIPs to sit. Blake's voice could barely be heard above the flutter of conversation, singing, and movement about the National Mall.

Blake's embrace of direct action had happened almost accidentally. When he attended the first meeting of the Commission on Religion and Race in New York, he told a press conference that preachers had to do more than preach—they had to *act*. Resolutions weren't enough anymore.

"How?" a reporter asked.

"Well, there's going to be a demonstration on the Fourth of July and we're investigating it to see . . ."

By the time the story appeared, Blake had committed himself to civil disobedience at the Gwynn Oaks Amusement Park in Baltimore.

On the Fourth of July, he joined a group of 500 people at the amusement park. Blake stood in line with his new friend Furman Templeton, a black active in a local Presbyterian church, and asked for tickets. The ticket seller said Blake could go, but not his black friend. Blake pushed the matter. Within minutes he was arrested, with 282 others, and taken to the station for booking. The next day, newspapers and TV stations carried images of the preacher in a collar, wearing a straw hat, getting carted away.

Protesters faced little real danger that day. They got arrested, processed, moved to an auditorium, then moved to a prison. "We didn't know if we were going to be released," one of the protesters, D'Army Bailey, remembered. "That was the only thing. We were released the next day and never went to court."

Even as Blake felt a rush of radicalization—risking his own safety for the cause, confronting someone on the question of race—he felt sorry for the owner of the amusement park. Racism is ignorance, after all. Even though the owner might be too callow to integrate his park, he had fears too. He was scared that integration would ruin his business.

Later, he told Blake: "When the Protestants and Catholics and the Jews are against me, I give up."

Now Blake had come to Washington to confess his own shortcomings, and those of the churches across white America. If white churches had followed Christ's teachings, he said, the civil rights struggle "would be already won."

"Our official pronouncements for years have called for a nonsegregated church in a segregated society," he said. "But as of August 28, 1963, we have achieved neither a nonsegregated church nor a nonsegregated society. And it is partly because the churches of America have failed to put their own houses in order . . . We do not therefore come to this Lincoln Memorial in any arrogant spirit of moral or spiritual superiority, to set the Congress or the nation straight, or to judge or denounce the American people in whole or in part."

Fifty thousand whites in the March on Washington, he said, symbolized a new commitment to civil rights.

"We come, and late we come, but we come to present ourselves this day, our souls and bodies to be a living sacrifice, holy and acceptable to God . . . a kind of tangible and visible sacrament . . . [that] can manifest to a troubled world the grace that is available in communion table and high altar."

TEARS HAD STREAKED MARIAN ANDERSON'S FACE earlier in the day. Scheduled to begin the March on Washington's afternoon program by singing the national anthem, she could not hustle to the podium fast enough. Camilla Williams, who studied music through a scholarship named for Marian Anderson, sang the anthem in her place.

Now, the most famous singer in the history of the nation's capital got a second chance. This time, she would sing "He's Got the Whole World in His Hands."

In another scenario, the marchers would hear another version of that song. Before the Great March, the Justice Department assigned John Riley to sit by a switch on the platform. If John Lewis used his fiery language and the crowd responded with anger, or violence, he would cut off Lewis's mike and put on a record of Mahalia Jackson singing "He's Got the Whole World in His Hands."

But it was Marian Anderson's turn now. She stood at the podium, dark dress and white gloves. In a girlish squeak, she announced her number. She closed her eyes, raising her hands as she moved into the song.

Before the March on Washington, only one event had ever attracted as many as 75,000 people to the National Mall—the free concert by Marian Anderson on Easter Sunday of 1939.

Anderson was, at the time, the premier female concert vocalist in the world. A contralto, she sang the full repertoire of gospel and folk music born of the African American experience. She also sang a full repertoire of classical music—Bach, Verdi, Schubert, Sibelius, Dvorak, Donizetti. Arturo Toscanini declared her voice "such as one hears once in a hundred years." That voice, a reviewer wrote, "sounds more like an exquisite wind instrument than like the human voice, the tones ringing out like a clarinet."

In the summer of 1938, Anderson's agents sought a venue for an Easter Sunday concert on April 9, 1939. Washington offered few concert halls for serious music. The best was probably Constitution Hall, owned by the Daughters of the American Revolution. Second best, probably, was the auditorium at Central High School.

The DAR refused to book Anderson. The DAR said that no dates were available and, besides, the organization's charter stipulated that "whites only" perform at the hall. Later, when the DAR's stance sparked an international controversy, the group said race wasn't the main issue. But when an agent privately inquired about booking a white performer, the DAR offered ten open dates, including April 8 and 10. Anderson's agents said they would agree to either of those days, but the DAR said no again.

Anderson's agents also tried booking a concert at the all-white Central High School, but the school board twice rejected booking requests. The board finally offered to allow Anderson to sing "only under positive and definite assurance and agreement that the concession would not be taken as a precedent." In other words, opening the school to Anderson would close it for all other blacks. No deal.

Finally, someone suggested that she sing at the Lincoln Memorial. In the seventeen years since its dedication in 1912, few groups had assembled there for public events. A public gathering on hallowed ground made sense. Franklin Roosevelt quickly approved the idea.

On a frigid Easter Sunday, Marian Anderson made history. She sang Donizetti's aria "O mio Fernando," Schubert's "Ave Maria," Harry Burleigh's arrangement of "Gospel Train," Edward Boatner's "Trampin'," and Florence Price's arrangement of "My Soul Is Anchored to the Lord."

Marian Anderson's opening number at that concert was what everyone always remembered. As the crowd waited expectantly, Anderson closed her eyes, tilted her head back, and sang:

> My country 'tis of thee
> Sweet land of liberty
> Of thee we sing . . .

That moment was frozen in history. One hourlong concert on a chilly day in 1939 demonstrated the power of mass gatherings at places like the Lincoln Memorial.

The concert lasted less than an hour, but the moment stayed in the bones of black Americans—and anyone who loved music and beauty, or cared about basic fairness—for generations.

Now, almost a quarter century later, Marian Anderson stood before a throng three times as great. Her role was small, a last-minute improvisation. But she provided a link to the past. And she took ownership of the Mall one more time.

> He's got the whole world in his hands,
> He's got the big round world in his hands
> He's got the wide world in his hands
> He's got the whole world in his hands
>
> He's got the wind and the rain in his hands
> He's got the moon and the stars in his hands. . . .

Ralph Matthews, a reporter for the *Afro-American,* knew Marian Anderson's voice was past its prime. But "I closed my eyes and saw her not as she appeared today, but as she sang in the same spot many years ago."

———

RUMORS OF CENSORSHIP WERE CIRCULATING ACROSS the National Mall by the time A. Philip Randolph introduced "Brother John Lewis."

The activists from the Student Nonviolent Coordinating Committee spread out below the Lincoln Memorial knew that the Catholic Church had threatened to pull out of the event unless Lewis tempered his rhetoric. The media knew, too. If Archbishop Patrick O'Boyle's intention was to direct global attention to the twenty-three-year-old civil rights worker from Troy, Alabama, he couldn't have done any better.

But the speech was still strong—unflinching—and the sound of agony gave Lewis a poignancy that no one else had that day. Someone said his voice was a "pained cracking."

The cunning Jim Forman, the man who tapped out a new version in the custodians' room under Abraham Lincoln's statue, actually *sharpened* the rhetoric. Forman took out two passages objectionable to the Catholics and the Kennedys—the refusal to support Kennedy's civil rights bill and the vow to march like Sherman. But he replaced every objectionable phrase with equally strong rhetoric.

When Lewis stood in front of 250,000 people on the Mall, and millions across the world, he did not flinch from complaining about sharecroppers working for three dollars a day . . . the "police state" in Danville, Virginia . . . peaceful protesters being arrested on "trumped-up charges" . . . activists facing the death penalty for demanding their God-given rights.

Lewis adopted the battle cry of colonial struggles in Africa—"One Man, One Vote!" Could any statement be more critical of America? America, the oldest modern democracy, needing to learn basic lessons on democracy from African colonies? And he complained about politicians who "build their careers on immoral compromises and ally themselves with open forms of political, economic and social exploitation."

But it was the *voice*—anguished, weary, and quivering, yet also resolved, defiant, and strong, even soft, loving, and hopeful—that gave the speech its power. From his opening words, spoken without any ice-breaking pleasantries, Lewis expressed weariness about the battle over civil rights. "We march today for jobs and freedom, but we have nothing to be proud of," he said. Immediately, he invoked the struggles of people across the South, ordinary laborers as well as civil rights workers, who could not indulge a midweek trip to the nation's capital.

"Hundreds and thousands of our brothers are not here," he said. "For they are receiving starvation wages—or no wages at all. While we stand here, there are sharecroppers in the Delta of Mississippi who are out in the field working for less than three dollars a day, twelve hours a day. While we stand here, there are students in jail on trumped-up charges. Our brother James Farmer, along with many others, is also in jail."

Lewis did not come for a celebration. And he certainly did not come to praise or thank the Kennedy administration or the mandarins of Capitol Hill, who grudgingly deliberated over every partial grant of basic rights. Even if the administration's bill somehow passed, it would still offer no real protections to many real people.

Unless Title III is put in this bill, there is nothing to protect the young children and old women from police dogs and fire hoses in the South when they engage in peaceful demonstrations. In its present form, this bill will not protect the citizens in Danville, Virginia, who must live in constant fear in a police state. It will not protect the hundreds of people who have been arrested on trumped-up charges. What about the three young men, SNCC field secretaries in Americus, Georgia, who face the death penalty for engaging in peaceful protest?

The most basic of all rights were missing in the Kennedy solution. Lewis cried out, with no false sense of optimism: "'One man, one vote' is the African cry. It is *ours,* too. It *must* be ours."

The hypocrisy of white liberal reformers, offering partial redress of centuries-old grievances, was especially painful in the case of Albany, Georgia—the place where a wily police chief defeated Martin Luther King's campaign in 1962, the place where, now, the Kennedy Justice Department indicted civil rights workers for picketing a store downtown.

"Do you know that in Albany, Georgia, nine of our leaders have been indicted not by the Dixiecrats but by the federal government for *peaceful* protest? But what did the federal government do when Albany's deputy sheriff beat attorney C. B. King and left him half dead? What did the federal government do when local police officials kicked and assaulted the pregnant wife of Slater King, and she lost her baby?"

And what party was willing to stand for the basic rights of blacks? Both parties were fatally compromised. "What political leader here can stand up and say 'my party is the party of principles'?" Lewis asked. "The party of Kennedy is also the party of Eastland. The party of Javits is also the party of Goldwater.

"Where is *our* party?"

The Washington police chief and television commentators were already calling the March on Washington a "church picnic." Malcolm X called it a circus, with the "We Shall Overcome"–singing Negroes and their white allies the clowns. But to John Lewis, the march was not a celebration, but a time to serve dire notice.

"We do not want to go to jail, but we will go to jail if this is the price we must pay for love, brotherhood, and true peace," he said.

"They talk about slow down and stop. We will not stop. All of the forces of Eastland, Barnett, Wallace, and Thurmond will not stop this revolution."

All right! Say it!

"If we do not get meaningful legislation out of this Congress, the time will come when we will not confine our marching to Washington. We will march through the South, through the streets of Jackson, through the streets of Danville, through the streets of Cambridge, through the streets of Birmingham."

Yes! We'll march!

In his first draft, Lewis vowed to have a modern, nonviolent, loving version of Sherman's March to the Sea. "We will march through the Heart of Dixie, the way Sherman did," he planned to say. "We shall pursue our own scorched-earth policy and burn Jim Crow to the ground—nonviolently."

Those words were now gone. But their power was felt even more with their absence, like a phantom limb. Anyone who heard reports about the "censored speech" felt the presence of the phrases that were no longer in the speech.

Now he promised to "splinter the segregated South into a thousand pieces and put them together in the image of God and democracy."

And then a plea: "We must say wake up, America, wake up, for we cannot stop and we will not and cannot be patient."

WALTER REUTHER BATHED IN APPLAUSE after delivering his speech and worked his way back to his seat. He reached out, instinctively, for hands and hugs. And then he sat down.

Carson Blake leaned toward him.

"How do you *do* that?" he asked.

Easy, Reuther said. When you speak at union halls—for conferences and conventions and board meetings—you're always competing with people talking at tables, waiters coming and going, doors opening and closing, plates crashing, and union members heckling, and you still have to keep people listening. It's a formula, Reuther told Blake. You get the audience with jokes. Joke, laugh, make a point; joke, laugh, make a point; joke, laugh—and then give the message of the day.

Whatever you do, Reuther told Blake, don't write out a text. Reading kills a speech. When you script a speech, you talk to your text. But you need to talk to the audience.

But even the best speech will only carry people so far.

"You're having the same problem as me," Reuther told Blake.

"Yeah, how's that?"

"Well, the leadership says all the right things but the locals haven't heard yet."

Walter Reuther, the president of the United Auto Workers, thrived in chaos—negotiating contracts with the Big Three, addressing rebellious affiliates, confronting the white racism in union locals, engaging in Democratic Party intrigue, collaborating behind the scenes with the president, battling other labor leaders like George Meany for primacy. Sometimes explosive, Reuther found ways to assert himself in a noisy environment.

Since A. Philip Randolph first announced plans to hold a massive March on Washington, Reuther had played a major role. Labor had two resources the march would need—money and bodies. Reuther also had an extensive political network and a close working relationship with President Kennedy.

The White House asked him to infiltrate the march and steer it away from radical rhetoric and direct action. And so he did. During the planning meetings in New York, Reuther wondered aloud about where to put two hundred thousand people in Washington. Pennsylvania Avenue and Capitol Hill—where the march was originally planned to take place—could never hold such a throng. Might it be better to move the march to the National Mall, between the Washington Monument and Lincoln Memorial? That was sly.

But Reuther could also be combative. When John Lewis hesitated to alter his speech earlier that day, Reuther played the goon. Everyone else, besides Roy Wilkins, was delicate.

For years, Reuther had made civil rights a central part of his politics. Labor unions were almost as lily white as Southern schools and Sunday church services. Workers in factories, mines, and furnaces and at construction sites often considered civil rights a zero-sum game. *If blacks get the jobs, we don't.* But Reuther worked hard to convince laborers everywhere, including the South, to accept blacks. Workers are workers, he said, and need to stick together. "Make up your mind whether you want your paycheck or your prejudice," he said.

By appearing at the march, Reuther defied the don of the labor movement, AFL-CIO president George Meany. In a four-hour meeting, Reuther and Randolph begged the union's executive committee to endorse and contribute to the march. "The labor movement is about the struggle of the people who are denied their measure of justice," Reuther later said, "and if the labor movement is not in the front rank [it] begins to forfeit the loyalty of the people whom I profess to lead and represent."

Meany argued that the march would produce riots and bloodshed. Reuther pointed out that more than a hundred thousand people had rallied in Detroit the previous week without any disorder.

"But George Meany made this a personal thing," Reuther told his UAW board. "You were either voting for him or against him. It had nothing to do with the idea, and four hours of this, it was quite obvious that George Meany did not want the council to authorize participation."

Meany allowed a special committee to draft a statement of sympathy for the march, then ripped it up and substituted his own statement lauding the AFL-CIO's leadership in civil rights. After the meeting, Reuther told reporters that that official statement "is so weak they will have to give it a blood infusion to keep it alive long enough to mimeograph it."

Reuther frequently complained that the labor movement had gotten sluggish and bureaucratic, lacking the daring of a quarter century before, when sit-down strikes forced automakers to capitulate to union demands. In his own union, he battled Southern whites who opposed working with blacks and civil rights. When he sent $50,000 to bail out civil rights protesters, white locals burned with anger. For years, the labor movement assumed that progress for all workers would eventually lift up the black worker. Reuther rejected that idea and spoke out for civil rights before most other prominent white leaders. After the 1954 *Brown* decision, Reuther warned Democrats against "straddling" on the issue. Straddle is exactly what the Democrats did. Civil rights laws were essential to prodding everyone—business firms, unions, local government—to do the right thing.

Meany and Reuther had long been rivals. The two battled for the attention of the president and congressional leaders. As head of the UAW, Reuther was part of the AFL-CIO executive board. Meany regularly thwarted Reuther's efforts to speak for labor and assume policy positions (like the post Reuther craved as a labor delegate to the United Nations). Reuther's many contacts with the Kennedy administration only increased Meany's ire. Reuther regularly met with the president, for hours at a time. In those White House meetings Reuther sometimes lamented the way Meany treated him; Kennedy sympathized but said Reuther had to accept Meany's status as the top labor leader.

As Reuther became a national spokesman for civil rights, he also struggled to address the UAW's own problem of black exclusion. Reuther had promised blacks a leadership position in the UAW back in 1936; twenty-three years later, when no blacks sat on the UAW board, a rebellion took place. A leader of the black uprising attacked the UAW leadership for talking a good game on civil rights while resisting, "with every means at their disposal, any efforts to change the lily-white character of their own international executive boards."

On this day, Walter Reuther could bask in the sun as the most significant white figure in the March on Washington. He had mobilized organized labor, served as a conduit between the Kennedys and the movement, contributed financially, and helped to resolve the John Lewis crisis.

When he spoke, he stated the matter simply.

"We must determine now—once and for all—whether we believe in the United States Constitution."

Reuther called civil rights the key to America's credibility in the Cold War.

"We can make our own freedom secure only as we make freedom universal so that all may share its blessings. We cannot successfully preach democracy in the world unless we first practice democracy at home . . . There is no halfway house to human freedom. What is needed in the present crisis is not half-way and half-hearted measures, but action, bold and adequate to square American democracy's performance with its promise.

"If we fail, the vacuum created by our failure will be filled with the Apostles of Hatred, who will search for answers in the dark of night, and reason will yield to riot, and the spirit of brotherhood will yield to bitterness and bloodshed and the fabric of our free society will be torn asunder."

As Reuther spoke, he pumped his left arm, pointing with his forefinger. One of Reuther's assistant's at the UAW, Irving Bluestone, stood nearby on the platform. Bluestone overheard two black women talking.

"Who is that white man?" the first asked.

"Don't you know him? That's Walter Reuther. He's the white Martin Luther King."

IN A SQUAT, SQUARE TWO-STORY BRICK BUILDING, in the sweltering Louisiana town of Donaldsonville, James Farmer sat, Buddha-like, in captivity.

Farmer was a round man with a pudgy face and a honeyed baritone voice.

For years, Farmer was the leading apostle of nonviolent direct action for civil rights. Back in 1941, he founded the Congress of Racial Equality, an integrated organization, to fight for black rights. Now, for the first time, CORE was active all over the nation, organizing people in Louisiana, Mississippi, Georgia, North Carolina and up north, in New York, Philadelphia, Chicago, and San Francisco.

Farmer's jailing came after a summer of demonstrations in Plaquemine, an old French settlement on the Mississippi River, twenty miles south of the state capital of Baton Rouge. CORE and the Student Nonviolent Coordinating Committee had targeted different congressional districts in the Black Belt for voter registration. Jim Farmer's CORE organization got the Sixth Congressional District of Louisiana.

After the wildest protest in Plaquemine's history, police rounded up 230 protesters. They separated Farmer from his people and put him in jail in Donaldsonville, twenty miles down the road, in a historic old building adjacent to City Hall—notorious for one of the 291 lynchings in Louisiana from 1876 to 1946.

It would have been easy to put up the $300 bail Farmer needed to get out of the Bayou and come to Washington. But Farmer said no—or, more specifically, the staffers at CORE, the people risking their lives for the movement, said no.

"We decided at CORE that we would make a better statement with Jim in jail than at the March on Washington," said Lolis Edward Elie, the group's lawyer. "Anybody with an ounce of ego would want to be in Washington. Jim always rivaled Martin Luther King as a speaker. He wanted to be there. But the group made that decision not to be there."

Rudy Lombard, one of the leaders of CORE's Louisiana campaign, insisted that Farmer stay in jail.

"We had to be careful about having one standard for community people and another for the leaders," he said. "So the disposition was it made a lot more sense for Farmer to stay in jail. Anything that needed to be said, Martin Luther King and the others would say it.

"We would not ask the local people to do anything that the CORE representatives would not do. That would apply to all of us, including Jim. We didn't think that going to Washington and participating in the march was any more important than staying involved with the community. It was very critical, the more we took action, the more Gordon West [a federal judge who ordered a halt to protests] and the others [opposed] us, that we all stay together and fight."

Farmer argued with the others in CORE.

"It's important for CORE to be there," he said. "And I *am* the titular head of the organization."

But the will of the group was that he stay. So he stayed.

For days, Farmer took calls from the march organizers. With each call, the tone got sharper. It started with friendly pleas. Then the talk turned to Farmer's *responsibility* to be in Washington. *What are you doing down there? You're one of the leaders. You should be here.*

Whitney Young called Farmer's wife, Lulu, and Young and Roy Wilkins sent telegrams. Privately, Roy Wilkins and other march organizers complained that Farmer was grandstanding. By staying away, Farmer elevated himself over the others. He made the silent statement that his cause—his campaign down in Iberville Parish, Louisiana—was more important than the national movement.

"If I get out on bail, I have to make sure the others get out too," he said. CORE didn't have the $33,900 in bail money—for more than two hundred prisoners, each held at $300 bail—needed to free everyone. Besides, emptying the jails would take the pressure off Plaquemine's mayor and police chief, who had arrested demonstrators for singing "We Shall Overcome."

Pleading with Farmer on the telephone did not help anyone. Local police and the FBI—who knows, maybe the White Citizens' Council and Ku Klux Klan, too—listened in on his phone calls. Every time people from the march called, they fed information to the enemy.

"I was a little embarrassed about this because the whole conversation was being tapped," Farmer later recalled. "Here were these sheriff's men sitting around grinning. They knew they were recording the conversation. There was just no reticence on the part of the caller. He was talking at length about internal civil rights business."

Caught between the CORE purists and the March on Washington organizers, Farmer finally got exasperated.

"Go to hell," he told one caller. "I'm not going to leave here when I have 225 people here. You can't get them out, so I stay here."

The police still thought Farmer might pay bail to get out. Maybe he'd surprise everyone, leave Louisiana, and show up in Washington a hero. So the police got an injunction against him, forbidding him to leave the state. That settled it—he had to stay, or else face contempt of court charges for fleeing the jurisdiction.

Farmer said he wanted someone to speak for CORE at the march. He suggested Bertrand Tyson, the only black doctor in Plaquemine. The response:

No way. It had to be someone from CORE's leadership. Farmer then suggested Floyd McKissick, the North Carolina lawyer who was now CORE's national chairman. Randolph said McKissick would be okay—as long as he delivered *Farmer's* message.

Jim Farmer was born to be a civil rights leader. Like Martin Luther King, he was a "PK," a preacher's kid. His father sternly directed his every action, to make sure he got the tools to survive in a white world. Junior pleased his father by overachieving. At age fourteen, he enrolled at Wiley College in Texas. Junior was a member of the first black college debate team ever to compete against a white school, defeating the University of Southern California back in 1935.

The Congress of Racial Equality, which he founded six years later, became the first civil rights organization to embrace nonviolence as an *aggressive* political tactic. Long before anyone knew about Martin Luther King, Jim Farmer began using direct-action tactics—marching, sitting in, sitting in white sections of segregated buses, defying Jim Crow in every way possible —to fight segregation.

Iberville Parish—the Louisiana equivalent of a county, where Plaquemine was located—recalled the days of Reconstruction. A few lavish plantation mansions occupied prominent high spots, with shacks for workers scattered in the invisible countryside. Workers were indentured for a few dollars a day, supporting the vast system that imprisoned them. They could work for only a couple months a year, at most, when cane needed to be harvested. Even that field work was getting more difficult to land, though, since the advent of mechanization in the late 1950s.

The mayor and local businessmen couldn't understand why CORE targeted Plaquemine. Race relations were "very pleasant," the mayor said, until "outside agitators and rabble rousers" came to town.

Iberville Parish was, in fact, one of the most integrated communities in all of Louisiana. A black middle class, with doctors and teachers and preachers, lived an active church and civic life. Whites and blacks worked together, shopped together downtown—and even went to school close to one another. Whites lived near Plymouth Rock Baptist Church, the most active black church in town.

Even though blacks were allowed to register to vote, they didn't elect anyone. And since 1958, parishes across Louisiana had purged blacks from voter rolls. In West Feliciana, where 60 percent of all people were black, not a single black was registered to vote.

But voting rights were just part of CORE's campaign. Blacks also wanted to redraw the map of the area. They pressed to annex two black communities—Dupont and Seymourville—to Plaquemine. CORE leaders said they wanted those communities to get their fair share of services, like roads, sewers, and streetlights.

Power was the real issue, always. With annexation, the community would have a black majority. Blacks could take over the town.

When black leaders met Mayor Charles Schnebelen, the mayor told them to make a presentation at the next city council meeting on August 29. But nothing would come of that. The activists told Schnebelen to forget it— and get ready for raucous protests. "There [won't] *be* any Plaquemine by the twenty-ninth of August," one of the CORE men told the mayor. And the protests began.

On Monday, August 19, police lobbed tear-gas canisters into the cluster of a couple dozen marchers, burning eyes and dispersing them—and then arrested fifteen for disturbing the peace. On Tuesday, CORE sent four groups of ten activists to sit in at cafés and restaurants and demand service. The eateries closed down, stranding the protesters outside—where police arrested them.

On Wednesday, after protests in the afternoon produced eighty-five more arrests, the mayor got a restraining order from U.S. District Judge E. Gordon West against any kind of demonstration. The judge interrupted his vacation to issue an order, effective "without notice," banning protests by members of CORE "and John Doe and Jane Doe and others acting in concert with them." Seventy protesters gathered at the Iberville Parish Court House and sang "We Shall Overcome"—and promptly got arrested. Six blocks away, at Plaquemine City Hall, eighty more sang songs and got arrested. By the weekend, 250 people had gotten arrested.

Plaquemine's police learned the lessons of Laurie Pritchett, Albany's police chief. Knowing that civil rights activists pressured small towns by overwhelming their jails, Pritchett borrowed cells from surrounding communities before Martin Luther King's protests started in 1962. Rather than pressuring Albany to change, the jailings removed King and his followers from the streets and churches. King finally posted bail and left Albany. It was his greatest defeat.

By staying in jail—when the eyes of the world focused on the March on Washington—Farmer kept his people together.

On the day of the Great March, as Jim Farmer sat in a sweltering jail cell in Louisiana, he did get one privilege. His jailers allowed a group of women to bring a TV into the jail. There, the group—the civil rights leader, his supporters, and his jailers—watched the March on Washington. And they heard the message of the missing man.

―――――

THROUGH HIS INTERMEDIARY, JAMES FARMER MADE the nuclear age the center of his civil rights analysis.

Floyd McKissick was allowed to deliver Farmer's statement at the March on Washington.

Leaning forward with helicopters hovering above—*thwap-thwap-thwap*—McKissick spoke with a high-pitched voice.

"In the age of thermonuclear bombs," McKissick said for Farmer, "violence is outmoded as the solution to the problems of men. It is a truth that needs to be shouted loudly, and no one else anywhere in the world is saying it as well as the American Negroes through their nonviolent direct action . . .

"Our direct action method is bringing down barriers all over the country, in jobs, in housing, in schools, in public places. It is giving hope to the world, to people who are weary of warfare and who see extinction hanging over their future like a mushroom cloud. If we can solve our problems and remove the heavy heel of oppression from our necks with our methods, then man has no problems anywhere in the world which cannot be solved without death.

"So we are fighting not only for our rights and our freedom, we are fighting not only to make our nation safe for [the] democracy it preaches, we are fighting to give the whole world a fighting chance for survival."

"GET A BISHOP IN THE EAST," Bayard Rustin told Mathew Ahmann.

When the March on Washington's steering committee decided to invite religious leaders to become cosponsors, Bayard Rustin had a problem. Getting a Protestant took little effort—Eugene Carson Blake, the head of the National Council of Churches, was an easy choice. The Jews were split into three branches—Orthodox, Conservative, and Reform—but Rustin had lots of plausible choices.

But the Catholics—divided among themselves about civil rights, notoriously hierarchical, and intensely traditional—offered no obvious choice. Ahmann approached Cardinal Francis Spellman of New York, but he said no. He said he didn't want to ride into another bishop's territory, when "God knows what" could happen. Archbishop Patrick O'Boyle, long a supporter of civil rights in Washington, would not agree to join the Big Ten, but he said he would deliver the invocation. There was no other obvious candidate, and no one considered a woman, like Dorothy Day of the Catholic

Worker movement, who was controversial across the country for her un-flinching radicalism.

Catholics had formed their first interracial councils back in 1934, mostly at the parish level, but did not convene a full national gathering on civil rights until 1958. By the summer of 1963, though, priests started to partici-pate in protests. Alarmed by the massive street crowds for Malcolm X in Harlem, Father Philip Murnion created a new program for young people and embraced gospel music in some services. So the Catholic Church was awakening to its mission beyond the parishes, but finding a national spokes-man proved difficult.

"We tried but it was too late in the game," Ahmann said. "Some of the bishops in the diocese opposed participation in the march by priests and nuns. Bishop O'Boyle wrote a letter directing nuns in the Washington dio-cese to stay home even though he participated in the march."

When no bishop emerged to participate on the March committee, Ah-mann took on the role. And when he took his place at the Lincoln Memorial to speak, he asked for basic empathy and a willingness to match words with deeds. By the time he spoke, the crowd was restless. Some started to gather their belongings to leave. Others talked among themselves. Some slept.

"Where is the man—white or Negro—whose heart has not been touched by the revelation in the past months of racial sores among the people of our country?" he asked. "Where is the man so callous that in some deep way his conscience has not yet been moved to see the civil effects of racial discrimi-nation upon both the Negro and the white man?

"Who can call himself a man, say he is created by God, and at the same time take part in a system of segregation which destroys the livelihood, citizenship, family life, and the very heart of the Negro citizens . . . which frightens the white man into denying what he knows to be right, into deny-ing the law of his God?"

"YOU CAN HOLLER, PROTEST, march, picket and demonstrate, but some-body must be able to sit in on the strategy conferences and plot a course. There must be strategies, the researchers, the professionals to carry out the program."

Whitney Young, the most conservative figure in Big Ten, was the move-ment's ultimate professional man. But in a curious way, he was also the most radical.

As the civil rights debate advanced in 1963, Young became the leading voice for the most controversial solution to the race problem, this side of Malcolm X's call for separatism. Young wanted to guarantee blacks a quota of jobs, positions in schools and colleges and unions.

The idea of quotas was bound to explode. At a press conference on August 20, President Kennedy rejected the idea: "I don't think we can undo the past." Up until now, the civil rights movement focused on moral issues, matters that could not be compromised—the rights to assemble, march, get served, and vote. Now Young wanted the movement to embrace a whole set of material issues, those in which one person's gain was another's loss.

Since John Kennedy took office, Young had maneuvered to get the administration's attention on race and urban issues. A month after Kennedy's election, the Urban League sent Kennedy a memo calling for a new approach to the racial crisis. Rather than emphasizing race alone, the Urban League urged attention to the problems where most blacks lived.

In May 1962, Young brought Urban League officials to the White House for three days of meetings to formulate policy strategies. Young developed close ties with the departments of Labor; Health, Education, and Welfare; and Justice; with the Pentagon; and with the Housing and Home Finance Administration. He was an early voice for creating a cabinet-level housing department. He pushed hard for hiring blacks in the administration. He helped design VISTA. He also served on a committee that banned military use of segregated facilities, and cultivated a relationship with Vice President Lyndon Johnson. Young became an insider, very much in the tradition of his father and of Booker T. Washington. Washington had argued that blacks would benefit more by accommodating segregation: "We can be as separate as the fingers, yet one as the hand in all things essential to our natural progress."

Young's father, Whitney Senior, was a student, then a teacher and coach at, and finally president of the Lincoln Institute near Louisville. The institute was founded when segregationists forced Berea College, which accepted both blacks and whites, to go all white. In the tradition of Booker T. Washington, the institute offered vocational training. Whitney Senior worked with the whites on their own terms. When he wanted to offer a course on electrical engineering, he called it a course for janitors. White benefactors could not object to keeping blacks at that lowest rung.

Early in his career, young Whitney Young supported boycotts and protests of all kinds. But as head of the National Urban League he grew uneasy about protest. Demonstrations—like the March on Washington—were fine as long as they just expressed collective longing.

Young usually ignored racist slights. On a trip to Atlanta, Young met a manufacturer to talk about getting better jobs for blacks. As they toured the plant, the executive pointed out individual workers, saying "This nigger over here" and "That cracker over there." Young debated whether to correct his language. "But there was nothing served by that," he said later. "I'm trying to get jobs for *my people*. I've *got* a job. Why just make myself feel good? I better keep my eye on the ball."

But his personal mildness contrasted with his proposals for remaking American social policy. Not only did Young propose quotas to guarantee blacks positions in every realm of American life, he also proposed that the federal government give reparations to blacks for more than three hundred years of servitude. If blacks had not been forced into slavery, then forced into near slavery on sharecropping plantations, and then shut out of political and social life by Jim Crow, they could have claimed their share of the American Dream. But centuries of racial discrimination and terror had shut blacks out. The American system, then, needed to make amends.

Now Whitney Young got up to the podium at the Lincoln Memorial and offered the broadest agenda of anyone for black issues:

They must march from the rat-infested overcrowded ghettos to decent wholesome unrestricted *residential areas dispersed throughout our city.*
They must march from the relief rolls to the *established training centers.*
From underemployment as unskilled workers to *high occupations commensurate with our skills.*
They must march from cemeteries, where our newborn die three times sooner and our parents die seven years earlier, to establish *health and welfare centers.*
They must march from the congested ill-equipped schools which breed dropouts and which smother motivation, to the *well-equipped integrated facilities throughout the city.*
They must march from play areas in crowded and unsafe streets to the *newly opened areas in the parks and recreation centers.*

Young called his ambitious program a domestic Marshall Plan. If any president adopted his agenda—most of which was incubating in federal agencies, foundations, and universities—it would be the biggest expansion of government since Franklin Roosevelt took office in 1933. Whitney Young wanted government programs for every moment of life, from cradle to grave.

Whitney Young got only a soft patter of approval from the throng. He didn't preach. He didn't bring down the house. He just laid out the agenda that would change the American landscape for generations to come.

THE DAY WAS HOT AND LONG and marchers grew weary from a night of bus travel and walking in tight Sunday shoes.

The speeches ran long. Speakers were asked to limit their remarks to four minutes, but they could not restrain themselves. Most were preachy, and they used the language of insiders. All this talk of FEPC and Title III was beyond the ken of most listeners. And the delivery could be stiff, monotonic.

The lines for food and bathrooms were hundreds of people long. Thousands sought relief by sitting at the edge of the reflecting pool—but the sun glared off the pool, turning it into a reflector oven. The water was warm and dirty. Still, marchers rotated positions by the pool, so they could dangle their swollen and hot feet into the water for relief.

The lucky ones found shade under the trees about a hundred feet away from the pool, but they didn't get a good view. People in the sun used umbrellas and newspapers for protection and wet towels and shirts to cool their temples.

Dorothy Cotton, who spent the early morning hours typing Martin Luther King's speech, worked her way close to the stage with her husband. Squeezing hands, the couple almost made it. "We were friends and wanted to see Martin," she said. But they decided they were too tired to stay, so they worked their way out of the crowd and went back to the Willard Hotel to watch the event on TV.

Elliott Linzer, one of the interns for the March on Washington staff, stayed in the staff tent for most of the day. He did odd jobs and watched the parade of politicians and celebrities. By mid-afternoon, he was too tired to stay awake. So he crawled under a table, lay down near a pretty black girl, and fell asleep. And he dreamed . . .

D'Army Bailey, one of a group of six or seven marchers that spent the night by the Washington Monument in sleeping bags, was not only tired but also upset that the march wasn't more radical. "We were tired of the humdrum rhetoric, so we left," he said. "We were aware of how the march had been compromised. We were not in tune with being led like sheep and we walked back to the car and drove back to the townhouse."

By noon, people started collapsing from heat exhaustion and dehydration. A fourteen-year-old girl from Washington named Sylvia Johnson collapsed near the Lincoln Memorial platform shortly after twelve thirty. A TV cameraman wrapped ice in tissue paper and cooled her temples, wrists, and ankles. Martin Luther King came over to comfort her, and she smiled as she left on a stretcher. Some passed out in the dense crowd and got passed above the crowd like hot dogs at a ball game. By the end of the day, thirty-five Red Cross stations treated 1,335 people.

One person died. After walking to the Lincoln Memorial, a fifty-six-year-old New Yorker named Charles Schreiber had a heart attack. He died at George Washington University Hospital.

The author Norman Mailer looked out on the crowd and sensed a letdown.

There was also an air of subtle depression, of wistful apathy which existed in many—one felt a little of the muted disappointment which attacks a crowd in the seventh inning of a very important baseball game when the score has gone 11–3. The home team is ahead, but the tension is broken: one's concern is no longer noble.

It was an agreeable afternoon, but it had a touch of the cancerous to it—the toxic air of totalitarianism. Because 200,000 people had come down, some in fear, some in all courage, but they had come with the memory of the summer behind him, that historic summer of television when revolution for the first time had been created in part by the indignation of all those militant millions who had seen Bull Connor's police using fire hoses on Negro children, yes, a revolution created in part by television, that instrument of social control which had been used since its inception precisely to dull and/or end forever the possibility of revolution.

Yes, the seed of dialectics was stirring again, a shade of Marx, the ghost of Lenin. Many, maybe most of those 200,000 people came to Washington expecting danger, looking secretly for an historic issue that day. And they were disappointed. Considering the heat and the depressed fury of the history which had created this March, it was probably the most peaceful large assemblage in the history of the republic.

Never had one seen people so polite to one another. The iron word had gone out: no violence today! And there was none. That took its toll. That put the hand of a powerful depression into the agreeableness of the afternoon.

———

WESTERN UNION DELIVERED HUNDREDS OF TELEGRAMS of congratulations to the March on Washington tent. One came from W. E. B. Du Bois.

"One thing alone I charge you, as you live, *believe in Life!*" Du Bois said in a final message composed two months before, during his final illness. "Always human beings will live and progress to greater, broader and fuller life. The only possible death is to lose belief in this truth simply because the Great End comes slowly, because time is long."

Then came the news that Du Bois had died the day before in Accra, Ghana, at the age of ninety-five. Maya Angelou led a group of Americans and Ghanaians to the U.S. embassy in Accra, carrying torches and placards reading "Down with American Apartheid" and "America, a White Man's Heaven and a Black Man's Hell."

In Washington, the news fluttered through the audience and onto the platform.

Over a seventy-year career, Du Bois took every conceivable approach to the race problem. He was a provocative propagandist and measured scholar. He was for integration and then for separation. He believed in the American dream and disdained it. He believed in the power of politics and the ambiguity of culture. He brawled and he stood aloof. He embraced indigenous liberation and global communism.

Du Bois wrote thirty-eight books on the experience of race—on slavery and reconstruction, rebellion and war, psychology and economics, America and Africa, war and democracy, ideology and crime. He wrote thousands of articles and reports. He debated Booker T. Washington and coined the expression "the talented tenth," to describe the vanguard that could lead the black race out of bondage. As an American facing the cruelty and degradation of Jim Crow, Du Bois embraced the pan-African ideal of a global race.

Lifetimes ago, in 1909, Du Bois helped create the National Association for the Advancement of Colored People. He left the NAACP in 1948 when he was rebuked for holding a civil rights march in Washington. In 1961 he became a Communist Party member, renounced his American citizenship, and became a citizen of Ghana.

When Bayard Rustin got news of Du Bois's death, he worked his way across the crowded stage to deliver the news to Roy Wilkins. As the head of the NAACP, surely Wilkins would want to say a few words about this historic figure.

"I'm not going to get involved with *that Communist* at this meeting," Wilkins told Rustin. "I'm not going to announce that Communist's death."

So Rustin crossed back to confer with Phil Randolph. How to announce Du Bois's death?

"Tell Roy that if he doesn't announce it, I will."

Rustin crossed the stage again. He told Wilkins that Randolph was ready to speak.

"I don't want Phil Randolph doing it," Wilkins said.

But someone had to announce the death of the century's most enduring civil rights leader at the nation's greatest demonstration.

"Well, you tell Phil I'll do it," Wilkins said.

That was the ornery Roy Wilkins—the same Wilkins who had attempted to block Rustin's appointment as the organizer of the March on Washington . . . who insulted Martin Luther King at Medgar Evers's funeral . . . who complained bitterly about the attention given the younger activists in the Deep South . . . who poked John Lewis . . . who dismissed the possibility of change resulting from demonstrations.

But a sweeter Roy Wilkins also showed up that day. For a man who did not believe in the power of mass demonstrations—who believed that real progress happened when elites lobbied presidents and congressmen and filed lawsuits against carefully selected targets—Roy Wilkins was positively buoyant on the day of the march.

His whole life, Roy Wilkins had been determined to live within the system. The grandson of former slaves, Wilkins was raised by an aunt in Duluth after his mother died of tuberculosis and his father abandoned him. After studying sociology at the University of Minnesota, he took a job in Kansas City with the black newspaper the *Call*. "Kansas City ate my heart out," he said. "It was a Jim Crow town through and through. There were two school systems, bad housing, police brutality, bombings in Negro neighborhoods. Police were arresting white and Negro high school kids just for being together."

Early political victories forge political character. Wilkins's first victory came in 1930, when he joined the successful effort to defeat President Herbert Hoover's nomination of John J. Parker to the Supreme Court. A coalition of labor and civil rights organizations targeted Parker for his yellow-dog contracts and his opposition to black suffrage. Later that year, blacks cast the decisive votes to defeat Senator Henry Allen of Kansas, who supported Parker. "I was ecstatic," Wilkins said. "Here at last was a fighting organization, not a tame band of status-quo Negroes." Fighting, though, was confined to the formal arenas of politics. Like intellectuals of the period, including William Kornhauser and José Ortega y Gasset, Wilkins believed that Hitler had forever discredited mass politics. Besides, he said, protest didn't work.

Even the protests in Birmingham and other cities, he said, "didn't influence a single vote by a congressman or senator . . . not a single one."

Wilkins moved to New York to write for the NAACP's magazine the *Crisis* before getting promoted to assistant to Walter White, the NAACP's executive secretary. Wilkins's efforts followed the contours of the movement—first he took on lynching, then school segregation, then public accommodations and voting rights. *Brown v. Board of Education* illustrated the NAACP's model of racial progress. The NAACP chipped away at the edifice of segregation—first gaining blacks admission to professional and graduate schools, where the idea of "separate but equal" was impossible to implement because of the complete absence of programs for blacks, and then moving on to universities. Only when the courts had embraced the idea of blacks and whites going to universities together did the *Brown* case move forward.

Tenacious, pragmatic, distrustful of radical approaches, Wilkins became the head of the NAACP in 1955. Wilkins helped create a black-owned bank to assist blacks in starting their own businesses and avoid reprisals for civil rights activism. He embraced the NAACP's emphasis on judicial and legislative strategies. But by the summer of 1963, he embraced direct action. On June 1, he was arrested for picketing a variety store in Jackson.

However mainstream in his approach, Wilkins maintained a hard line against segregation. "It's just poison and no matter whether you have a teaspoonful or you have a barrelful of it, it ain't no good," he said. "Self-segregation is worse than another kind because your own eyes ought to be wide open. Segregation ought to be seen for what it is. It is not, necessarily, the division of people according to color. It can . . . and it does take that [form] in America; it is a device for control, for isolation and control. . . . A segregated group can always be cut off, be deprived, be denied equality."

Now, standing before this integrated throng—tan and relaxed, wearing a royal blue overseas hat with the letters NAACP stitched in gold—he began to talk with "my people." He paused, smiled, looked out on the throng that extended down the Mall, out back under the trees by the snow fence, even up in the tree branches. He was in the mood to play.

"I want to thank you for coming here today," he said, like a friendly uncle, "because you have saved me from being a liar. I told them that you would be here. They didn't believe me . . . because you always make up your mind at the last minute. And you had me scared! But isn't it a great day?"

Laughter rippled across the Mall. Then Wilkins called for silence down the middle of the Mall. "I want everybody out here in the open to keep quiet, and then I want to hear a yell and a thunder from all those people who are out there under the trees."

Suddenly, like magic, the crowd quieted.

And then he commanded the people on the edges of the Mall, sitting under the trees, to shout out. The Mall filled with cheers. And Wilkins laughed.

"There's one of them *in* the tree!"

Wilkins suddenly reveled in mass politics. And humor leavened even his dead-serious points.

"We want freedom now!"

"We come here to petition our lawmakers to be as brave as our sit-ins, and our marchers, as daring as James Meredith, to be as unafraid as the nine children of Little Rock, and to be as forthright as the governor of North Carolina, and to be as dedicated as the archbishop of St. Louis.

"All over the land, especially in parts of the Deep South, we are beaten, jailed, pushed, and killed by law enforcement officers. The United States government can regulate the contents of a pill, but apparently has no power to prevent these abuses of citizens within its own borders."

He endorsed President Kennedy's civil rights legislation but insisted on strengthening it. "The president's proposals," he said, "represent so moderate an approach that if any part is weakened or eliminated, the remainder will be little more than *sugar water.* Indeed, the package needs strengthening. The president should join us in fighting for something more than *pap.*"

After a day of somber and contentious rhetoric, Wilkins chose to be light.

He turned toward Congress: "We commend Republicans, north and south, who have been working for this bill. We even salute those Democrats from the South who want to vote for it and don't dare. We say to these people, 'Give us a little time, and we'll emancipate *you*—get to the place where they can come to a civil rights rally *too!*"

Then he spoke about W. E. B. Du Bois: "Regardless of the fact that in his later years Dr. Du Bois chose another path, it is incontrovertible that at the dawn of the twentieth century his was the voice that was calling to you to gather here today in this cause. If you want to read something that applies to 1963 go back and get a volume of *The Souls of Black Folk* by Du Bois, published in 1903."

Half a world away, Shirley Graham Du Bois, his widow, wept in appreciation.

"Now, my friends, you got religion today. Don't backslide tomorrow.

Remember Luke's account of the warning that was given to us all. 'No man,' he wrote, 'having put his hand to the plow, and looking back, is fit for the kingdom of God.'"

MAHALIA JACKSON TOTTERED TOWARD the podium, a dark blue dress wrapped around her ample body, with an oversized peach-colored corsage, and a blue hat with a flower that seemed poised to fly off. She ambled up, smiling the whole time.

The NAACP's John Morsell winced, anticipating her collapse.

"Huge as she is, unsteady in her high heels standing on the steps," he said later, "I was sure she would stumble and wind [up] down at the bottom."

Cameras snapped. All three national networks trained cameras on her. Mahalia was the beginning of the prime-time show. She would set the stage for Martin Luther King.

For Mahalia Jackson, the day was one long celebration. Onstage, she used an eight-millimeter camera to film the day's events. She saw a celebrity and turned the camera. "Wait a minute," she told a visitor on the platform. "I have to get Sammy Davis."

She swayed with the music, clapping. She paused for interviews with TV and radio stations.

"The congressmen are smiling at all the people," Mahalia Jackson told one interviewer. "It's the realization of everything we've been striving for such a long time. Whatever masses of people like this want to be done has got to be done by the people they put in office. . . . People were afraid before, but there's nothing to fear now. I have high hopes that everything is going to come out all right."

When Mahalia got onstage, the pianist scattered notes for a prelude. She leaned to the left, looked down, then forward. Someone moved the microphone down.

And now she sang.

The words were simple: "I been 'buked, and I been scorned." But she stretched those words out, making them deeper and more resonant as they reached out across time. Each syllable was a symphony, full of sounds and emotions.

> *Iyeeeeeeee*
> *been a-buked, Lord . . .*
> *I*

Been scorned.
Ohhh,
Been 'buked, Lord
And I been scoooooorned.
You knowwwww, ohhhh, been buked, Lord
And I-yeeee beeeen scoorrrrrrned.

Mahalia's long stretching of a syllable into many notes—in the traditional black melismatic style—created a world of sound and color. Every line was full of diverse sounds, musical ornamentation. With this approach, Mahalia created the effect of a whole congregation singing in one voice. Using the "Dr. Watts" style—common in black churches when Mahalia was growing up—a song leader sings or chants a line of a hymn, and the congregation elaborates the line over an extended riff. Rather than unified voices, the effect is a soulful jangle of sounds. The coming together of different voices accentuates the solemn or ecstatic emotions of the moment. But Mahalia brought these many sounds and emotions into one voice.

The second line roused the crowd with its hushed promise of passion. The Mall was all quiet. "Yes, I—" All still quiet. She riffed, got more focused, gathered her passion: "You know I'm going to *tell* my Lord." She smiled a sweet smile, with an open mouth.

As she moved deep into song, Mahalia merged that ample body and that even more ample soul. She corralled all her power, then she unleashed that power into the song.

"I want my hands . . . my feet . . . my whole body to say all that is in me," she once explained. "I say, 'Don't let the devil steal the beat from the Lord!' The Lord doesn't like us to act dead. If you feel it, tap your feet a little—dance to the glory of the Lord."

Music saturated Mahalia's life. She grew up in New Orleans, in a neighborhood by the levee. The Front of the Town was a stew of blacks, Creoles, Italians, and French. Growing up, she heard exultant and mournful and bacchanalian sounds wherever she went—blues from Jelly Roll Morton and King Oliver in cafés and nightclubs, great female vocalists like Bessie Smith and Ma Rainey and Mamie Smith, brass bands playing dirges on the way to cemeteries and celebrations on the way back, Caruso blaring from the windows of white folks' homes, clapping and screaming in the Baptist churches, the drums, cymbals, and triangles of the Sanctified Church.

Her mother died when she was five. Her aunt raised her, abusing her when she didn't keep house well enough. Music was her refuge. She listened to Bessie Smith on the record player and sang in two church choirs.

To escape her aunt's abuse, she went to Chicago in 1926. Just sixteen years old, she took in laundry and worked as a hotel maid. But when she sang at the Greater Salem Baptist Church, she got the attention of Thomas Dorsey, the modern father of gospel music. Mahalia and Dorsey performed at churches all over the city and became a sensation. By 1948 her recording of "Move On Up a Little Higher" would become a best seller, selling 8 million copies.

Mahalia arrived in Chicago at the beginning of the gospel movement. Charles Tindley had already started to revolutionize music. Gospel formalized the old Negro spirituals—it was composed music, precise in its earthly, heavenly sorrow and ecstasy. The slow roll of the music invited call and response, just as the ministers' slow drive into preaching pulled in the congregation like a slow movement of the tide.

The old slave songs focused on the world to come, a salve for the repression and sorrow of life on earth. Gospel put the focus on *this life,* right now, on earth.

You may talk about me sure as you please
Talk about me sure as you please
Children, talk about me sure as you please
Your talk will never drive me down to my knees.

The people on the National Mall craned their necks, shifted their bodies, to see her. Eyes were wide open, to hear her better. People covered their faces with their fingers. People wept, bobbed in joy, leaned in toward their mates. They shaded themselves from the sun with newspapers, programs, cupped hands. They threw their heads back in laughter.

This was catharsis. Mahalia expressed the deepest suffering of the black race, reaching back to the slave ships and centuries of bondage and broken hopes and dreams—but also painting the brightest picture of the Exodus and a better world.

But it was not just catharsis. It was *collective catharsis.* Everyone heard it together, looked around, felt what others felt. Crowded together, everyone touched somebody, who touched someone else. . . . The electricity traveled down from Mahalia to hundreds of thousands of souls, connected to each other.

I've been 'buked and I've been scorned,
I've been 'buked and I've been scorned,
Children, I've been 'buked and I've been scorned,
Tryin' to make this journey all alone

Music was a calling of the Lord. She got offers to play in juke joints and with jazz and blues musicians, but she refused any offer that did not glorify God.

Other great artists sang gospel, then moved on to other music—the blues or classical pieces—but when they wanted to sing gospel again they had lost that old feeling. Mahalia Jackson never wanted to sing anything but gospel.

Jesus died to set me free
Jesus died to set me free
Children, Jesus died to set me free
Nailed to that cross on Calvary

In a matter of seconds, people cried and smiled, leaned forward to listen, and threw their heads back in laughter.

Gospel—and Mahalia—had everything that all music and all performance could offer. The precision of classic composition. The involvement of the audience. Improvisation, making each performance new. Flattened thirds and sevenths, surprising the audience and pulling them into music almost beyond their control. Shouting and whispering. Influences not only of the old spirituals, but also small combos and big bands, vocal and orchestral music, jazz and the blues. Percussive but also rolling like molasses. Slow- and then fast-moving crescendos, with an intensity that grew as sweet entreaties gave way to shrill, raspy, hard, full-throated hollers.

As she sang, Mahalia listed to the right, as if the power of her words would tip her over. But she got stronger as she went.

I've been 'buked and I've been scorned
I've been 'buked and I've been scorned
Children, I've been 'buked and I've been scorned
Tryin' to make this journey all alone

For the first time all afternoon, Bayard Rustin stood still. All day, he bounded from one end of the stage to the other, chain-smoking, reaching over people, leaning in to confer with Randolph, passing notes, curling his body around speakers and singers . . . *running things.*

Now Rustin stood to Mahalia's side. He held his notebook like a hymnal. He closed his eyes, then opened them again, barely, and looked over at Mahalia. He was perfectly still. The former singer smiled. He sang along, softly.

"I've been 'buked and I've been scorned . . . Your talk will never drive me to my knees . . . Tryin' to make this journey all alone."

"I WISH I COULD SING!"

Rabbi Joachim Prinz moved onto the stage where Mahalia Jackson had just performed one encore, a buoyant number called "How I Got Over," and declined roaring chants for another.

Whenever Joachim Prinz spoke—in his synagogue, the Temple B'nai Abraham in Newark, or on one of his tours of the United States or Europe; in English or German or French or Hebrew—he spoke without a script. Communication happens best when the speaker and audience establish a rapport, not when the speaker *delivers remarks.*

In synagogue, he always gave sermons after music. The music created a buffer between the sermon and the rest of the service. As the music played, he looked over his notes, thought about the congregation, what was happening in the community.

And then the words came tumbling out, forceful, intellectual but usually simple too, with the trill of the German refugee's accent. He often spoke about contemporary events—racism, poverty, the duty to stand up to tyranny. He dug into his reservoir of knowledge about his faith, but also about art and music and food.

Prinz had traveled around Europe all summer, as he did every summer. He gave lectures, visited museums and concert halls and vineyards, and visited his homeland of Germany. He had flown home to New York just a couple days before, and then down to Washington the day before the march.

Now Prinz paused before the crowd at the National Mall and said: "I wish I could sing!"

Joachim Prinz was a short man, about five feet, six inches, and he carried a few extra pounds. He had a chiseled face, with gray hair spread across his forehead. When Prinz arrived in Washington, the American Jewish Congress gave him a speech. Angry, he told the AJC staff that he would write his own speech. He hid in his hotel room at the Statler, distilling his life as a Jew—from outspoken rabbi to exile to full-fledged American—into a few minutes of rabbinic wisdom.

On this one day, Prinz used a script. He knew he would never ascend a bigger stage. Limited to seven minutes, he needed to make his point quickly—with heart, but without any wasted words. He had to compose a kind of prose poem.

"I speak to you as an American Jew."

Joachim Prinz lived his first thirty-five years in Germany, the last four under Hitler's Nazi rule. Before other German Jews took Nazism seriously,

Prinz organized Jews to create safe zones and escape near-certain death. His family died in the Holocaust. For some reason, no one knows, the Gestapo let him leave Germany in safety. The best guess is that one of the Gestapo agents liked him, an accident of history. And so in 1937, he and his pregnant wife took a French luxury vessel to the United States.

From the time he arrived in the country, Prinz thought of himself as an American. He was not a German refugee or immigrant or alien, but an American—as if his family had lived there for generations. The figures who defined his history were George Washington, Abraham Lincoln, Theodore Roosevelt, W. E. B. Du Bois, Franklin Roosevelt, Martin Luther King. And American racism and discrimination were his problems, too.

But he still bore his history in Germany. And he drew from that experience to make sense of the race crisis in America.

"When I was the rabbi of the Jewish community in Berlin under the Hitler regime, I learned many things. The most important thing that I learned under those tragic circumstances was that bigotry and hatred are not the most urgent problem. The most urgent, the most disgraceful, the most shameful, and the most tragic problem is silence."

The crowd came alive. They applauded. "There you go!" someone called out. Rabbi Prinz was now preaching in a massive outdoor Negro church.

"A great people which had created a great civilization had become a nation of silent onlookers."

Yeahhhh!

"They remained silent in the face of hate, in the face of brutality, and in the face of mass murder."

Back in his own temple, in Newark, New Jersey, a new crisis was developing before the old one was resolved. Before blacks across America could win the basic rights of citizenship—voting, access to public accommodations, protections against job discrimination—his beloved Jewish community was breaking apart in his own city.

White flight was emptying Newark of its middle class. The black middle class was starting to move out as well. Left behind was the toughest of all communities—poor blacks, discriminated against for centuries, lacking basic skills, desperately in need of the middle class that just left.

At the same time, blacks started to turn against Jews, their longtime allies in the civil rights struggles—both of their peoples had been captives of ghettos, both victims of lynchings, both strangers in their own lands, both subject to vile caricatures and quack science.

Before coming to the March on Washington, Prinz encountered Martin

Luther King in an airport. They talked about the Jewish slumlords in Harlem, how angry blacks were blaming Jews for the problems of the ghetto. Legitimate grievances against specific businessmen more and more frequently took on anti-Semitic tones. King expressed horror at the development. Prinz asked him to do something about it, to confront his people about their own prejudices.

Prinz told King: *We—you—cannot be silent.*

Whatever the problem, Prinz told his newly aroused audience, the problem was disengagement. The answer was to be involved.

"America must not become a nation of onlookers. America must not remain silent. Not merely black America, but all of America. It must speak up and act, from the president down to the humblest of us, and not for the sake of the Negro, not for the sake of the black community, but for the sake of the image, the idea and the aspiration of America itself."

AS HE MOVED TO THE PLATFORM, Martin Luther King saw Harry Belafonte and shot him a smile.

"I wonder if the president will really understand what this day is all about, if he will really see its significance," King said.

"If he doesn't understand this one," Stanley Levison said, "he'll understand the next one."

"I guess that's what it's about, isn't it?"

By the time King looked out, the crowd had thinned. Hours before, people packed the Mall tight as rush-hour commuters. Just leaning over to pick something off the ground jostled four or five others. And even though the heat was not too oppressive—eighty-seven degrees at noon—the humidity hung heavy. So people started to break away from the throng's edges. The groups from Connecticut started leaving at two thirty in the afternoon, not long after the speakers started the afternoon program.

As he listened to other speakers, King scribbled notes on his prepared text. Always, until the last minute, King adjusted what he wanted to say. Those notes read:

We must live with the same people from whom we are demanding our right.
Today the whirlwinds of revolt are shaking our nation.
Then America will be the home of uncompromising loyalty to social justice.

Never again must our nation cast the mantle of its sanctity over the system of segregation.

Through our actions we will subpoena the conscience of men to appear before the judgment seat of morality.

Everyone waited. At the long press tables, which cut into the slopes just below the Lincoln Memorial, the reporters looked up. The crowd made a ballpark buzz, then quieted. And then A. Philip Randolph introduced King.

"At this time I have the honor to present to you . . . the *moral leader* of our nation—"

With every moment of pause, emphasizing the British trill of Randolph's words, the cheering rose.

"—a great, dedicated man—"

Clapping.

"—a philosopher of a nonviolent system of behavior in seeking to bring about social change—"

Cheers swelled.

"I have the pleasure to present to you Dr. Martin Luther King . . . *Jun-ior!*"

The crowd sent a thunderclap down the Mall. A chant rose from the apron of humanity in front of the Lincoln Memorial.

Hip, hip . . . hooray!
Hip, hip . . . hooray!
Hip, hip . . . hooray!

The chant got louder and louder. Sounds of people laughing filled the spaces between chants. By the sixth round, the chant reached its peak. It was like a cheer at a baseball game or a retirement picnic. Joyous. Finally, by the tenth round, the chant dissolved to a few stray voices.

"We were levitating," one marcher said. "We weren't on the ground anymore."

King peered across the bobbing crowd. Sitting behind her husband, Coretta saw "from the line of his back" that the ovation stirred him. King looked buoyant. He bounced softly on the balls of his feet.

"The next president of the United States!" someone shouted.

Martin's thin smile revealed, faintly, the dimples on his soft, round face. He had already waved, his right arm extended and sweeping, when he first approached the wooden podium. He did not stoke the chant. He mouthed "thank you" a couple times and waited for quiet.

———

ALWAYS, HE BEGINS SLOWLY, like thunder rolling from a distance before a great storm.

Martin Luther King speaks deliberately, like a 45 rpm record being played at 33⅓ rpm speed. His long, thick, baritone words stretch out to establish a new mood. In a low drawl, he emphasizes syllables to create his own cadence, to bring his audience into the flow of emotions.

"I am *happy* to *join* with you to*day*," he says, sounding mournful, "in what will go *down* in *his*tory as the *great*est *demon*stration for *free*dom in the *his*tory of our *nation*."

Martin Luther King invokes Abraham Lincoln and tells the long, hard story of the subjection of American blacks.

"Five score years ago, a great American, in whose symbolic shadow we stand today, signed the Emancipation Proclamation. This momentous decree came as a great beacon light of hope to millions of Negro slaves who had been seared in the flames of withering injustice. It came as a joyous daybreak to end the long night of their captivity."

King's Southern accent, softened by time spent in his family's bourgeois circles and tempered by years in the North, put a special emphasis on his words: "in the *his-tor-eh* of our *ow-a* nation" . . . "a *gret* American" . . . "symbolic *shadda*" . . . "*gret beckon* light."

Long night of captivity. King's brooding voice tells two parallel stories of exile and return. For hundreds of years, Jews were held in captivity, as slaves, in Egypt—like blacks in America. They struggled to maintain their own identity—like blacks in America. They endured because of their faith in God—like blacks in America. And then one day, they freed themselves from bondage—like blacks will, one day, as well.

His voice is steady, but King wants to find his pacing. If he moves slowly, he will not falter, and he will find a way to bring the crowd with him.

Right away, King uses anaphora, the repetition of key words and phrases at the beginning of successive statements. Repetition brings the listener back to a familiar place, then connects to a new thought or image. Repetition keeps the audience involved. Repetition makes it easy to remember the words and to get into a rhythm, as they become familiar. Repetition invites the call and response in black churches across the South. *Yeah! Uh-huh! Amen! That's right!*

After recalling the story of Lincoln freeing the slaves, with the simple stroke of a pen in the middle of a bloody war, King laments the inferior position of blacks a century later. Each mournful repetition deepens the pain, raises the dramatic tension. Each repetition condemns the oppressor. The oration becomes poetry:

> But one hundred years later, the Negro still is not free.
> One hundred years later, the life of the Negro is still sadly crippled by the manacles of segregation and the chains of discrimination.
> One hundred years later, the Negro lives on a lonely island of poverty in the midst of a vast ocean of material prosperity.
> One hundred years later, the Negro is still languished in the corners of American society and finds himself in exile in his own country.

King looks down at his text, shakes his head as he speaks. He rocks back and forth on the balls of his feet as finds his rhythm.

Every invocation of "one hundred years" emphasizes the horrors of the black's position in American life. *Not free. Crippled. Manacles. Chains. Lonely island of poverty. Languished in the corners. Exile in his own country.*

And then King introduces Clarence Jones's metaphor of the bad check, so simple and so basic. A bad check represents bad faith, failed promises, broken contracts.

> In a sense we have come to our nation's capital to cash a check. When the architects of our republic wrote the magnificent words of the Constitution and the Declaration of Independence, they were signing a promissory note to which every American was to fall heir. This note was a promise that all men—yes, black men as well as white men— would be guaranteed the unalienable rights of life, liberty, and the pursuit of happiness.
> It is obvious today that America has defaulted on this promissory note insofar as her citizens of color are concerned. Instead of honoring this sacred obligation, America has given the Negro people a bad check, a check which has come back marked "insufficient funds."

The first burst of applauses rises up from the crowd.

"But we *refuse* to believe that the bank of justice is bankrupt. We *refuse* to believe that there are insufficient funds in the great vaults of opportunity of this nation."

Laughter from the crowd. Shouts: "Uh huh!" "Yeah!" "Sure enough!"

"So we have come to cash this check—a check that will give us upon demand the riches of freedom and the security of justice."

A second, greater burst of applause.

Now King honors his country, calling attention to the civic power of Lincoln's monument. He rejects calls to "go slow" and "cool off."

"We have also come to this hallowed spot to remind America of *the fierce urgency of now*. This is no time to engage in the luxury of cooling off or to take the tranquilizing drug of gradualism."

The crowd ripples with recognition, then knowing laughter. A thin black man sitting close to the stage hears the tranquilizer reference, looks down for a moment, thoughtfully, then looks up and explodes in laughter. King's line releases some toxin from the body.

For this one moment, the stubbornness of racism lifts and the people revel in a moment of integrated community.

Now is the time to make real the promises of democracy.

Now is the time to rise from the dark and desolate valley of segregation to the sunlit path of racial justice.

Now is the time to lift our nation from the quicksands of racial injustice to the solid rock of brotherhood.

Now is the time to make justice a reality for all of God's children.

Each invocation pulls the audience into the future. And people in the crowd respond. *You got it! Yes it is! Yeah! Amen! Now is the time! Now! That's right!*

Across the Mall, people have quieted down. King's voice echoes, his baritone voice triumphing over the tinny sounds of the loudspeakers. Whispers can be heard in spots. A soft breeze, occasionally rippling over the crowd, is louder than the sounds of the masses below.

King now warns the Washington establishment—and the vast middle class, what one politician would call the "forgotten middle class" and the "silent majority"—that gradual improvements will not satisfy blacks anymore. Conflict could turn into a bloodbath unless the American people redeem the promise of freedom.

It would be fatal for the nation to overlook
the urgency of the moment.

This sweltering summer of the Negro's legitimate discontent will not pass
until there is an invigorating autumn of freedom and equality.

Nineteen sixty-three is not an end,
    but a beginning.
Those who hope that the Negro needed to blow off steam and will now
    be content
    will have a rude awakening if the nation returns to business as usual.
There will be neither rest nor tranquility in America
    until the Negro is granted his citizenship rights.
The whirlwinds of revolt will continue to shake the foundations of our
    nation
    until the bright day of justice emerges.

Subtly, King conjures images of apocalypse. The "whirlwinds of revolt" echo the countless moments where the Bible talks about staggering catastrophe, when evil brings forth flood, famine, drought, a plague of locusts, and the chaos of the Tower of Babel. As Jeremiah (4:20) teaches: "Disaster on disaster is proclaimed / For the whole land is devastated."

King warns his people to maintain their own dignity, to avoid the temptation to embrace bitterness or violence. He speaks to the followers of Malcolm X, who offers a simpler, purer, solution—*fighting back, by any means necessary.*

"But there is something that I must say to my people who stand on the warm threshold which leads into the palace of justice. In the process of gaining our rightful place, we must not be guilty of wrongful deeds.

"Let us not seek to satisfy our thirst for freedom by drinking from the cup of bitterness and hatred."

O Lord! Amen! Yes! Sure enough!

"We must forever conduct our struggle on the high plane of dignity and discipline. We must not allow our creative protest to degenerate into physical violence. Again and again, we must rise to the majestic heights of meeting physical force with soul force.

"The marvelous new militancy which has engulfed the Negro community must not lead us to a distrust of all white people, for many of our white brothers, as evidenced by their presence here today, have come to realize"—his voice rises—"that their destiny is tied up with our destiny."

Marvelous militancy. All summer, critics of the civil rights movement have wondered why blacks cannot be more patient. The president, congressmen, newspaper publishers, TV commentators, professors, mayors, unions, corporate CEOs, churches, social organizations—everyone seemed to be saying to go slow. But the time for patience is over. Militancy—*marvelous militancy,* borne of great patience and suffering, expressed with love, and applied with the tools of nonviolence—is now the movement's watchword.

Cheers rise up, louder and more sustained than before. People smile.

"They have come to realize that their freedom is inextricably bound to our freedom. We cannot walk alone.

"As we walk, we must make the pledge that we shall always march ahead. We cannot turn back. There are those who are asking the devotees of civil rights, 'When will you be satisfied?'"

Not everyone could hear King's words. The sound system, the best available, still crackled and blanked out. Far from the Lincoln Memorial, people followed the words on transistor radios—and by watching the movement of bodies ahead. "Down near the front there were people jumping up, waving hands and flags and signs," Elsa Rael said. "We were a little out of it, so we had to make our own joy—so we were singing. We got small bursts of words from King and shut up."

> We can never be satisfied as long as the Negro is the victim of the un-speakable horrors of police brutality.
> We can never be satisfied, as long as our bodies, heavy with the fatigue of travel, cannot gain lodging in the motels of the highways and the hotels of the cities.
> We cannot be satisfied as long as the Negro's basic mobility is from a smaller ghetto to a larger one.
> We can never be satisfied as long as our children are stripped of their self-hood and robbed of their dignity by signs stating "For Whites Only."
> We cannot be satisfied as long as a Negro in Mississippi cannot vote and a Negro in New York believes he has nothing for which to vote.
> No, no, we are not satisfied, and we will not be satisfied until justice rolls down like waters and righteousness like a mighty stream.

With each line, King increases the stakes for his movement. He begins with police brutality, the search for night lodging and food, and life in the ghetto. He moves on to children's dignity and the right to vote. He ends with the prophet Amos's great image of the Kingdom of Heaven on earth.

Each round gets cheers. First scattered clapping and cheers and calls. *Yes!* Then more. *That's right!* Finally, huge applause. *My Lord!*

Every good preacher—every good leader—connects with the real circumstances of his audience's lives. *I know your pain. I have shared in your pain. I have been beaten and jailed and reviled. I have not forgotten how you have suffered. I know, so you can trust me.* King has spent a decade learning about the problems of the people assembled before him. He has worked, intimately, with people at the highest and lowest levels of society.

I am not unmindful that some of you have come here out of great trials
    and tribulations.
Some of you have come fresh from narrow jail cells.
Some of you have come from areas where your quest for freedom
    left you battered by the storms of persecution and
    staggered by the winds of police brutality.
You have been the veterans of creative suffering.
Continue to work with the faith
    that unearned suffering is redemptive.

That brief phrase—*unearned suffering is redemptive*—strikes Harold Bragg "like an electric shock."

Harold and his wife, Lynn, traveled all night from Kent, Ohio, in their VW Beetle. Harold sits on a stool, holding an umbrella over Lynn's head to block the sun. For the first part of King's speech, they listen to King "like it was a lesson from a great master."

Now the idea of suffering for redemption surges through Harold's body. He remembers his father telling him about his grandfather—one of the few black landowners in Alabama—sitting on a horse, getting shot by a white farmer who was jealous that a colored man could command such an expanse. His father, five years old when this happened back in 1917, saw his father fall dead off the horse.

The lesson his father and mother passed on when he told their children that story was: "You return hatred with love."

King's whole speech has told of the hard, violent, brutal, unfair, unjust life of blacks in America. The wrong people have suffered. So many people have been teargassed, beaten, kicked, burned, bombed, shot.

But that suffering—like Christ's suffering on the cross—can bring a better day. That suffering can change people's hearts. That suffering can clear poison from the system.

Then change can come.

Unearned suffering is redemptive. Believe it, and you will fight on—with Martin. Disbelieve it, and you will be gripped by despair—or the combative, uncompromising, separatist jingoism of Malcolm.

For now, the crowd stands with King. Even the separatists stand with King, now.

For that redemption to happen—to change the world—people need to return to their homes to fight and suffer, still more, for the cause of justice. So:

> Go back to Mississippi,
> go back to Alabama,
> go back to South Carolina,
> go back to Georgia,
> go back to Louisiana,
> go back to the slums and ghettos of our northern cities,
> knowing that somehow this situation can and will be changed. Let us not
>   wallow in the valley of despair,
> I say to you today, my friends.

Just feet from King, Mahalia Jackson calls out. Mahalia is an old family friend of the Kings. She has been a guest in the Kings' house. She was with King in Detroit about a month ago when King talked about a dream.

"Tell them about the dream, Martin!" she shouts. "*Please . . .* tell them about the dream!"

King does not hear her, but he doesn't need to hear her. He already knows he's going to talk about the dream. He shouted out his dream last night, in his hotel room, after everyone else went to bed.

Clarence Jones, sitting about fifteen feet away, sees King grab the podium, lean back, and turn over his prepared text. "These people don't know it," Jones says, "but they are about to go to *church.*"

> So even though we face the difficulties of today and tomorrow,
> I still have a dream.
> It is a dream deeply rooted in the American Dream.

"Aw, s——," Wyatt Tee Walker says when he hears the phrase from out on the Mall. "He's using the dream." Somewhere around here, someone shouts from behind King: "F—— that dream, Martin! *Now,* goddamn it! *Now!*" But King continues.

> I have a dream that one day this nation will rise up and live out the true
>   meaning of its creed: "We hold these truths to be self-evident: that all
>   men are created equal."
> I have a dream that one day on the red hills of Georgia the sons of former
>   slaves and the sons of former slave owners will be able to sit down
>   together at the table of brotherhood.

> I have a dream that one day even the state of Mississippi, a state sweltering with the heat of injustice, sweltering with the heat of oppression, will be transformed into an oasis of freedom and justice.

Richard Pritchard, a skinny white preacher from Wisconsin who returned to the United States from Africa just last night, sits by the reflecting pool. When his wife told him about the march, he jumped into a car at his family's home in New Jersey. All day he's been jet-lagged and weary from his early morning drive.

But now, lightning shoots through his body as he hears about the dream. He remembers—*feels*—his own dream, which called him to the ministry decades before.

Pritchard became a minister because he believed God saved him as a small child, when he spent three years in the hospital with tuberculosis. And then, as a young priest, he saw racism in God's own flock. White priests wouldn't take assignments in black churches—and so he decided to become the pastor of a black parish in Kansas City. Later, at a different church, members of his own parish made racist statements. Didn't they understand that God loved blacks as much as whites?

"My dream was to make Christ more realistic," he says. "I used to talk about it—*my dream*. When I was a kid I used to hear how the English talked about the Welsh as savages in the hills, and that's what they were saying about blacks. I could feel how blacks would feel. In Christ there is no Jew or Greek, slave or free, male or female. We are all free in Christ."

So skinny you can see his bones, the Reverend Pritchard dangles his feet in the water. He is being baptized anew. King's dream is his dream. The image almost removes him from the throng, and at the same time connects him even more with the throng.

"It's funny, it hit me with such force."

> I have a dream that my four little children will one day live in a nation where they will not be judged by the color of their skin but by the content of their character.
> I have a dream today.
> I have a dream that one day, down in Alabama, with its vicious racists, with its governor having his lips dripping with the words of interposition and nullification; one day right there in Alabama, little black boys and black girls will be able to join hands with little white boys and white girls as sisters and brothers.
> I have a dream today.

> I have a dream that one day every valley shall be exalted, every hill and mountain shall be made low, the rough places will be made plain, and the crooked places will be made straight, and the glory of the Lord shall be revealed, and all flesh shall see it together.

Talk about the dream transforms time and space. What might come to pass, later, seems at hand, *now*. With faith, ideals can be more real than the pain or poverty of the here and now.

Sitting on a patch of grass far from the Lincoln Memorial, sipping cold drinks from thermoses, Ruth bat Mordecai and some kids from a New York–based American Jewish Congress youth group listen to Martin Luther King's dream.

As King gives voice to his dream, Ruth watches some black boys nearby. The boys laugh as King's voice climbs the ladder, higher and higher. They laugh so freely that their bodies shake. Ruth knows the crowd includes cynics, and she resents having her experience of King's dream ruined by *these ones*. How can you openly mock *Dr. King*—at an event like *this*? And nobody seems to care!

"Suddenly," she recalls, "we understand. The black boys are laughing not in mockery but in joy—at the utter preposterousness of what Dr. King promises, and at its unutterable beauty."

Across the Mall, people call out the lines to each other.

"I have a dream," one says.

"That *one* day, little black boys and black girls . . ." says another. "I have a *dream!*" someone else says.

"*Dowwwn* in Ala*bama* . . ." comes the response.

Strangers shout out: "I have a *dream!*"

Tears fill Harold Bragg's eyes. "It's like being before the pearly gates, as though we had reached the Promised Land," he says, "even though King was laying out what was *to come.*"

With this dream, King brings his audience into a separate world, a distant, far-off place, but still so familiar. What is unreal is also very real.

Then King moves to sustain his people for the hard journey ahead. He reminds the crowd that they need faith—stronger than any troubles of the moment—to realize the dream.

> This is our hope.
> This is the faith that I go back to the South with.
> With this faith we will be able to hew out of the mountain of despair a stone of hope.

With this faith we will be able to transform the jangling discords of our
    nation into a beautiful symphony of brotherhood.

With this faith we will be able to work together, to pray together, to strug-
    gle together, to go to jail together, to stand up for freedom together,
    knowing that we will be free one day.

King connects simple statements, repeated again and again—"One hundred years later," "Now is the time," "We cannot be satisfied," "Go back," "I
have a dream," "With this faith"—to America's true national anthem.

"This will be the day," he says, "when all of God's children will be able
to sing with a new meaning, 'My country, *'tis* of thee, sweet land of *liberty*,
of *thee* I sing. Land where my *fathers* died, land of the *pilgrim's* pride, from
every mountainside, *let freedom ring*.' And if America is to be a great nation
this *must* become true."

If . . .

Then, full of the passion of the words of that simple anthem, King imag-
ines freedom ringing—a dreamlike image—and exhorts the crowd to make
this vision happen. He sings out lines full of sounds and sights—postcards
from the American Dream.

So let freedom ring from the prodigious hilltops of New Hampshire.
Let freedom ring from the mighty mountains of New York.
Let freedom ring from the heightening Alleghenies of Pennsylvania!
Let freedom ring from the snowcapped Rockies of Colorado!
Let freedom ring from the curvaceous slopes of California!

All of these are Northern places, and their images are ones of pure beauty.
But that's not enough. King now invokes the sites of repression across the
South.

But not only that.
Let freedom ring from Stone Mountain of Georgia!
Let freedom ring from Lookout Mountain of Tennessee!
Let freedom ring from every hill and molehill of Mississippi!
From every mountainside,
let freedom ring!

Those lines come from one of King's old friends, a preacher from Chicago
named Archibald Carey. In a speech at the 1952 Republican Convention,
Carey sang "My Country, 'Tis of Thee" and cried "Let freedom ring!" and
issued some of those same postcards.

Finally, dizzy from the view of a nation teeming with freedom, King offers the moment of deliverance.

He sways now. He lifts his whole body with the speech. The people in the crowd follow their King. They sway, they smile, and they laugh with anticipation of every new image.

And when this happens,
when we allow freedom to ring,
when we let it *ring* from every village and every hamlet,
from *every* state and *every* city,
we will be able to speed up that day when all of God's children,
black men and *white* men,
Jews and *Gentiles,*
*Prot*estants and *Catholics—*

Martin Luther King turns to his right and raises his right arm high, his elbow bent slightly, blessing the congregation at this great mass.

"—will be able to join hands and sing in the *words* of the old Negro spiritual, "Free at *last!* Free at *last!* Thank God Al*might*y, we are *free at last!*"

PART 5

Onward

EXPLOSION.

Instantly, the crowd yelled and cheered. *Yeahhh! Heyyyy!* Heads tilted back, bodies went liquid, hands raised high. The sound system could not capture the clamor. The crowd's noise wrapped around the long National Mall. The cheers rose up and hung in the air. People hugged strangers, like on V-J Day at Times Square. Smiles covered their faces. Eyes glistened. Weary old men and angry young men cried and smiled. Women and children embraced. Others just moved in circles, looking for some way to express themselves.

Clarence Jones, Martin Luther King's consigliere, embraced him. "You was *smoking*," Jones told him. "The words was so hot they was just *burning* off the page!"

Marcus Wood, King's classmate at Crozer Theological Seminary, watched the speech from his VIP seat about thirty feet away from King. As he watched his old friend, he wondered about the stress and strain of delivering such a big speech.

When King finished—his arms lifted high, blessing the crowd—police surrounded him to usher him back toward the massive statue of Abraham Lincoln. The march leaders would meet there, then depart for the White House.

Wood saw a look of fear on King's face.

"He was frightened," Wood said. "He didn't know what could happen in a crowd like that. I could tell from the expression and body language, he was scared. He had aroused the congregation. With the dream, he knew he was bringing down some people who disagreed. They didn't mind him having a thought, but they *did* mind him having a dream. If he just said, 'The day will come,' that would have been accepted. But he said 'I have a dream,' and that links him to a divine realm."

Since their days together at Crozer Theological Seminary, King had talked about martyrdom. He now spoke so much about dying for the cause that his friends ceased to be alarmed. And the reality was that King came under attack frequently. Racists bombed his home, a deranged woman stabbed him at a book-signing event, a Kluxer punched him on a stage. He got death threats almost daily.

"He knew somewhere down the line, something was going to happen," Wood said. "His attitude is, I'm going to turn it loose and hope the audience responds." And so he wrote all his major speeches to sound like prophetic last words.

Toward the end of the day, a group of Young Jacobins gathered in the March on Washington staff tent. They leaned back in the foldout chairs and mocked the whole event. They complained about President Kennedy's takeover of the march, the censoring of John Lewis, the sickly sweet sentiments of the crowd, the U.S. Information Agency shooting scenes for propaganda films. All day the Jacobins openly mocked Martin Luther King—"De Lawd," they called him, mocking his messianic airs.

But as King finished his oration, they celebrated.

"We were on our feet, laughing, shouting, slapping palms, hugging, and not an eye was dry," says Michael Thelwell. "What happened in that tent was the most extraordinary, sudden, and total transformation of mood I have ever experienced."

At the White House, President Kennedy turned to an aide. "He's damned good," he said. "Damned good."

BAYARD RUSTIN GOT A MOMENT TO BASK when Phil Randolph asked him to get pledges to fight for civil rights from the hundred thousand or so marchers still paying attention to the program.

Randolph was scheduled to read the demands of the march, but he was tired. Tears streamed down his cheeks as he asked Rustin to take the stage.

A stranger to all but the real activists, "Brother Outsider" stood at the podium and punched the air. He read the demands and asked for assent from the assembled.

"It is time for you to act," Rustin shouted. "I will read each demand . . . and you will respond to it:

"That we have effective civil rights legislation, no compromise, no filibuster, and that it include access to decent housing, integrated education, FEPC, and the right to vote. What do you say?

"The withholding of federal funds from all programs in which discrimination exists. What do you *saaaaaaay?*"

The crowd roared.

"We demand that segregation be ended in every school district in the year 1963."

The audacity of that one—in a year in which only about 150 districts took new steps to desegregate, in a nation of 36,000 districts—aroused the crowd as never before.

Aroused himself, Rustin leaned into the microphone with gusto.

"*Weeeeeeee demannnnd . . .* the enforcement of the Fourteenth Amendment, the reducing of congressional representation of states where citizens are disenfranchised."

Another never-gonna-happen demand excited the crowd anew.

"An executive order banning discrimination in all housing supported by federal funds."

Roar.

"*Weeee demannnnd . . .* that every person, black or white, be given training and work with dignity to defeat unemployment and automation."

Roar.

"We demand that there be an increase in the minimum wage so that men may live in dignity."

Roar.

"All rights given to any citizen be given to black men and every minority group—including a strong FEPC."

Roar. And with that, Bayard Rustin's job—which began when he hitchhiked up and down the eastern seaboard, recruiting churches and unions to rally at the 1941 March on Washington—ended.

Minutes later, Rustin spied Phil Randolph standing alone, tears welling. "Mr. Randolph," he said, "it looks like your dream has come true." Randolph called it "the most beautiful and glorious day" of his life.

BENJAMIN MAYS, WHO HAD INSPIRED Martin Luther King and his classmates at Morehouse College to take up the civil rights struggle—when he fought segregation on trains, Walter McCall says, "that made a terrific imprint on us"—stood to deliver the benediction.

"Here we are, God, confused, baffled, floundering, afraid, faithless, debating whether the Congress of the United States should pass legislation guaranteeing to every American the equal protection of the law, debating whether a bus should have the right to discriminate against a man because thou, oh God, made him black.

"Please God, in this moment of crisis and decision, give the United States wisdom, give her courage, give her faith to meet the challenge of this hour. God, keep, sustain, and bless the United States and help the weary travelers to *overcome,* some day soon."

THE GUARDIANS, THE NEW YORK COPS trained to use nonviolent techniques to contain disorder at the March on Washington, stood on the sidelines, watching the Young Jacobins. After a few minutes, the Guardians decided to move in and contain the crowd. They made a ring around the demonstrators, then pressed in—pushing, pushing, pushing—until the demonstrators were under control.

And then everyone laughed.

In July and August, the Guardians had trained to isolate troublemakers, but they did not have a chance all day to act. Now, they acted.

Those Young Jacobins were mostly twentysomethings from the Student Nonviolent Coordinating Committee. They were the radicals, the ones who wanted to challenge the Washington establishment with protests on Capitol Hill, sit-ins in the offices of Strom Thurmond and James Eastland, lie-ins at National Airport—something to disrupt the normal operations of the capitol.

But they were on their best behavior all day, letting the anguish of the summer turn to joy, for one day.

Bob Moses in his white T-shirt and Julian Bond in his casual collar shirt, Dorie Ladner and Rachelle Horowitz in dresses—they all formed a circle that stretched to half the length of a football field. Crossing one arm over the other, each gripped the hands of the people on either side. They swayed back and forth, singing "We Shall Overcome," the song that Pete Seeger adapted from an old Negro spiritual.

We are not afraid,
We are not afraid,
We are not afraid today.
Oh, deep in my heart,
I do believe
We are not afraid today.

That's when the security forces laughingly moved in. Wearing gold armbands, the specially trained police surrounded the singers and pressed inward, creating a tight nest.

———

BEFORE LONG, THE NATIONAL MALL WAS EMPTY. The evening breeze tossed around thousands of signs, newspapers, cups, and wrappers. Rooftop security forces, guns once pointed toward the middle of the Mall, were gone. Helicopters no longer hovered. Police dispersed. Only a few stray marchers remained, wandering around the Mall in search of souvenirs.

The March on Washington left more than four hundred tons of debris. The march organizers had offered to recruit a gang of a thousand volunteers to clean up, but the District of Columbia government declined the offer. More than four hundred city workers began to clear the garbage after five o'clock. They dismantled the podium and the scaffolding for TV cameras and packed 120 portable toilets onto trucks. Garbage trucks backed onto the grass to haul away the garbage. Workers gathered the packaging and remnants of eight thousand box lunches, fifty thousand hot dogs, and a hundred thousand bottles of soda. They hosed the rest of the trash into drains, where it would wash into the Potomac River.

Bayard Rustin walked around the Mall, drawing on his cigarettes, tired but needing to work off the day's high. He moved around, picking up posters and newspapers, cups and wrappers.

"LOUIS, SHOW US HOW MUCH INFLUENCE you got."

Louis Martin spent most of the day on the Mall, roaming the crowd and visiting with politicians and celebrities. He thought everything was set, but he never considered that the leaders of the March on Washington would be hungry after a day of standing in Washington sun.

Louis Martin was an old newspaper publisher who had become a policy adviser to President John F. Kennedy. Back in the 1960 campaign, he was part of a group of advisers who convinced Kennedy to call Coretta King to express his concern when Martin was imprisoned in Georgia—a call that many credit with swinging the black vote to Kennedy. That spring, Martin urged President Kennedy to propose major civil rights legislation, against the advice of other aides. He stayed in constant contact with activists throughout the South.

Today, Martin would act as a party host.

Toward the end of the program, Martin jumped in a White House car and raced back to the mansion, where officials were watching Martin Luther King on TV. When the march was done, Martin ran out to the northwest gate of the White House compound to greet the leaders. Dave Powers, an old Boston pol who was now the official presidential greeter, joined him.

Walter Reuther walked directly to Martin. For all to hear, he said, "Louie, show how much influence you got and get us some food."

For a moment, Martin panicked. The White House mess was closed for the day. "For some minutes there, I was really in a stew," he later said. "This is something I didn't think about."

So he called President Kennedy's secretary, Evelyn Lincoln, and the two went to the White House mess downstairs for sandwiches and coffee. Whitney Young joked that he wanted Scotch instead.

Besides offering advice on civil rights and domestic policy, Martin's job was to tend to the needs of the Kennedy brothers. In one White House meeting with civil rights leaders, the president greeted the group and asked Vice President Lyndon Johnson to take over. "At one point Bobby looked up at me and motioned for me to come over," Martin remembered. "So I went over, and he whispered into my ear: 'I've got a date, and I've got to get on this boat in a few minutes. Can you tell the vice president to cut it short?'" Part of the job.

Now President Kennedy walked in. He walked directly to Martin Luther King.

"*I* have a dream," he said.

The group posed for pictures. At one point, Floyd McKissick was asked to step aside for a word or two. He suspected someone was taking the group picture—and trying to exclude him. But he got in the group picture.

Phil Randolph and Walter Reuther pushed Kennedy to support the FEPC. "A job is really basic," Reuther said. Kennedy said he supported FEPC and Title III but could not get the votes to pass the bill in Congress. Kennedy's tally showed only 144 Democrats supporting these provisions in the House. Some Republicans would add their votes—but not enough to get to a majority of 218.

Kennedy steered the conversation toward family values. "Isn't it possible for the Negro community to take the lead in committing major emphasis upon the responsibility of these families, even if they're split, and the rest of the problems they have, on educating their children?" Echoing Booker T. Washington, Kennedy said blacks could help themselves by keeping families together, getting jobs, and tending to children. But Floyd McKissick countered the president. "Parents are not able to stay home," he said. "I mean they have to work, get out and do some kind of work, and there is a lack of parental control in many of the homes."

Carson Blake pointed out the deficiencies in education. He also highlighted the 13 percent black unemployment rate. "If 13 percent of the general population were unemployed like the Negro, you'd have a shooting revolution," he said.

Blacks' real problems, Whitney Young said, were up north. Young renewed his push for a raft of social programs—not just civil rights, but jobs, vocational training and apprenticeships, education, health care, and housing. He wanted nothing less than a New Deal for blacks and the poor.

Kennedy handicapped the chances for the civil rights legislation.

The president warned against false optimism. The bill would not have an FEPC or give the Department of Justice broad authority to intervene on civil rights cases. Congressional committees would also cut or neuter provisions for equal access to public accommodations.

When the meeting ended, President Kennedy left for a six o'clock meeting with foreign policy advisers. They debated, again, whether to assist generals planning a coup against Ngo Dinh Diem, America's ally in South Vietnam.

The march leaders went out to the White House portico and talked to media.

"We have developed new unity among the leadership of the civil rights movement," Phil Randolph said. "We subpoenaed the conscience of the nation," Martin Luther King said. "It did something for Negroes to see white people there with them, and not in any condescending relation," Roy Wilkins said.

All over Washington, other civil rights figures granted interviews and analyzed the event—and what would come next. Fred Shuttlesworth suggested that more marches would take place throughout the Black Belt communities of Alabama, Mississippi, Georgia, and Louisiana.

"The kind of trouble we've been having must be overcome by creative tension," he said. "The people of the North must come and finish the business of the Civil War."

ON THE TRIP HOME TO QUEENS, the old school bus without shock absorbers carried Elsa Rael through the same streets she had seen that morning.

At dawn, when the bus came into town, those streets were empty. The long blocks of brick row houses looked buttoned up, as if they were expecting a tropical storm. They only people she saw outside were cops and National Guardsmen. Washington looked like a city under martial law—grim and closed.

Coming home, she noticed something different. The windows and doors

of those row houses opened, people stood on the stoops, waving and jumping up and down. Kids swarmed into the street, as if to hug the buses. The
drive became a parade, an emancipation celebration. It was like a homecom-
ing after war.

That's when Elsa Rael decided to write a cantata. She wanted to capture
the transformation that she saw on these streets of poor black people, who
now laughed and celebrated in the city where they had even less right to vote
than the people of Mississippi or Alabama.

> *On the road, they passed the same faces*
> *They had passed that morning at summer's end.*
> *The same faces which had watched their*
> *Procession into Washington with fear,*
> *And doubt and misgiving, now smiled.*
> *The same windows which had that morning*
> *Been shuttered against them, were now flung open!*
> *And people waved, and sang, and cheered!*

Gone was the trepidation, the sense of battening down the hatches. She felt
like celebrating.

Buses had little trouble getting out of town. Some of those buses, though,
got attacked on the way home.

On Maryland's Northeast Expressway, buses returning to Philadelphia
were ambushed with rocks and rifle shots. Windows in three buses were
smashed and the taillights in a fourth smashed. Police reported that a .23-
caliber rifle bullet hit one of the buses.

Riders on one of the buses from Jackson, Mississippi, were roughed up at
a stop near Meridian. One required medical attention—and police threatened to arrest him before other members of the group protested. Charles
Evers, the brother of the slain NAACP leader Medgar Evers, demanded an
investigation.

"Our people were returning from a tremendous affirmation of faith in
democracy and received wonderful treatment in the nation's capital," he
said, "only to return to harassment, intimidation, and unjust treatment."

Some of the marchers couldn't get service at rest stops.

A bus from the Mamaroneck branch of the NAACP stopped at the Al-
cove Bar and Package Goods Restaurant in eastern Maryland. When passengers ordered a hot meal, waiters refused to allow blacks to sit; they had
to get takeout. A bus from White Plains stopped at the S&T Truck Center in

White Marsh. Marchers used the restrooms but could not buy drinks and snacks.

"Truckers only" was the reason. When a marcher from another bus showed his trucker's license, he was still refused. "You're not on duty," was the reason. When some demonstrators protested, the waiter said, "You *are* nonviolent, aren't you?"

On the plane back to Minneapolis, Mayor Arthur Naftalin's contingent wanted to convert the excitement of the march into commitments for future civil rights work. Matthew Little, the state's NAACP leader, who had organized the trip, got on the PA system and got unanimous agreement to make the local March on Washington committee an ongoing concern. Then he got young people to commit to going down to Mississippi the next summer. When they got home, they saw Louis Armstrong in the airport. He endorsed the march for the TV cameras and played a song.

BAYARD RUSTIN WENT BACK TO HIS HOTEL to watch the television coverage of the March on Washington.

For Rustin, the march marked the end of the modern civil rights movement. Until now, protests and demonstrations had been essential to force politicians and the public to face and address the horrors of segregation.

From the time the march was announced, people had debated its potential ripple effect. That morning, a *Boston Herald* editorial warned that if people could rally for civil rights, they could rally for other causes too: "What of a march in some tomorrow for a less intelligent cause—a march, say, for the abandonment of nuclear weapons?" That evening, a graduate student from Ghana told the Educational Radio Network that the march would give rallies greater legitimacy across the world, including South Africa. "With the publicity it has been given, the apartheid government of [Hendrik] Verwoerd, who replied to similar marches by shooting and killing people, would hesitate if not find it completely impossible to do what it did . . . There will be a chain reaction all over Africa."

Rustin wanted to turn the March on Washington into a permanent coalition. If Congress dragged its feet on civil rights—if the Senate held up legislation with a filibuster—the March on Washington Movement could mobilize, instantly, and descend on the capital, with activists demanding action. Rustin had already talked with Phil Randolph and Martin Luther King about sustaining the extraordinary energy of the March on Washington. To start, the march committee could conduct hearings to expose "the extent of terror and brutality in the South." And they could organize posses of a thousand or so to flood Capitol Hill if civil rights legislation got stuck in filibusters or committees.

Deep down, he knew it wouldn't happen. At least three people—Roy Wilkins, Whitney Young, and James Farmer—didn't like Rustin's plans. Wilkins and Young had already beaten back plans for a radical march. They still feared alienating their white supporters, their allies inside the system, by making a protest permanent. James Farmer saw, in Rustin's plans, a hidden plot to take over CORE. And, of course, Martin Luther King was a band of one.

In a way, it didn't matter. As soon as Congress passed civil rights legislation, the game would change. When blacks gained the right to vote, use public accommodations, get a job, buy or rent a house, and go to school, they would move "from protest to politics," as Rustin later argued.

For years now, blacks had had no choice but to challenge the system from outside. Because their demands were moral, absolute, they had to be uncompromising. But now they would enter the mucky process of bargaining. They would become part of an endless scrum with other groups—whites and Hispanics and Asians, business and labor, women and students and constituencies yet to be imagined. All of them, in shifting alliances, would battle over contracts, jobs, services, regulations. This was the everyday stuff of politics.

The very success of the civil rights movement would make it obsolete. But the legacy of a downtrodden and abused group rising up to claim its rights—and reconstituting the American regime—would endure forever.

"I happen to believe," Rustin told Robert Penn Warren, "the Negro . . . is, as it were, the *chosen people,* by which I do not mean that he is superior or that he is better or that he's any more noble. It means, I think, that he has now an identity which is a part of the national struggle in this country for the extension of democracy.

"He is in movement, like many who are at the bottom of the barrel. If he shakes, the barrel shakes. And I believe that we are chosen nonviolently to eradicate from this country the last vestiges of privilege and racism. *This is our destiny.* To the degree that the Negro goes into the streets or into courts or into restaurants, theaters, hotels, into the legislative halls, or marches before them, as a part of that he will find his true identity.

"Out of his absence of privilege, he moves beautifully and nonviolently. And in the process, he brings a great deal of beauty to this country."

ACKNOWLEDGMENTS

MY WORLD DURING THE WRITING of *Nobody Turn Me Around* didn't match the buzz of the March on Washington headquarters in Harlem. Bob Dylan never dropped by to say hi, for example. But my life still buzzed with creative and important people. I must thank them.

Greatest thanks, as usual, go to Isabel Chenoweth and her children, Walker and Leila, whose enthusiasm and support sustained me. John Adams took great interest in the project from the beginning and offered a place to stay in Atlanta. Richard Chenoweth and Jim Leeson, as always, offered their encouragement and friendship.

My editors at Beacon Press—Gayatri Patnaik, and also Joanna Green—embraced my vision for this book right away and helped me to realize it, along with others at Beacon Press, including Helene Atwan, Tom Hallock, P. J. Tierney, Pamela MacColl, and Susan Lumenello. My agent, John Silbersack of Trident Literary Group, saw the potential of both the topic and the approach and offered invaluable advice and encouragement.

My good friend Alex Heard, who was working on a fascinating study of the Willie McGee case as I worked on this book, taught me a lot about civil rights, research, and writing along the way. John Egerton shared some tricks of the writing trade. His own accomplishments gave his advice and support extra heft. Eric Etheridge also offered encouragement and contacts. Wayne Coffey, as always, cheered me on and talked writing.

A number of people offered priceless materials during my research. Walter Naegle allowed me to listen to tapes of Bayard Rustin's private conversations about the topics of this work. Keith Luf of WGBH-Boston set me up with recordings of the Educational Radio Network's coverage of the March.

Students in my writing classes at Yale always amaze me with their openness to learning and passion for civil rights.

And then there were the people in libraries and research centers—Greg Eow and Kevin Pacelli at Yale's Sterling Library; Cynthia Patterson Lewis and Elaine Hall of the King Center; Laura Anderson of the Birmingham

Civil Rights Institute; Craig Scott of the Gadsden Public Library; Andrea Blackmun of the Nashville Public Library; Wesley Chenault and Okezie Amalaha of the Auburn Avenue Research Library in Atlanta; Kathe Hambrick of the River Road African American Museum in Plaquemine; and the people at the University of North Carolina Library, the Duke University Library, and, most of all, the New York Public Library's Schomburg Center for Research in Black Culture.

My family also helped, in countless ways. Special thanks are due to my mother, Gale Euchner, and to those who read drafts and put me up, Jim and Dotty Eichner and Susan Cararez and her family. I drew special inspiration from Claire and Michael Giangrasso, who taught me about grace and courage as I was researching historic figures of grace and courage.

ABBREVIATIONS

AMP	August Meier Papers, Schomburg Center for Research in Black Culture, New York Public Library
BR	Bayard Rustin Papers, Library of Congress
BR-HW	Recorded conversations between Bayard Rustin and Harry Wachtel (private collection)
GP	Albert E. Gollin Papers, Schomburg Center for Research in Black Culture
KC	King Center for Nonviolent Social Change, Atlanta
LOC	Library of Congress
PCM	Paley Center for Media, New York
SFC	*San Francisco Chronicle*
WP	*Washington Post*
WRL	Walter Reuther Library, Wayne State University

PROLOGUE

ON A PITCH-BLACK NIGHT: Author interviews with Robert Avery, James Lawson, and Walter Fauntroy. Gadsden boys: "Three Teens Hitchhike to Hear About a Dream," *Gadsden Times,* February 17, 2002. Moore shooting: Mary Stanton, *Freedom Walk* (Jackson: University Press of Mississippi, 2003). Harris poll on race: "Majority of Whites on Discrimination," *WP,* August 26, 1963. Civil rights activity in 1963: "Driven By 100 Years of Frustration," *Atlanta Daily World,* December 10, 1963.

PART 1: NIGHT UNTO DAWN

MARTIN LUTHER KING SAT: Author interviews with Wyatt Tee Walker, Dorothy Cotton, and Harry Boyte Jr.; Symposium Commemorating the 1963 March on

Washington, Gilman Library, George Washington University, October 10, 1998. Andrew Young: Jonathan Rieder, *The Word of the Lord Is Upon Me* (Cambridge, MA: Harvard University Press, 2008), 58. "Sort of a Gettysburg Address": David Garrow, "Martin Luther King: The March, the Man, the Dream," *American History*, August 2003. Percy Green on Uncle Tom: "Says Uncle Tom Lived 'Hi on Hog,'" *Muhammad Speaks*, August 16, 1963. "Insufficient funds" analogy: Evan J. Charkes, "A Wintertime Soldier," *Columbia College Today*, January/February 2008. "Hate for hate": Clayborne Carson, ed., *The Papers of Martin Luther King, Jr.*, Vol. 4 (Berkeley: University of California Press, 2000), 320. Influences on King's preaching: Lewis Baldwin, *There Is a Balm in Gilead* (Philadelphia: Fortress, 1991), chapter 5. Prathia Hall and "I have a dream": Roger Fritts, "The Most Famous American Sermon of the 20th Century," Cedar Lane Unitarian Universalist Church, Bethesda, MD, undated. "Dreams are great": Mervyn A. Warren, *King Came Preaching* (Downers Grove, IL: InterVarsity Press, 2001), 192. King's Montgomery crisis: David Goldfield, *Black, White, and Southern* (Baton Rouge: Louisiana State University Press, 1991), 101. King's Detroit speech: Clayborne Carson et al., *Call to Conscience* (New York: Grand Central, 2002), 57–73. "Give us the ballot": BR-HW, October 31, 1985.

ALL THROUGH THE NIGHT: Author interviews with Walter Fauntroy and Rachelle Horowitz. Also see BR-HW; Rustin interview, GP; documents in March on Washington folders, BR.

CHARISMA MEANS, LITERALLY, "GIFT OF GRACE": Author interviews with Wyatt Tee Walker, Rachelle Horowitz, Marcus Wood, Walter Fauntroy, and Norman Hill; also see BR-HW, December 12, 1985. Johnnie Carr remark: Carr interview, KC. King in private: Rieder, *Word of the Lord*, 56. College memories: Walter McCall, interview, KC. Daddy King: Baldwin, *There Is a Balm*, 100. Schoolteachers' comments: Lewis Chandler and N. P. Tillman, interview by Donald Smith, KC. "We had no idea": Brailsford Brazeal, interview, KC. "I had doubts": "Man of the Year," *Time*, January 3, 1964. "He was storing up information": Herman Bostick, interview, KC. Maple Shade, restaurant incident: McCall, interview. Marriage to Coretta: Coretta King, interview by Donald Smith, KC. "His words flowed": Coretta Scott King, *My Life with Martin Luther King* (New York: Cappelen, 1969), 239. Montgomery bus boycott: Taylor Branch, *Parting the Waters* (New York: Simon & Schuster, 1988), chapter 5. Nonviolence as "geometry": James Bevel and Bernard Lafayette, interview, Nashville Public Library. Use of nonviolence: C. B. King, Albert Cleage, and Brailsford Brazeal, interviews, KC. "Martin, if you have desegregated *anything*": Drew Hansen, *The Dream* (New York: Ecco Press, 2003), 14.

A. PHILIP RANDOLPH FACED ONE SIMPLE CHOICE: Author interviews with Stanley Aronowitz, Norman Hill, James Lawson, Rachelle Horowitz, Courtland Cox, and Dorothy Cotton; also see Jervis Anderson, *A. Philip Randolph* (Berkeley:

University of California Press, 1986) and BR-HW. King urges new proclamation: "President Urged To End Race Laws," *New York Times*, June 6, 1961. "The march of technology": *Muhammad Speaks*, April 1, 1963. Kahn memo: Tom Kahn Papers, LOC. "Might so threaten the president": FBI file, June 1–2, 1963. "He who would be free": A. Philip Randolph Papers, LOC. Father's influence: *New York Post*, December 29, 1959. Working within democracy: *Norfolk Journal and Guide*, January 28, 1950. "Give us the ballot": BR-HW, December 12, 1985. JFK refuses King request: Simeon Booker, *Black Man's America* (New York: Prentice-Hall, 1964), 30–31. "More than ever before": FBI memo, June 10, 1963; FBI file, June 2, 1963. A. D. King calls Cleveland Robinson: AMP. Jones and King: David Garrow, *Bearing the Cross* (New York: Harper Perennial, 2004), 292. George Lawrence comments: Adam Fairclough, *To Redeem the Soul of America* (Athens: University of Georgia Press, 2001), 152; "Marchers' Master Plan," *Life*, August 23, 1963. JFK tries to dissuade: Garrow, *Bearing the Cross*, 271. Wilkins on "tinge of Harlem": ibid., 274.

TWENTY-FOUR BUSES IDLED: Marlene Nadle, "The View from the Front of the Bus," *Village Voice*, September 5, 1963, and Charles Portis, "Rolling Down from New York," *New York Herald-Tribune*, August 29, 1963. City Hall protests: "Mayor Ousts Sit-Ins After City Hall Clash," *Daily News*, August 23, 1963. Jim Peck: Raymond Arsenault, *Freedom Riders* (New York: Oxford University Press, 2006), 150.

A TARMAC FULL OF C-82S: Author interviews with Daniel Boatwright and Violet Finger; also see Joseph Califano, *Inside* (New York: Public Affairs, 2004), 110–14. Williams letter: KC.

GOING TO THE MARCH WAS A BIG DEAL: Bernard LaFayette, author interview, and FBI account of meeting, September 20, 1963.

THE ONLY PERSON ALLOWED A GOOD NIGHT'S SLEEP: Anderson, *Randolph*; Herbert Garfinkel, "Black March on the White House," University of Chicago dissertation, 1956; also see "A Post Portrait," *New York Post*, December 29, 1959. "Bayard, where have you been?": "A. Philip Randolph: Labor's Grand Old Man," *Ebony*, May 1969. Pullman organizing: "He Speaks for 15 Million," *New Leader*, September 2, 1950. "If we don't meet in this church": Larry Tye, *Rising from the Rails* (New York: Macmillan, 2004), 144. "In common parlance": *Chicago Defender*, February 8, 1941. Randolph planning and canceling marches: Lucy Barber, *Marching on Washington* (Berkeley: University of California Press, 2004), chapter 4; *Norfolk Journal and Guide*, January 28, 1950.

AFTER A TRIP OF MORE THAN 2,700 MILES: Documentary *The Bus* (1965), directed by Haskell Wexler; author interviews with Wexler, John Handy, and Franklin Chung. Also see "Journey Toward a Dream," *New York Times*, April 4, 1965.

"WHAT'S GONNA HAPPEN WHEN BIG BUBBA": Bill Perry, author interview. Route 40: Michael O'Brien, *John F. Kennedy* (New York: Macmillan, 2005), 595.

ALL NIGHT, PROTESTERS STAGED: Author interviews with Bob Moses, Sheila Michaels, Courtland Cox, and Dorie Ladner. "I was told not to fight back": "Notes on Civil Rights March," *Sunday News,* September 1, 1963. Americus case: Elizabeth Holtzman, *Who Said It Would Be Easy?* (Baltimore: Arcade, 1996), 19–21.

JUST AFTER TWO O'CLOCK ON THE MORNING: Author interviews with Courtland Cox, Rachelle Horowitz, and Norman Hill. Reuther's role: Walter Reuther, remarks to executive board of United Auto Workers, September 24–26, 1963, WRL. Ahmann's role: Mathew Ahmann, interview, AMP. Also see John Lewis, *Walking with the Wind* (New York: Simon & Schuster, 1998).

THE JOHN LEWIS CRISIS ROBBED BAYARD RUSTIN: Author interviews with Rachelle Horowitz, Norman Hill, Walter Naegle, Courtland Cox, and Roger Wilkins; also see BR-HW and Robert Penn Warren, interview, 1964 (*Who Speaks for the Negro?*; collected interviews online at whospeaks.library.vanderbilt.edu). Horn & Hardart strike: Bayard Rustin, interview, GP. Also see Daniel Levine, *Bayard Rustin and the Civil Rights Movement* (Piscataway, NJ: Rutgers University Press, 2000) and Jervis Anderson, *Bayard Rustin* (Berkeley: University of California Press, 1998). "Twoness": W. E. B. Du Bois, *The Souls of Black Folk* (Lawrence, KS: Digireads, 2005), 7. Activism and Quakerism: August Meier, interview, AMP. British accent: Horowitz and Cox. Police attack: Alfred Gollin, interview, GP. California speech: FBI memo to J. Edgar Hoover, October 19, 1942. "Completely defeated": Anderson, *Bayard Rustin,* 107. "If you deal creatively": "Brother Outsider," *POV,* Public Broadcasting System, 2003. Rustin on Young Communist League: Bayard Rustin, interview, BR-HW; Robert Penn Warren, interview, whospeaks.library. vanderbilt.edu.

THE FORMER STREET HUSTLER AND PIMP: Author interviews with Nat Hentoff, Courtland Cox, and Dorie Ladner. "Time to get a divorce": "The Black Muslims," *Sydney Morning Herald* (Australia), May 19, 1963. "We don't preach": "Malcolm X Starting Drive in Washington," *New York Times,* May 10, 1963. "Real men": "Malcolm X Terms Dr. King's Tactics Futile," *New York Times,* May 11, 1963. "The followers": Jack Bloom, *Class, Race, and the Civil Rights Movement* (Bloomington: Indiana University Press, 1987), 197. "God is about to eliminate": "Negro Leaders Disagree on Rights Methods," *Tennessean,* June 28, 1963. Harlem Unity Rally: "Malcolm X: All Time Greatest Speeches," Master Classics (MP3), 2008.

THE FBI ATTEMPTED TO EXPLOIT FEARS: FBI files of Martin Luther King and others. See also Sullivan memo and Hoover response, in Richard Gid Powers, "The FBI Marches on the Dreamer," *American History*, August 2003. Levison and O'Dell: Ronald Kessler, *The Bureau* (New York: Macmillan, 2003), 155–58.

WALTER FAUNTROY HAD REASON TO BELIEVE: Security meeting: Memo (unsigned), GP. Russell Long remark: "Police Wait for Marchers," *Raleigh News and Observer*, August 26, 1963.

CAN A DEMONSTRATION CHANGE: "The Impact of TV on Negroes," *SFC*, September 3, 1963. Gunnar Myrdal, *An American Dilemma* (New York: Harper & Row, 1944).

A KANSAS CITY MAN: Threat to King: FBI memo, August 28, 1963. Postcard threatening Wilkins: Roy Wilkins Papers, LOC. Kennedy threat: FBI files, June 21, 1963. Grounding planes: "The Psychiatrist Had a Head Start," *Washington Daily News*, September 29, 1963.

PART 2: INTO THE DAY

A HELICOPTER HOVERED OVER: Helicopter: "Rambler," *Washington Star*, August 29, 1963. Morning of march: "First Marchers Arrive," *Washington Daily News*, August 27, 1963. Holmes recollections: "March on Washington Looks at 40," *USA Today*, August 21, 2003.

BAYARD RUSTIN, WHO STAYED UP: Author interviews with Rachelle Horowitz, Norman Hill, Courtland Cox, Wyatt Walker, and Dorothy Cotton. Statler Hotel lobby: B. M. Phillips, "Free . . . dom . . . Free . . . dom NOW," *Afro-American*, September 7, 1963. Morsell on "sinking feeling": John Morsell, interview, GP.

IN THE GREEN-AND-WHITE-STRIPED PARTY TENT: Author interviews with Rachelle Horowitz, Elliott Linzer, Haskell Wexler, and Michael Thelwell. WUST headquarters operations: Carole Wolff notes, GP. Gadsden boys at WUST: Robert Avery and James Smith, author interviews.

PLANNING FOR THE MARCH ON WASHINGTON: Author interviews with Rachelle Horowitz, Norman Hill, Courtland Cox, Peter Orris, and Elliott Linzer; also, Rustin Papers and GP. John Williams account: *The God King Didn't Save* (New York: Coward-McCann, 1970), 60. "I simply don't know how": *New York Post*, August 25, 1963. Rustin's to-do list for the march: BR. Letter from Josephine Baker's manager: BR. Latrine letters: letter from Paul Douglas to Philip Randolph, August 9, 1963, March on Washington files, BR.

IN THE WAR ROOM AT THE PENTAGON: William Geoghegan, author interview.

ALL SUMMER LONG, THE MARCH GOT SOFTER: Author interviews with Rachelle Horowitz, Courtland Cox, Norman Hill, and Elliott Linzer. Lomax criticism: "Rights March is 'Fixed,' Says Negro Author," *SFC*, August 19, 1963. Whites dominating the march: FBI memo (August 14, 1963). Truman on civil rights: "President Truman's Speech to NAACP on Human Rights, *New York Times*, June 30, 1947. Wilkins on Washington turnout: Sterling Tucker, interview with Albert Gollin, GP.

WHEN THE BUSES ROLLED INTO WASHINGTON: Author interviews with Elsa Rael, Ericka Huggins, and Jack Shattuck, as well as media and book accounts. Jean Shepherd memories: WOR broadcast, August 29, 1963. Sterling Tucker, interview by Albert Gollin, GP.

PART 3: CONGREGATION

AS THE LEADERS OF THE MARCH ON WASHINGTON: McLaurin account: "The Psychiatrist Had a Head Start—And Few Men," *Washington Daily News*, August 29, 1963. Visit with Dirksen: "March Leaders Press Civil Rights Bill case," *Los Angeles Times*, August 29, 1963. Dirksen's views on civil rights: "Campaign for Integration," *New York Times*, June 9, 1963. Early civil rights laws as "crawl space": Bob Moses, author interview. "The Republican attitude has always been": "Rally Impact on Congress Still Doubtful," *WP*, August 29, 1963. Legislative prospects: Mathew Ahmann, interview, GP. "Southern people have never accepted": "Keeper of the Rules," *Washington Monthly*, July/August 1987, 59. Reuther strategy: Reuther, remarks to executive board, WRL. Railroad bill: "A Strike Postponed," *WP*, August 29, 1963.

WHEN BLACK LIMOUSINES TOOK THE BIG TEN: 1960 census: *Statistical Abstract of the United States 1961*, 82nd annual edition, section 13, "Elections, Composition of Congress," No. 476, "Composition of Congress by Political Party Affiliations, by States: 1957–1961" (Washington, D.C.: U.S. Department of Commerce, Bureau of the Census), 355, http://www2.census.gov/prod2/statcomp/documents/1961-02 .pdf. "The champion of the filibuster": Joshua Zeitz, "All Through the Night with Strom Thurmond," posted August 29, 2007, American Heritage.com, http://www .americanheritage.com/articles/web/20070829-strom-thurmond-filibuster-civil -rights-voting-1957-segregation-integration_print.shtml.

BONNIE PRINCE CHARLIE—CHARLIE GETER: Author interviews with Wynn Alexander, Charlie Geter, and Louise Williams. Philadelphia activism: "Dump-In Newest Civil Rights Wrinkle," *Afro-American*, August 31, 1963, and "150 march in CORE City Hall Protest," *Philadelphia Tribune,* August 27, 1963. Cecil Moore remark: "The Awful Roar," *Time,* August 30, 1963.

BY THE TIME HARVEY JONES GOT TO UNION STATION: Author interviews with Harvey Jones and David Sageser. Charleston trip: "I Woke Up With My Mind Set on Freedom," *Washington Daily News,* August 29, 1963. James Hauser: "Jim Won't Be Able to Wash His Hands," *Washington Daily News,* August 29, 1963. The Reverend Sageser's ambivalence: David Sageser, author interview. Sageser sermon: *CBS News Special Report: The March on Washington,* August 28, 1963, PCM.

HOLLYWOOD CELEBRITIES BUNDLED THEMSELVES: Author interviews with Dorie Ladner, Rachelle Horowitz, and Carol Taylor; March on Washington files, BR. Boycott talk: "Performers Eye Boycott of Segregated Theaters," *Los Angeles Times,* August 29, 1963. Jackie Robinson: Educational Radio Network live coverage, available at WGBH, Boston. Burt Lancaster petition: CBS live march coverage (videotape), PCM. Dick Gregory: "Gregory Elects to Stay in Jail," *SFC,* August 18, 1966; "Dick Gregory Says March is Beautiful," *Afro-American,* September 1, 1963; CBS march coverage, PCM; live radio coverage (audiotape), WGBH. Fair employment: *Los Angeles Times,* August 1, 1963. Grand Wizard plane crash: "Dick Gregory Says March is Beautiful."

WHEN HANK THOMAS CONFRONTED A RACIST: Author interviews with Hank Thomas, Rachelle Horowitz, and Courtland Cox. William Johnson message to King: Johnson letter, July 18, 1963, BR. March security trainer Julius Hobson: "FBI Records List Julius Hobson as 'Confidential Source' in '60s," *WP,* May 22, 1981.

ON THE EDGE OF THE NATIONAL MALL: Author interviews with Mark Levy, Mike Wenger, and Deborah Yaffe.

THE MUSIC WAS TOO CONTROLLED: Author interviews with Dorie Ladner and John Handy. "It was like a fire": Robert Simpson, interview, Birmingham Civil Rights Institute. "He is a strident, nasal wailer": "Freedom Songs Offer Rare Video," *Newsday,* August 27, 1963. Gregory on whites: Mike Marqusee, *Wicked Messenger: Bob Dylan and the 1960s* (New York: Seven Stories Press, 2005), 15. Absence of jazz at the march: John Handy, author interview.

ON THE EDGE OF THE TIDAL BASIN: Bob Moses, author interview; see also "For God's Sake Leave the Kid Alone," *Washington Daily News,* August 29, 1963. Monroe kidnapping incident: Robert Williams, *Negroes with Guns* (Detroit: Wayne State University Press, 1998), chapters 2–3.

NOT FAR FROM JIMMY PRUITT: Mae Mallory: Jack Claiborne, "Carolinas Contingent Aims Barbs at Ervin," *Charlotte Observer,* August 29, 1963. "I do not advocate violence": Williams, *Negroes with Guns,* 4. "I saw the circle closing": Williams, *Negroes with Guns,* 49.

"THE AUDIENCE IS SO OBVIOUSLY ONE-SIDED": Author interviews with Roger Mudd, Rachelle Horowitz, Norman Hill, and Courtland Cox; also, CBS march coverage, PCM. Thurmond attack: *Congressional Record,* August 13, 1963. Randolph answers Thurmond: John D'Emilio, "Invisible Man," *The Crisis,* July/August, 2003.

AS BLACKS DEMONSTRATED FOR EQUAL RIGHTS: "States Rights Amendments Debate Tonight," *Tennessean,* June 27, 1963. Electoral College: "Unpledged Electors Movement Feared," *Tennessean,* June 5, 1963. Barnett on relocation: "Equalize Negro Population in States, Barnett Urges," *Chicago Tribune,* August 20, 1963.

JEROME SMITH WAS PART OF A GROUP: Author interviews with Henry Morgenthau, Bob Moses, and Toby Stein. Paul Newman: "The Stars Just Marched, Too," *SFC,* August 29, 1963. "Race screen" bus incident: "A Young Boy's Stand," *Morning Edition,* National Public Radio, December 1, 2006. Meeting with Robert Kennedy: James Wechsler, "RFK & Baldwin," *New York Post,* May 28, 1963; Arthur M. Schlesinger Jr., *Robert Kennedy and His Times* (Boston: Houghton Mifflin, 1978), 330–35. "The rest of us were more genteel": Henry Morgenthau, author interview. Baldwin's reaction to meeting: Fern Marja Eckman, "James Baldwin," *New York Post,* January 13–16, 1964.

THE KENNEDYS HAD BEEN WARNED ALL YEAR: Martin memo: Russell Riley, *The Presidency and the Politics of Racial Inequality* (New York: Columbia University Press, 1999), 218. White House conversations: Jonathan Rosenberg and Zachary Karabell, *Kennedy, Johnson, and the Quest for Justice* (New York: Norton, 2003), 116–25. King jubilant: FBI file, June 12, 1963. Wiretapping: David Garrow, *The FBI and Martin Luther King Jr.* (New York: Norton, 1981), 94–95. The 1964 election: "How Much Will Rights Vote Cost President in Votes": *Arkansas Gazette,* August 18, 1963. Kennedy speech: online at millercenter.org/scripps/archive/speeches/detail/3375. "He was really great": FBI file, June 12, 1963.

A TYPICAL WASHINGTON RESIDENT: Simon Cloonan interview (audiotape), WGBH; Fletcher Knebel, "Washington, D.C.: Portrait of a Sick City," *Look,* June 4, 1963; Bill Davidson, "A City in Trouble," *Saturday Evening Post,* July 13–20, 1963. "All hell is going to break loose": "Hacker Chatter on the March," *SFC,* August 18, 1963. Dixiecrats: Irwin Ross, *The Loneliest Campaign* (New York: New American Library, 1968), 131. "It pains me to think": KYHV radio, Little Rock, Arkansas, August 21, 1963. Thanksgiving Day riot: "Fight at D.C. Grid Game," *Spokane Chronicle,*

November 29, 1962. Downtown Washington on day of march: "Capital to Pause," *SFC*, August 25, 1963; "Usually Busy Streets Deserted on March Day," *WP*, August 29, 1963; "Washington Discreetly Pulls Blinds," *Raleigh News and Observer*, August 29, 1963; "Downtown Sales Are Hard-Hit For a Day; Many Stores Close," *WP*, August 29, 1963. WUST janitor: notes, GP.

LENA HORNE APPROACHED: Ericka Huggins, author interview; James Gavin, *Stormy Weather* (New York: Atria Books, 2009).

A TRIM MAN WEARING A TIE AND BLAZER: Nazis and the march: William Schmaltz, *Hate* (Washington, DC: Brassey's, 1999), ch. 8. "My men will aid the police": "It Was a Fine Day for a March," *Washington Daily News*, August 28, 1963. Flyers: "A Plan to Combat Rights March," *SFC*, August 21, 1963. "But they will not be allowed": *WP*, August 2, 1963. William Pattison remarks: "U.S. Nazis' Command Post," *SFC*, August 21, 1963, and "A Hate Peddler's Strategy," *SFC*, August 25, 1963. McIntyre flyer threat: "Leaflet Rain," *Tennessean*, August 28, 1963. Allen speaks and is booked: live march coverage (audiotape), WGBH.

A HULKING FIGURE: Author interview with Ned O'Gorman; see also O'Gorman, "Freedom March," *Jubilee*, October 1963.

JACK TAKAYANAGI ALSO WENT TO WASHINGTON: Author interview with Jack Takayanagi. Japanese internment camps: Peter Wright et al., *Manzanar* (New York: Vintage Books, 1989); Masayo Duus, *Unlikely Liberators* (Honolulu: University of Hawaii Press, 2007). "Proof" of Japanese plot: Wright et al., *Manzanar*, 44.

THE BIG TEN LINGERED ON CAPITOL HILL: Author interviews with Norman Hill and Rachelle Horowitz; live march coverage (audiotape), WGBH.

NED O'GORMAN LOOKED OUT ON THE MARCHERS: Author interviews with Ned O'Gorman and Rita Hauser (formerly Schwerner). "Constitution Avenue is awash": Edward Morgan, transcription from diary, March on Washington files, BR. Helen Fineman remark: "200,000 People and Not a Single Incident, *Christian Science Monitor*, August 30, 1963. "No more Sam Ervin": "Carolinas Contingent Aims Barb at Ervin," *Raleigh News and Observer*, August 29, 1963. "I listened, as I never had before": Toby Stein, author interview, and "Notes on a Walk in Washington," *Interracial Review*, October 1963. "I'm too old to march": *Wider City Parish Newsletter* (New Haven, CT), September 1963. Outside the Navy Building: "200,000 People and Not a Single Incident." The Reverend Dukes for governor: Carole Wolff, notes, GP. Mailer: "The Big Bite" (column), *Esquire*, December 1963.

AS DEMONSTRATORS BROKE OFF: Notes from National Security Archive, www
.gwu.edu/~nsarchiv/NSAEBB/NSAEBB101/vn07.pdf. King's influence on monks:
Michelle Ho, conversation with author.

PART 4: DREAM

JAMES FORMAN OF THE STUDENT NONVIOLENT COORDINATING COMMIT-
TEE: Author interviews with Courtland Cox, Rachelle Horowitz, William van den
Heuvel, Dorie Ladner, and Will Campbell; also see Sam Hoskins, "Speech Too Hot
to Handle," *Afro-American,* September 14, 1963; Stokely Carmichael, *Ready for
Revolution* (New York: Scribner, 2003), chapter 15; Nelson Lichtenstein, *The Most
Dangerous Man in Detroit* (New York: Basic Books, 1995), 386; Reuther, remarks
to executive board, WRL; Carson Blake, interview by Albert Gollin, GP. Shuttles-
worth addresses marchers: videotape, WGBH. "Madam, stop now": BR-HW.

"WE ARE NOT A MOB": Phil Randolph, speech: audiotape, WGBH.

ONSTAGE, THE WOMEN OF THE MOVEMENT: Author interviews with Rachelle
Horowitz, Norm Hill, and Courtland Cox. Daisy Bates story: Belinda Robnett,
How Long? How Long? (New York: Oxford University Press, 1997), 77. Anna Hedge-
man and Pauli Murray protest lack of role for women: letters, BR. Maida Springer,
dispute with Murray: Yvette Richards, *Maida Springer* (Pittsburgh: University of
Pittsburgh Press, 2004), 263–64.

ALSO ABSENT FROM THE PROGRAM: Author interviews with Courtland Cox
and Norm Hill. Jane Stembridge remark: letter, BR.

"WE COME LATE": Author interviews with Danny Schechter and D'Army Bailey.
Amusement park arrest: "Eugene Carson Blake Among 283 Arrested in Baltimore,"
Presbyterian Life, August 1, 1963, and March on Washington files, BR.

TEARS HAD STREAKED MARIAN ANDERSON'S FACE: Reviews of Anderson's
singing: Raymond Arsenault, *The Sound of Freedom* (New York: Bloomsbury,
2009), 28, 23, 84. Ralph Matthews comment: "The Cast Has Changed," *Afro-American,* August 31, 1963.

RUMORS OF CENSORSHIP: Author interviews with Courtland Cox and Rachelle
Horowitz. Lewis's speech: James Forman, *The Making of Black Revolutionaries* (Se-
attle: University of Washington Press, 1997); audiotape, WGBH; videotape, PCM.

WALTER REUTHER BATHED IN APPLAUSE: Carson Blake, interview, GP. Walter Reuther's role and speech: Nelson Lichtenstein, *The Most Dangerous Man in
Detroit* (Champaign: University of Illinois Press, 1997), 274. "With every means at

their disposal": ibid., 376. "Who is that white man?": Irving Bluestone, interview, WRL.

IN A SQUAT, SQUARE TWO-STORY BRICK BUILDING: Author interviews with Lolis Elie, Rudy Lombard, Marvin Rich, and Sidney Marchand. Organizing in Plaquemine: *Louisiana Diary*, National Educational Television, 1964; Gordon Carey, interview, GP.

THROUGH HIS INTERMEDIARY, JAMES FARMER MADE: McKissick delivers Farmer's remarks: videotape, PCM; audiotape, WGBH.

"GET A BISHOP IN THE EAST": Mathew Ahmann, interview, GP; audiotape of speech, WGBH.

"YOU CAN HOLLER, PROTEST": Dennis Dickerson, *Militant Mediator* (Lexington: University Press of Kentucky, 2007); Whitney Young, interviews by David Rusk (for this book) and Albert Gollin, GP.

THE DAY WAS HOT AND LONG: Author interviews with Dorothy Cotton, Elliott Linzer, and D'Army Bailey. Sylvia Johnson collapses: "TV Cameraman Turns Ace First-Aid Hand as Heat Fells 150," *Afro-American*, September 7, 1963. Norman Mailer's impressions: Mailer, "The Big Bite."

WESTERN UNION DELIVERED HUNDREDS OF TELEGRAMS: BR-HW, October 31, 1985. "I was ecstatic": Roy Wilkins, *Standing Fast* (New York: Da Capo Press, 1994), 92, 93. Suspicion of mass politics, support of integration: Roy Wilkins, oral history, Ralph J. Bunche Collection, Howard University. Du Bois telegram: Elliott Linzer, author interview. Calvin Craig Miller, *Roy Wilkins: Leader of the NAACP* (Greensboro, NC: Morgan Reynolds, 2005). Wilkins speech: audiotape, WGBH.

MAHALIA JACKSON TOTTERED TOWARD: John Morsell, interview, GP. "Wait a minute": "Mahalia Focuses on Other Stars," *WP*, August 29, 1963. "Dr. Watts" gospel style: Gena Dagel Caponi, ed., *Signifyin(g), Sanctifyin', & Slam Dunking: A Reader in African American Expressive Culture* (Amherst: University of Massachusetts Press, 1999), 165.

"I WISH I COULD SING!": Jonathan Prinz, author interview; letter to Martin Luther King, September 8, 1967, American Jewish Archives, Cincinnati, Ohio.

AS HE MOVED TO THE PLATFORM: King scribbles on prepared text: original document, KC. "Next president": "The Best Behaved," *SFC*, August 29, 1963.

ALWAYS, HE BEGINS SLOWLY: Author interviews with Harold Bragg and Richard Pritchard. (Text of speech reproduced with permission from the King Estate.) "F—— that dream": Williams, *The God King Didn't Save*, 63. Ruth bat Mordecai recollections: "If Not Now, When," *Our Age*, October 6, 1963.

PART 5: ONWARD

EXPLOSION: Marcus Wood, author interview. "Why, why should": Gwyndolyn Meadowbrooks, interview, KC.

BAYARD RUSTIN GOT A MOMENT TO BASK: Rustin reads the demands: videotape, PCM; audiotape, WGBH. "Mr. Randolph": Thomas Gentile, *March on Washington* (Denver, CO: New Day, 1983), 250.

BENJAMIN MAYS, WHO HAD INSPIRED: Benediction: audiotape, WGBH.

THE GUARDIANS, THE NEW YORK COPS: Author interviews with Rachelle Horowitz, Dorie Ladner, and Sheila Michaels.

BEFORE LONG, THE NATIONAL MALL WAS EMPTY: "Washington—The Day After," *SFC*, September 1, 1963.

"LOUIS, SHOW US HOW MUCH INFLUENCE": Louis Martin, interview, GP. Martin role in 1960 campaign: Berl Bernhard, William Taylor, and Harris Wofford, "Civil Rights, Politics and the Law: Three Civil Rights Lawyers Reminisce," panel discussion, Woodrow Wilson International Center for Scholars, January 19, 2006. RFK's date: Louis Martin, interview, Lyndon Johnson Library. President Kennedy's meeting with march leaders: audio recordings, John F. Kennedy Presidential Library. Blake on education and unemployment: Thomas F. Jackson, *From Civil Rights to Human Rights* (Philadelphia: University of Pennsylvania Press, 2006), 182. March leaders meet with the press: videotape, PCM; audiotape, WGBH.

ON THE TRIP HOME: Author interviews with Matthew Little and Elsa Rael. (Rael cantata quoted with permission by author.) Attacks on returning marchers: letters, BR; "Shots, Rocks Hit 'Freedom' Buses," *Afro-American*, September 7, 1963.

BAYARD RUSTIN WENT BACK TO HIS HOTEL: Author interviews with Rachelle Horowitz and Norman Hill. Rustin remark to Warren: Robert Penn Warren, interview, whospeaks.library.vanderbilt.edu.